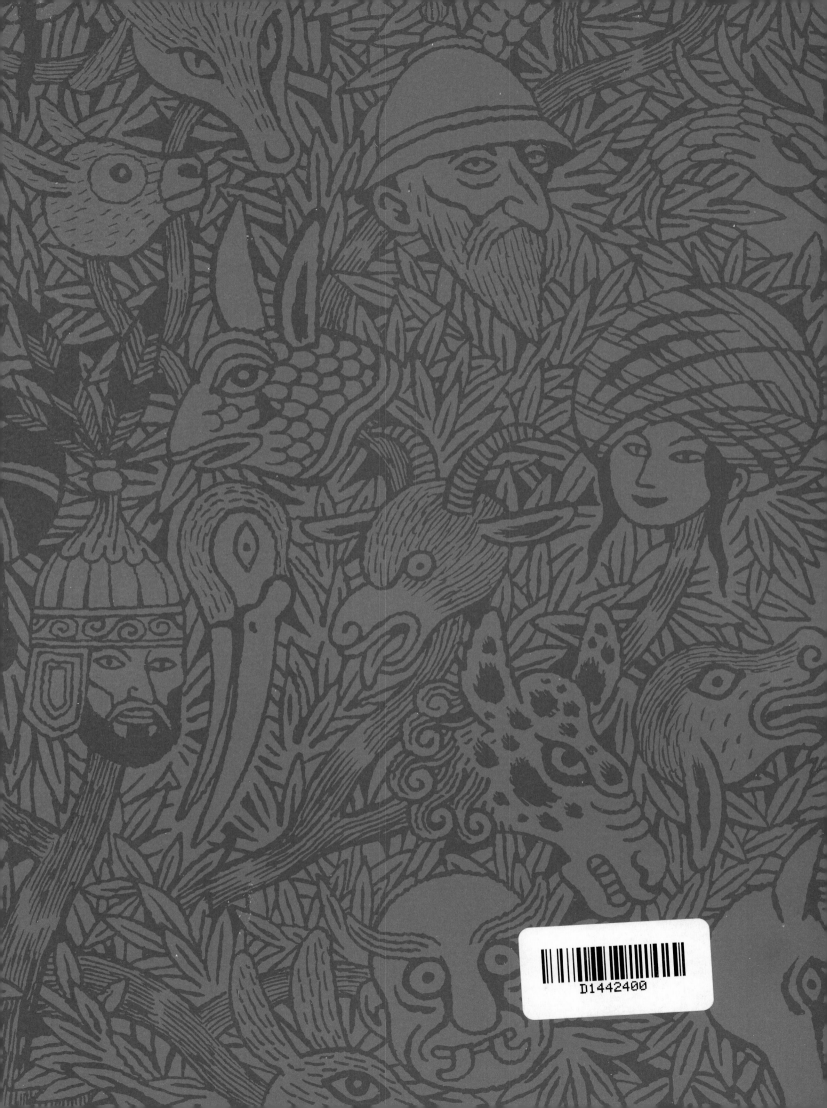

David B.

Hâsib

& the Queen of Serpents

To Ulysse and Tito

Special thanks to Impedimenta (Madrid) for helping with the files. Lettered with a font based on David B's hand lettering, created by Officine Bolzoni.

ISBN 9781681121628
Library of Congress Control Number: 2018936235
© 2015-2016 Gallimard Jeunesse
© 2018 NBM for the English translation
Translation by Montana Kane
Lettering by Ortho
Printed in China
1st printing June 2018

David B.

Hâsib

& the Queen of Serpents

A Tale of a Thousand and One Nights

nbm GRAPHIC NOVELS

Nantier · Beall · Minoustchine
NEW YORK

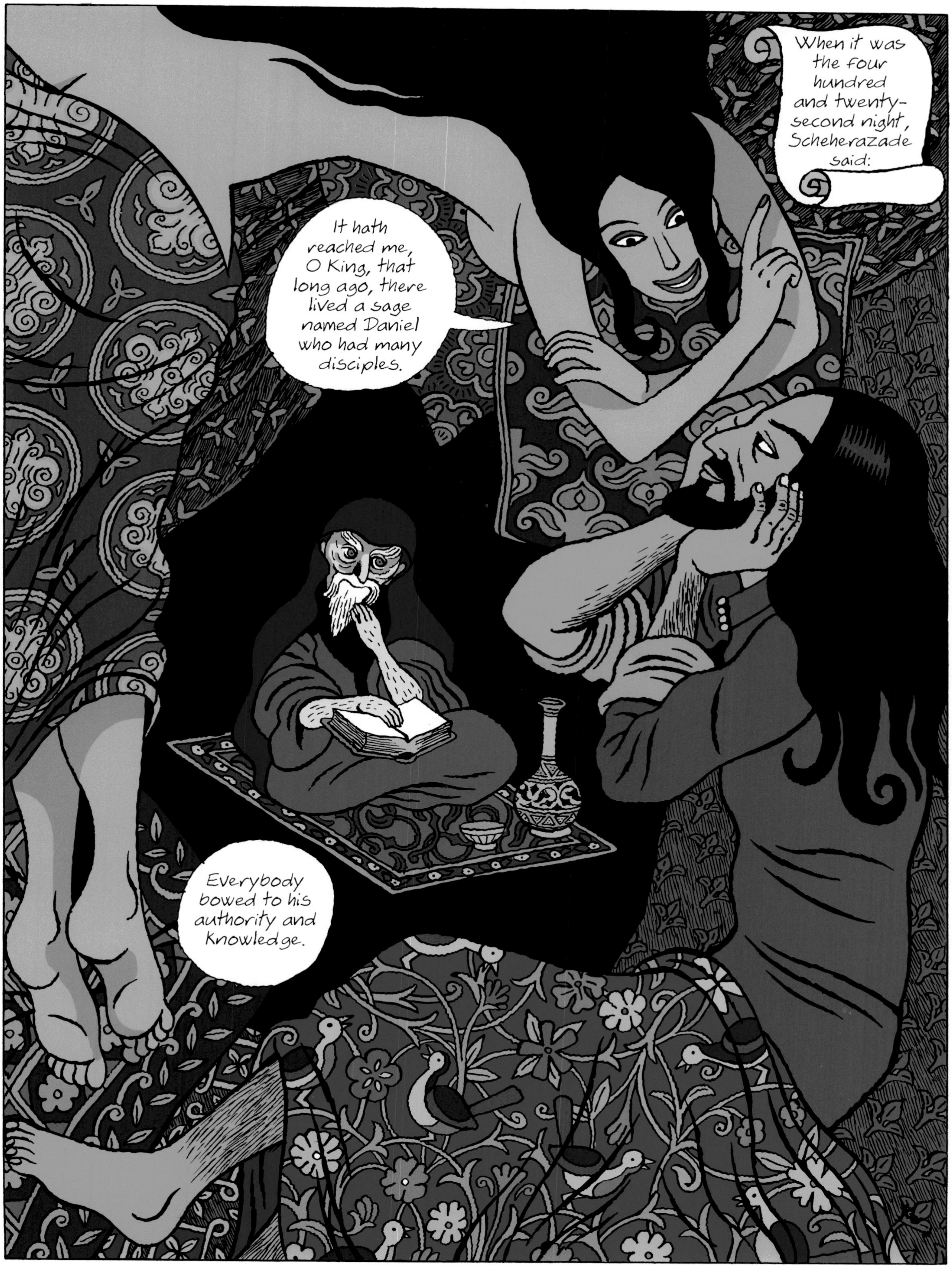
When it was the four hundred and twenty-second night, Scheherazade said:
It hath reached me, O King, that long ago, there lived a sage named Daniel who had many disciples.
Everybody bowed to his authority and knowledge.
1

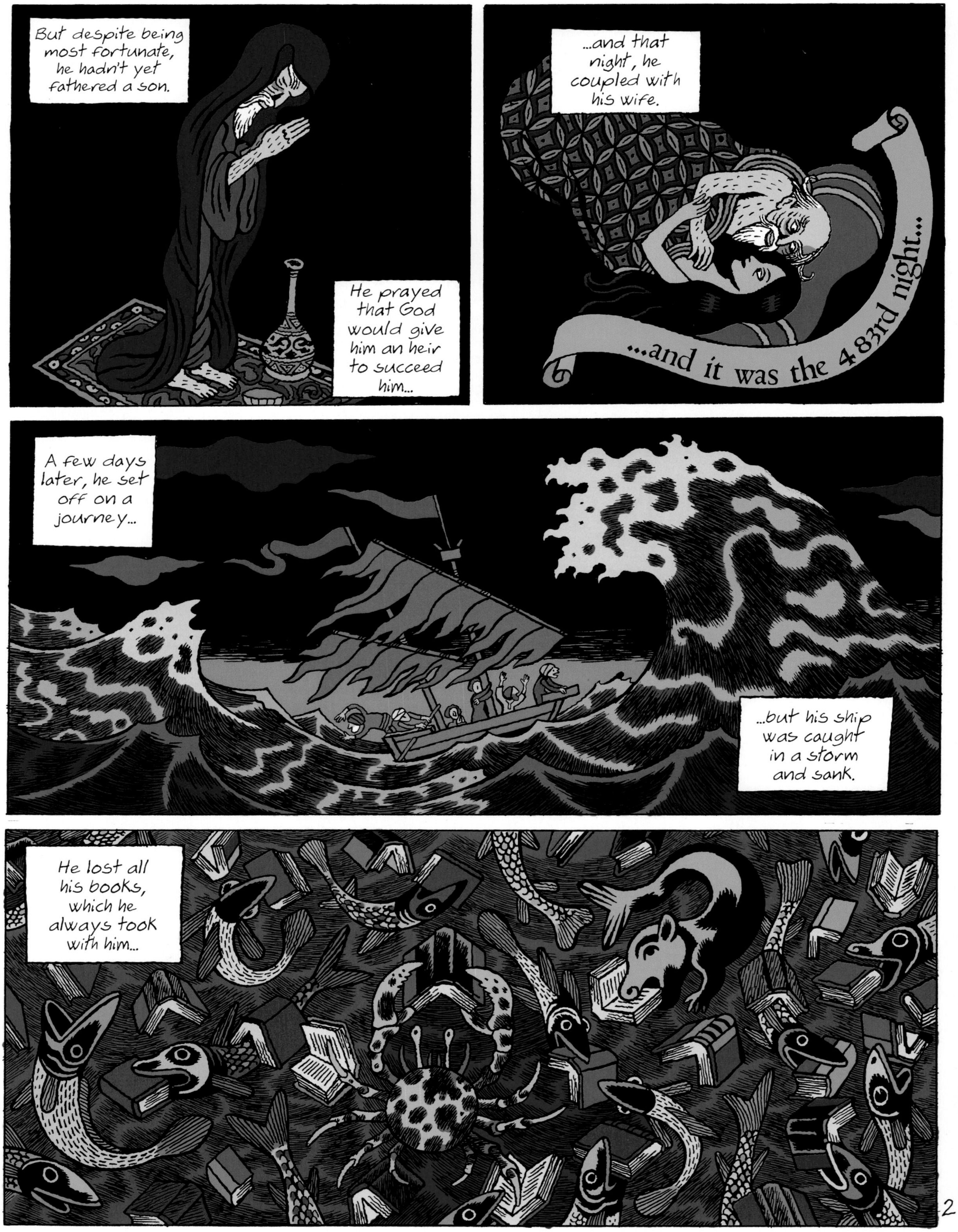
But despite being most fortunate, he hadn't yet fathered a son.
He prayed that God would give him an heir to succeed him...
...and that night, he coupled with his wife.
...and it was the 483rd night...
A few days later, he set off on a journey...
...but his ship was caught in a storm and sank.
He lost all his books, which he always took with him...

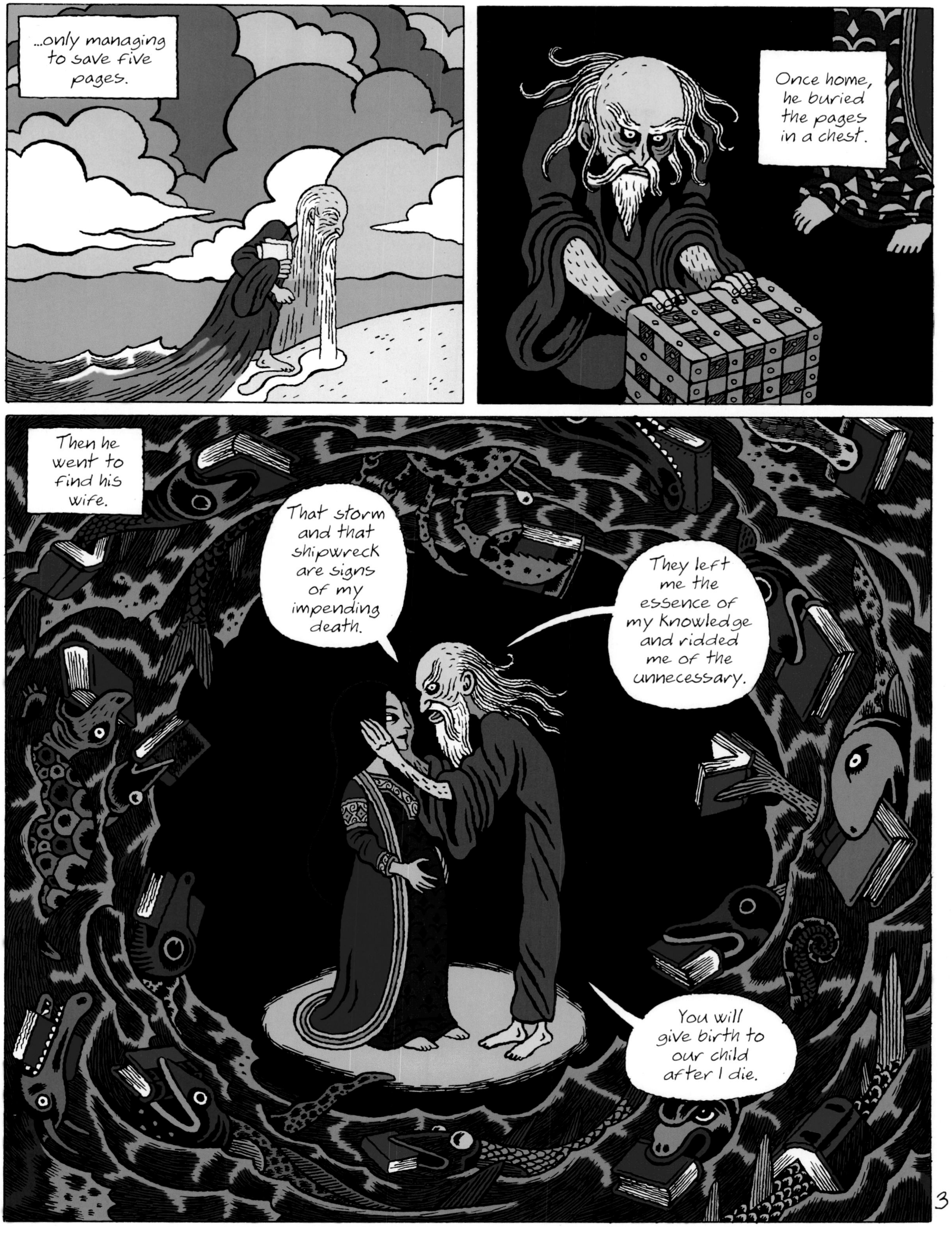
...only managing to save five pages.
Once home, he buried the pages in a chest.
Then he went to find his wife.
That storm and that shipwreck are signs of my impending death.
They left me the essence of my knowledge and ridded me of the unnecessary.
You will give birth to our child after I die.
3

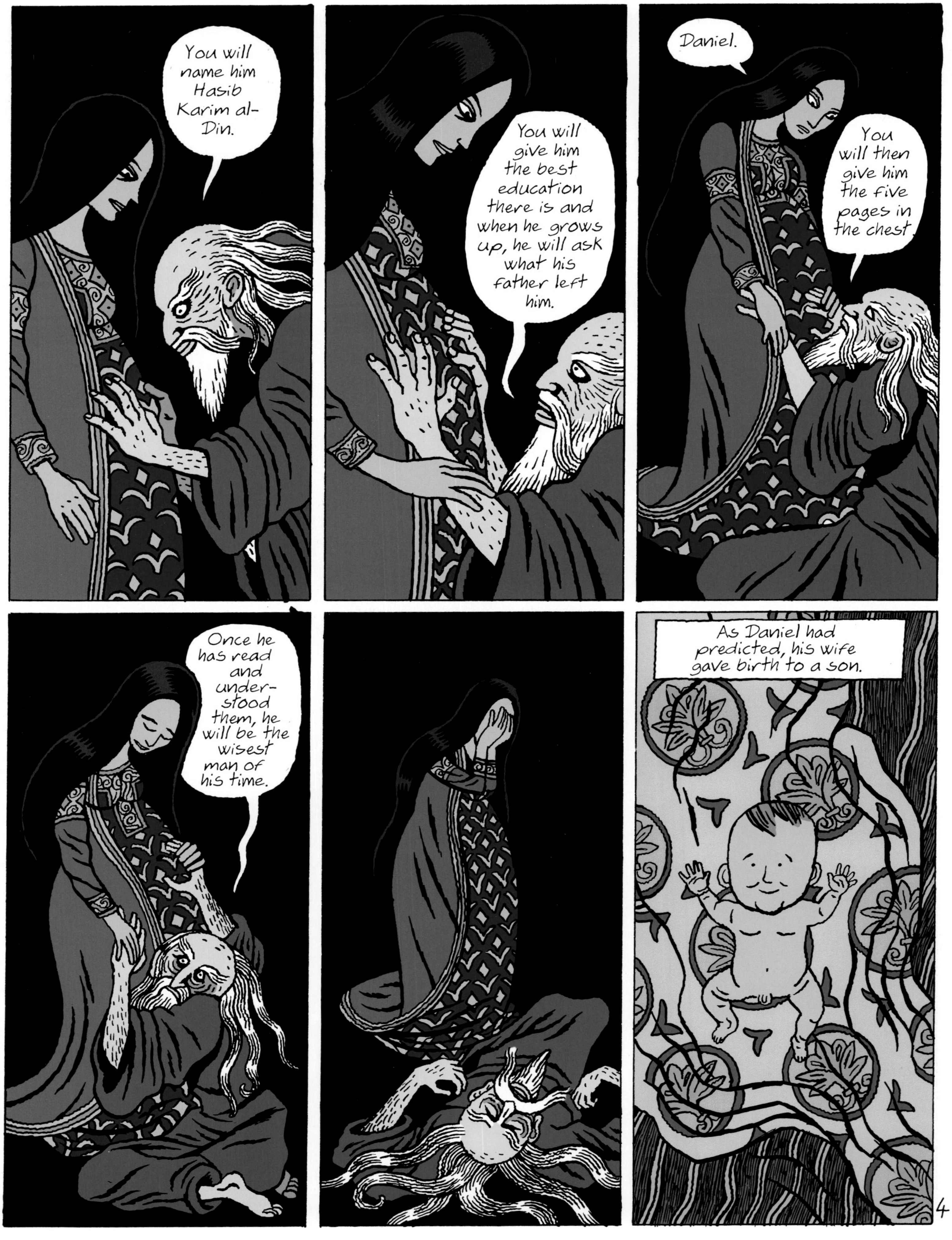

You will name him Hasib Karim al-Din.
You will give him the best education there is and when he grows up, he will ask what his father left him.
Daniel.
You will then give him the five pages in the chest.
Once he has read and under-stood them, he will be the wisest man of his time.
As Daniel had predicted, his wife gave birth to a son.
4

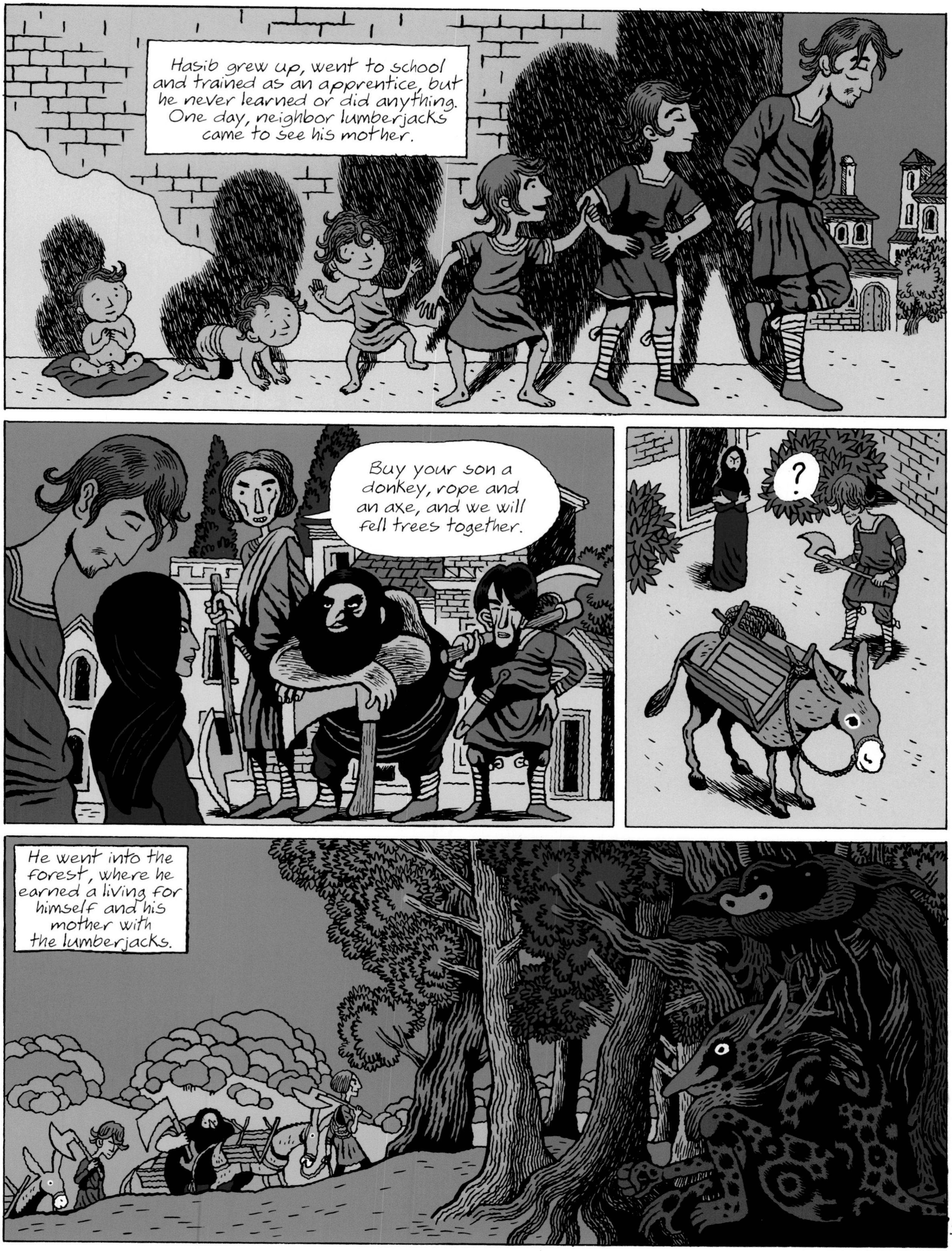
Hasib grew up, went to school and trained as an apprentice, but he never learned or did anything. One day, neighbor lumberjacks came to see his mother.
Buy your son a donkey, rope and an axe, and we will fell trees together.
?
He went into the forest, where he earned a living for himself and his mother with the lumberjacks.

5

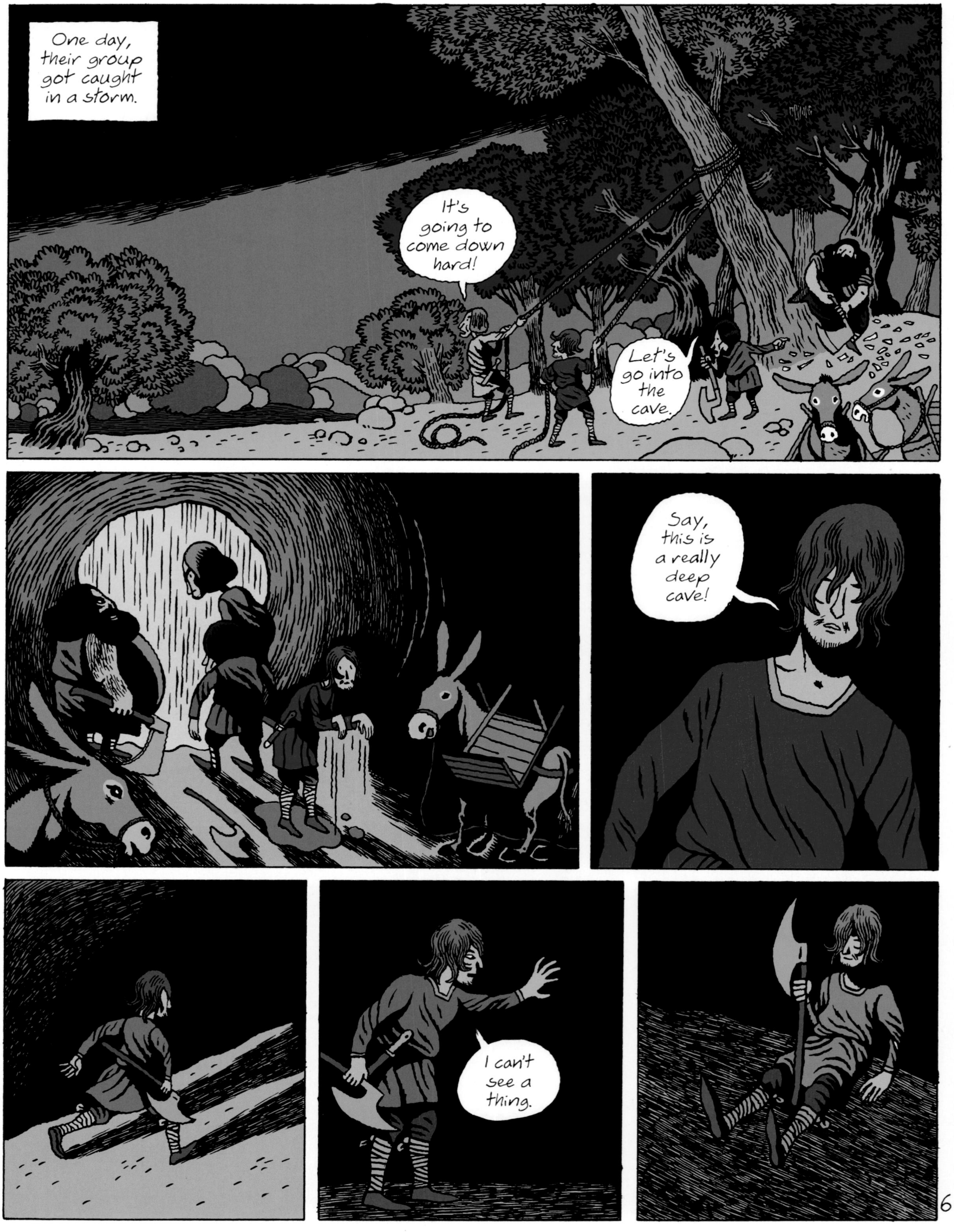
One day, their group got caught in a storm.
It's going to come down hard!
Let's go into the cave.
Say, this is a really deep cave!
I can't see a thing.

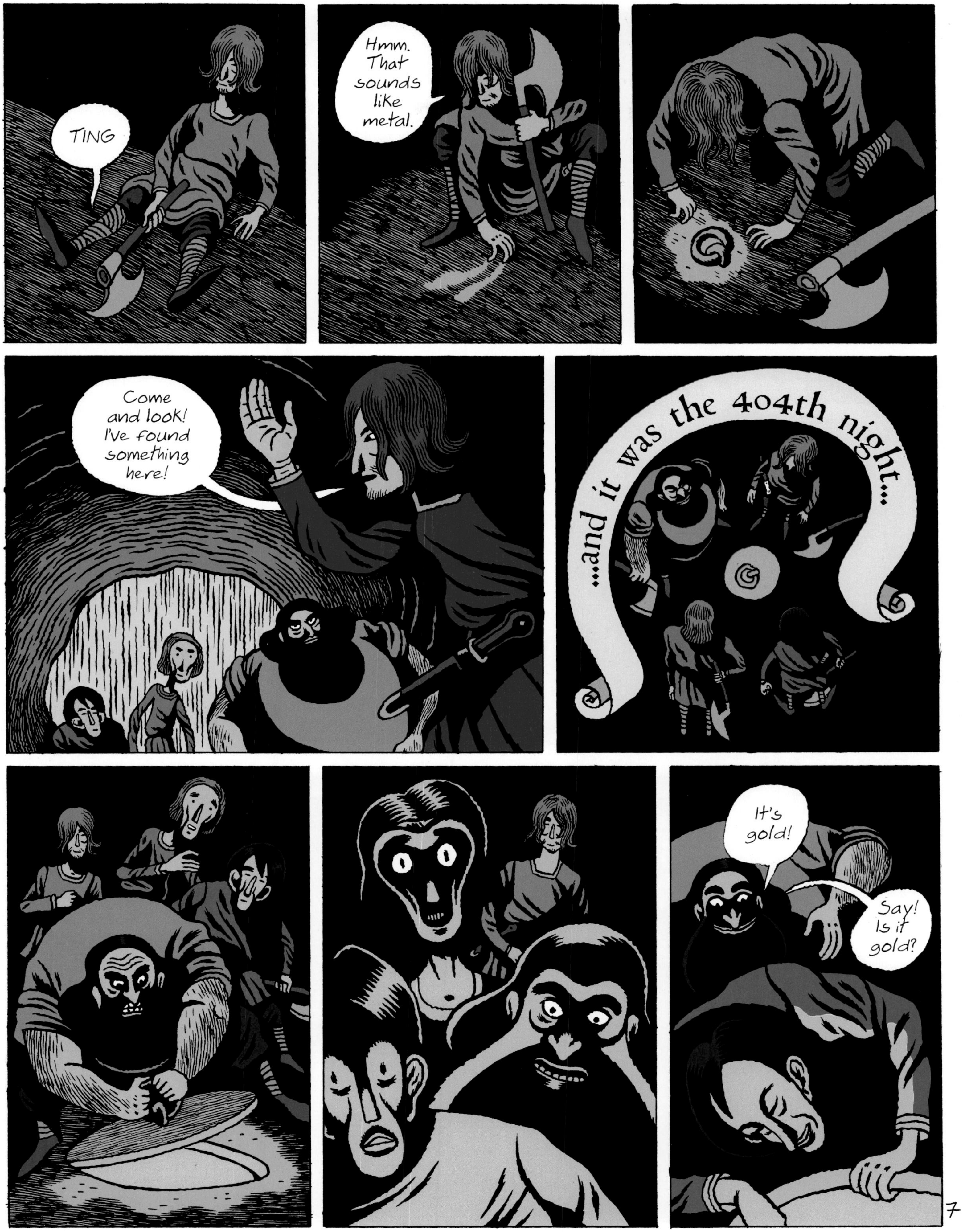
TING
Hmm. That sounds like metal.
Come and look! I've found something here!
...and it was the 404th night...
It's gold!
Say! Is it gold?
7

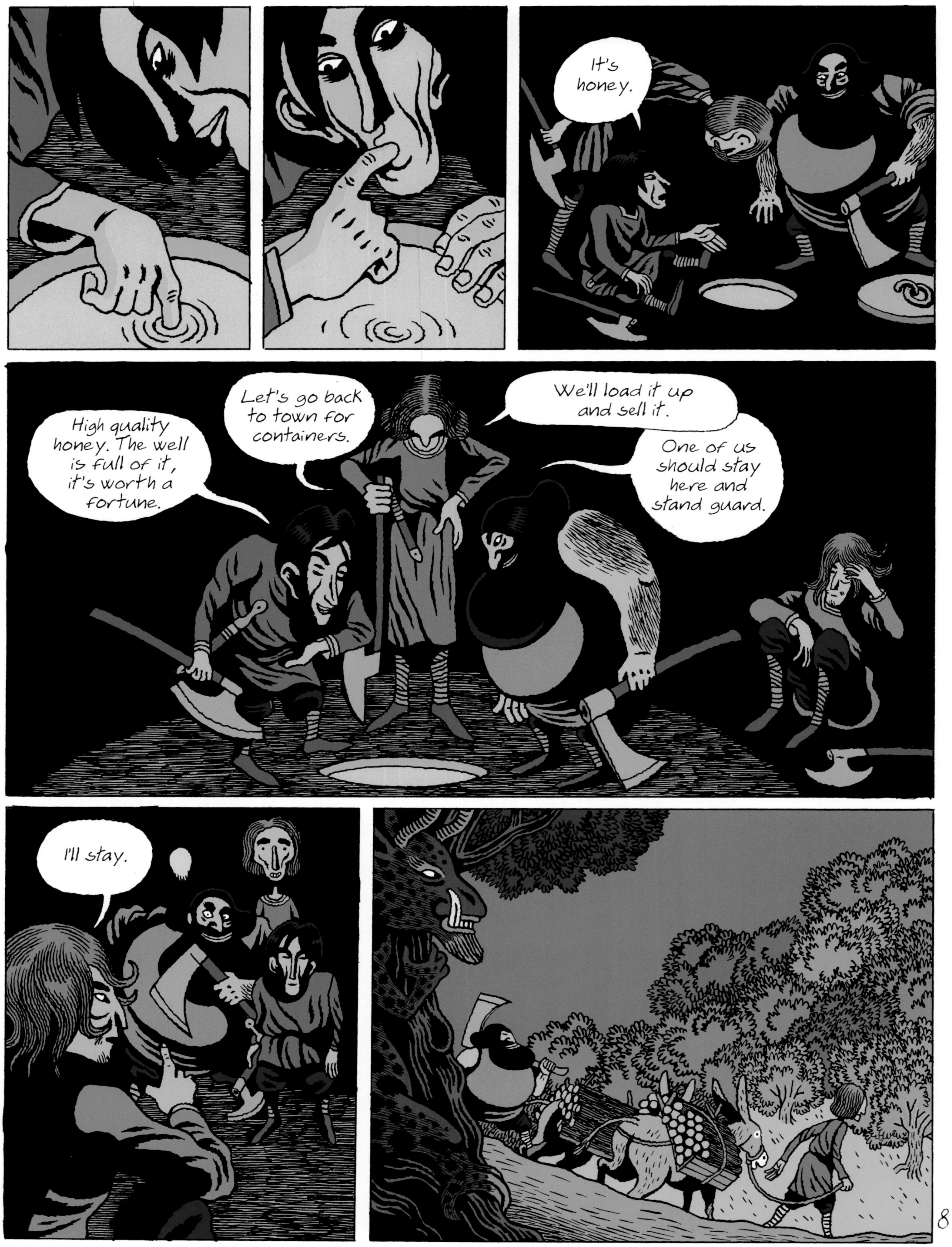
It's honey.
High quality honey. The well is full of it, it's worth a fortune.
Let's go back to town for containers.
We'll load it up and sell it.
One of us should stay here and stand guard.
I'll stay.
8

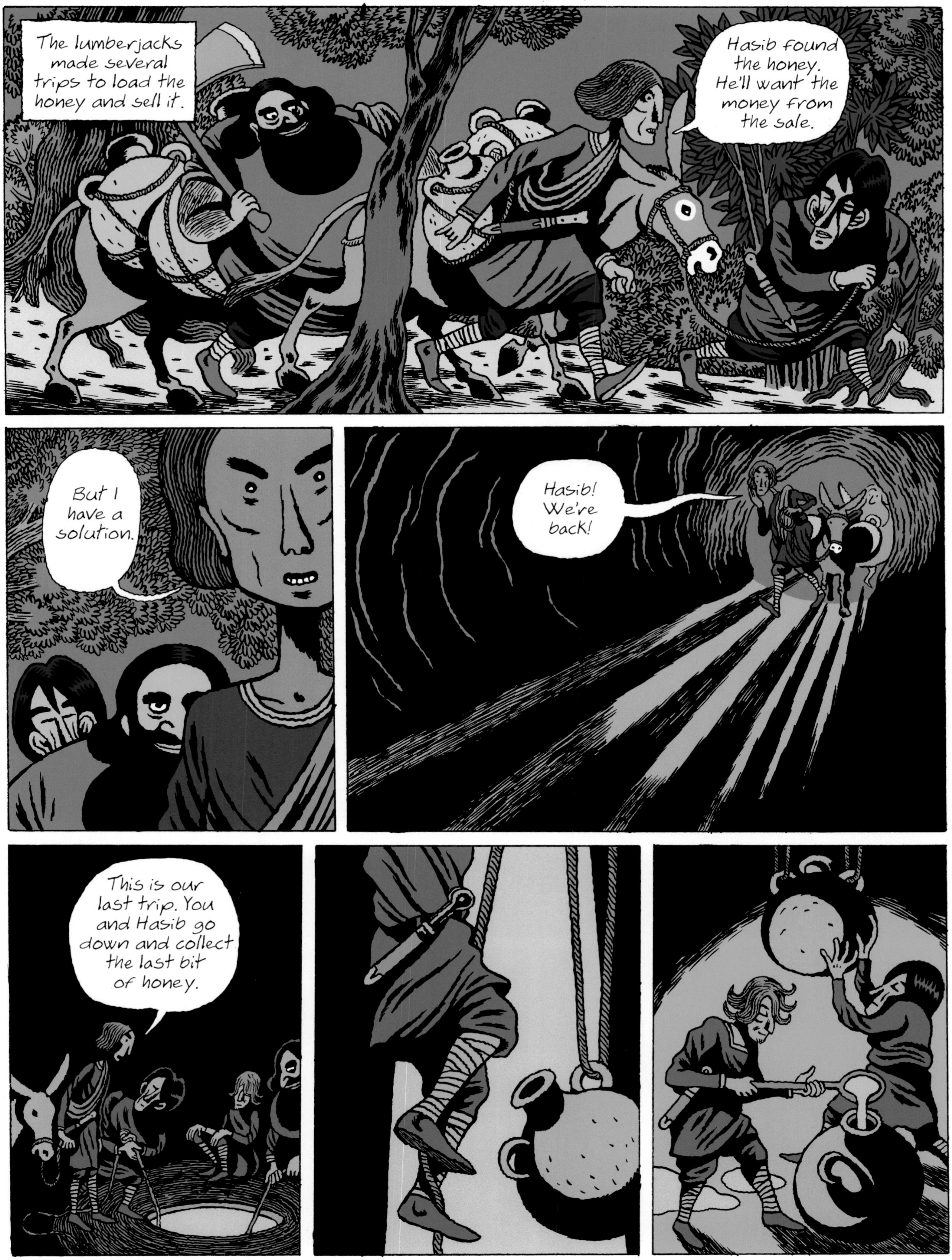
The lumberjacks made several trips to load the honey and sell it.
Hasib found the honey. He'll want the money from the sale.
But I have a solution.
Hasib! We're back!
This is our last trip. You and Hasib go down and collect the last bit of honey.
9

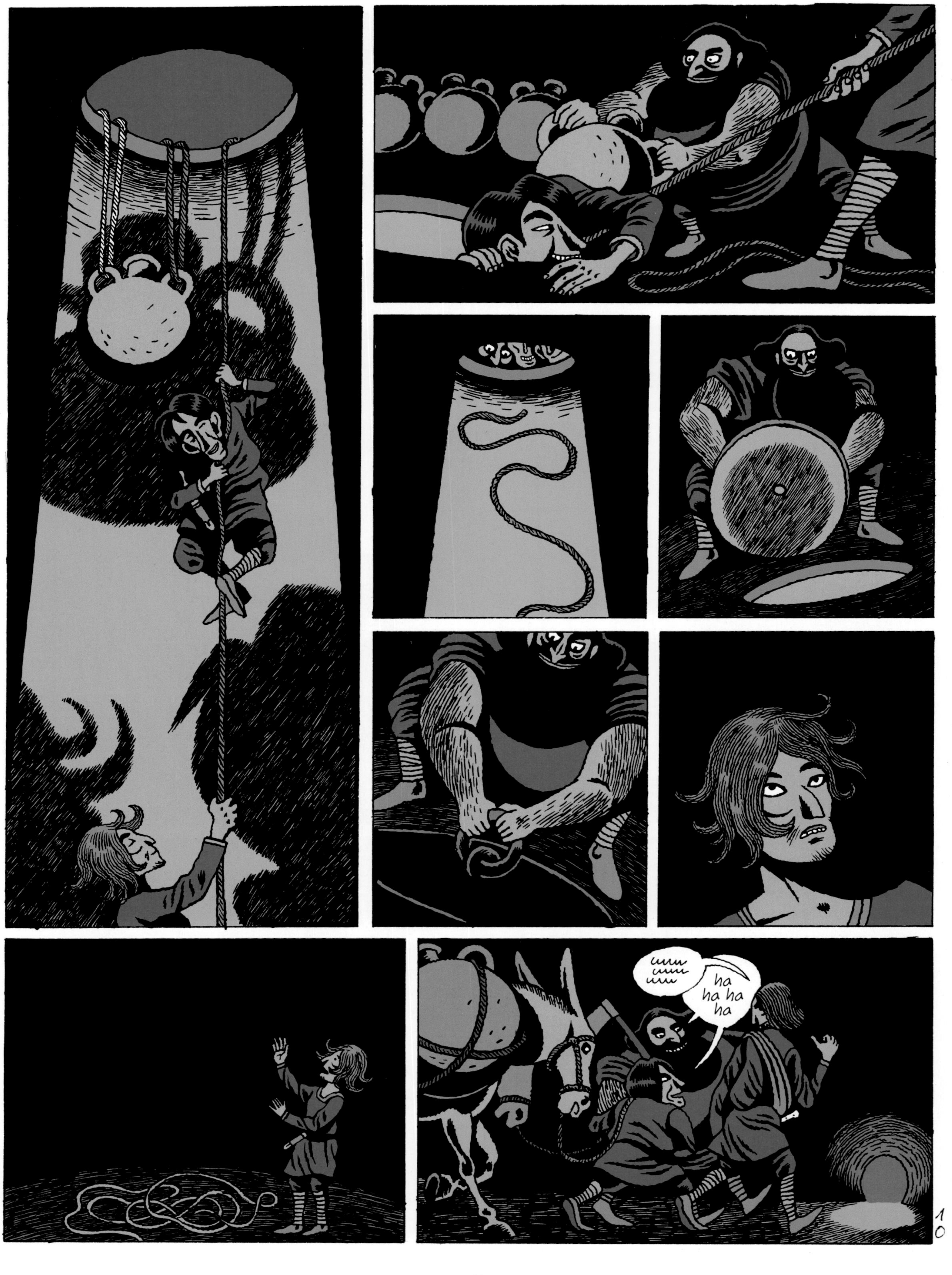
uuuu
uuuu
uuu
ha
ha ha ha
ha

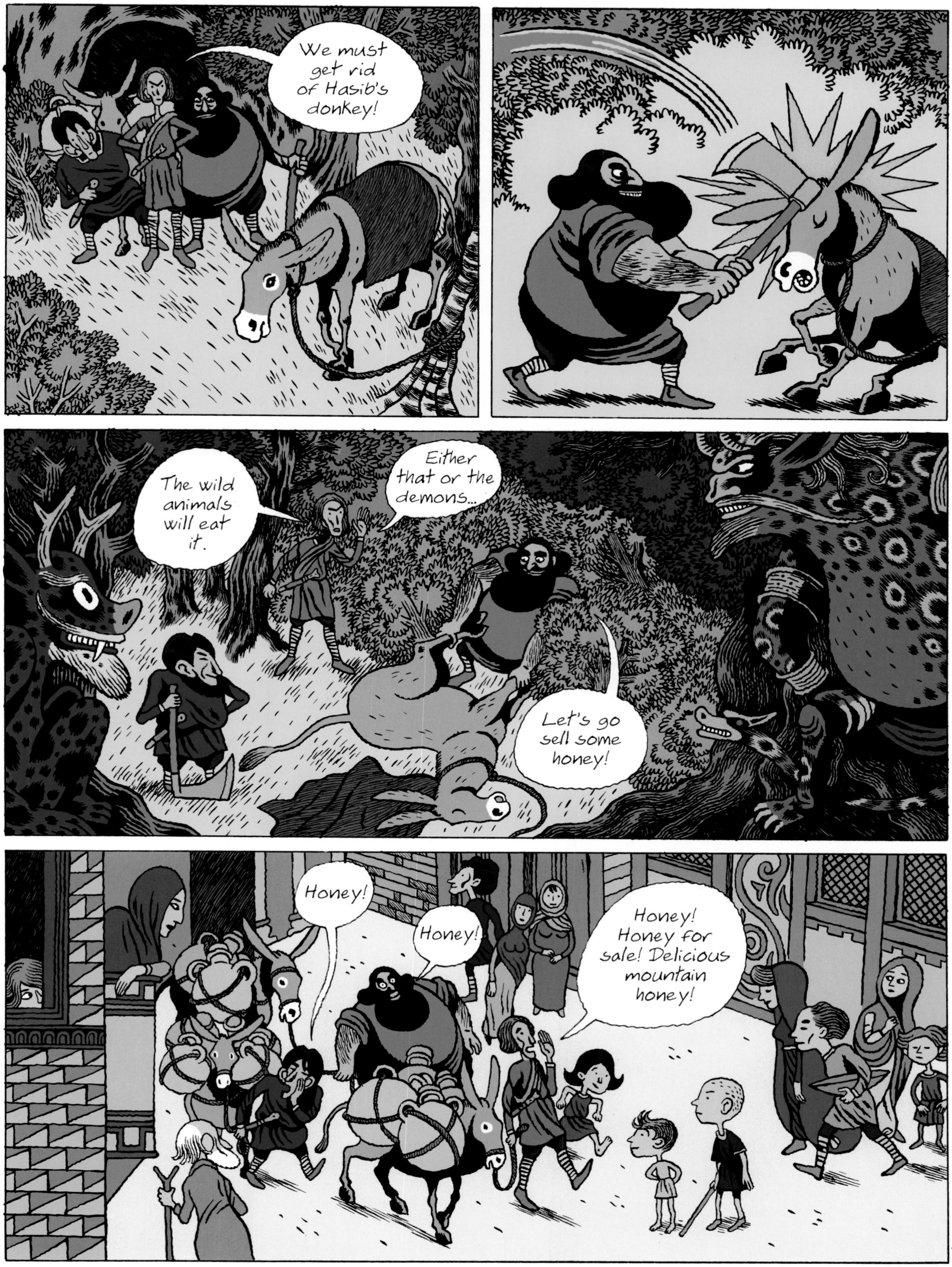
We must get rid of Hasib's donkey!
The wild animals will eat it.
Either that or the demons...
Let's go sell some honey!
Honey!
Honey!
Honey! Honey for sale! Delicious mountain honey!

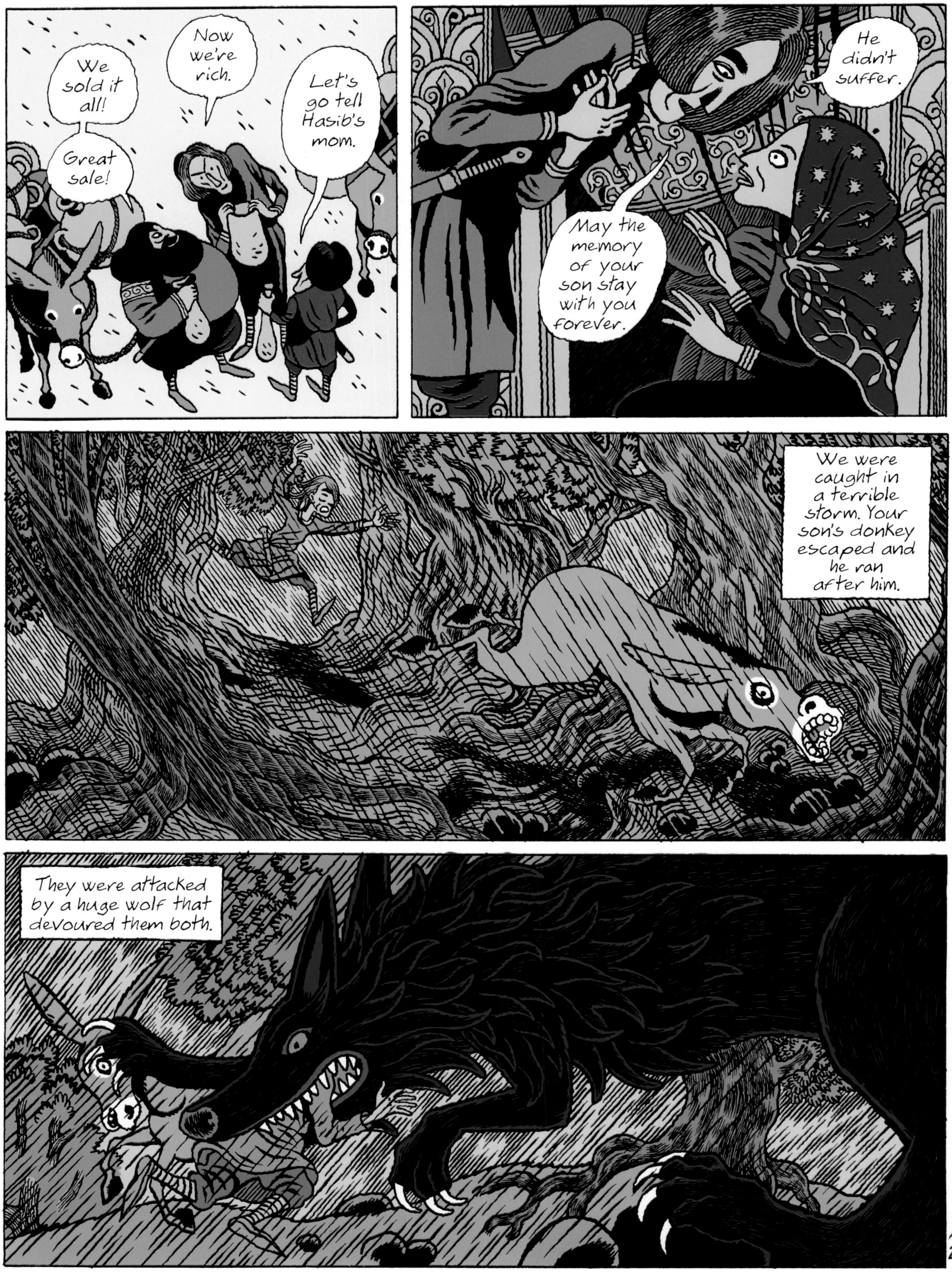
We sold it all!
Great sale!
Now we're rich.
Let's go tell Hasib's mom.
He didn't suffer.
May the memory of your son stay with you forever.
We were caught in a terrible storm. Your son's donkey escaped and he ran after him.
They were attacked by a huge wolf that devoured them both.

12

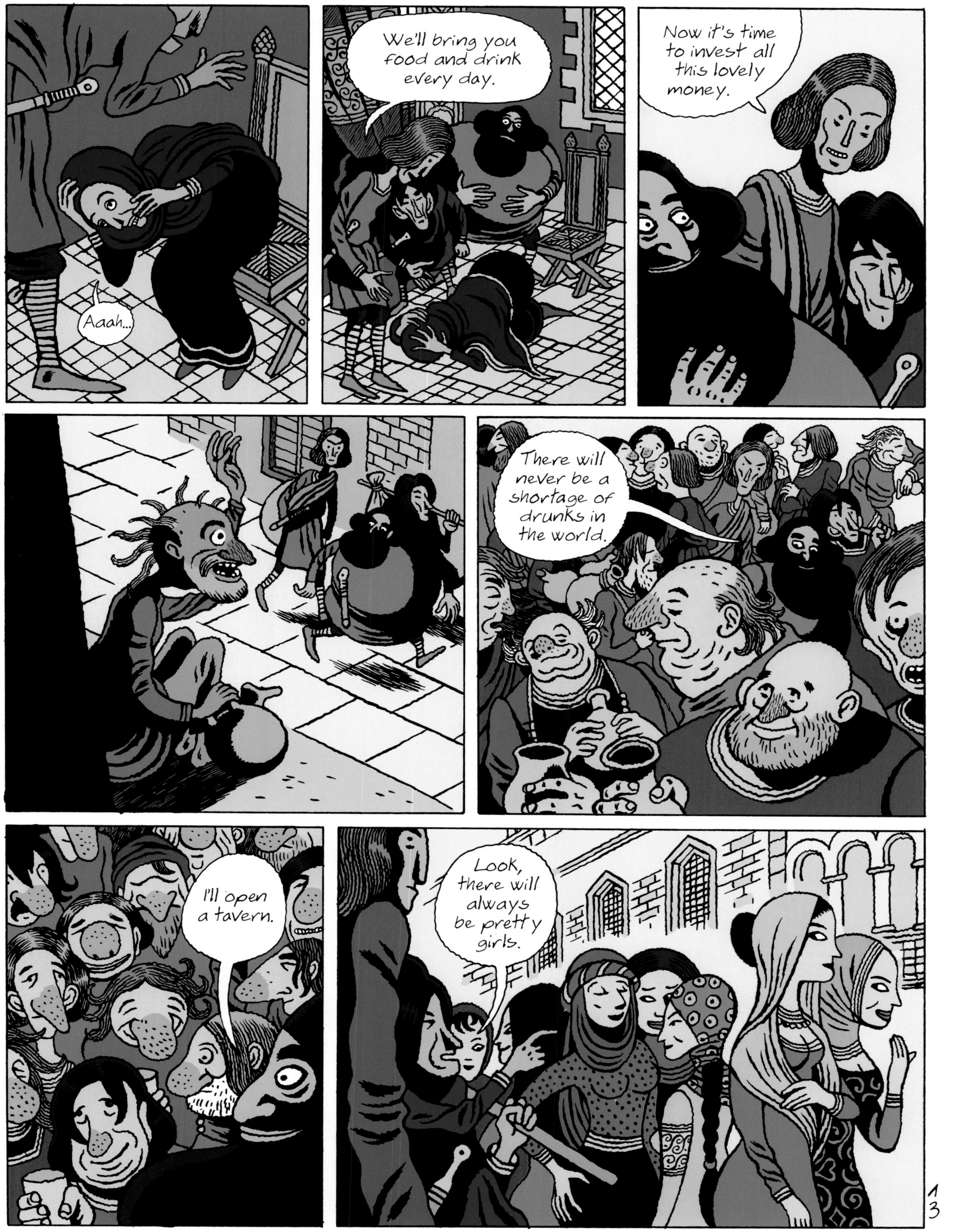
Aaah...
We'll bring you food and drink every day.
Now it's time to invest all this lovely money.
There will never be a shortage of drunks in the world.
I'll open a tavern.
Look, there will always be pretty girls.
13

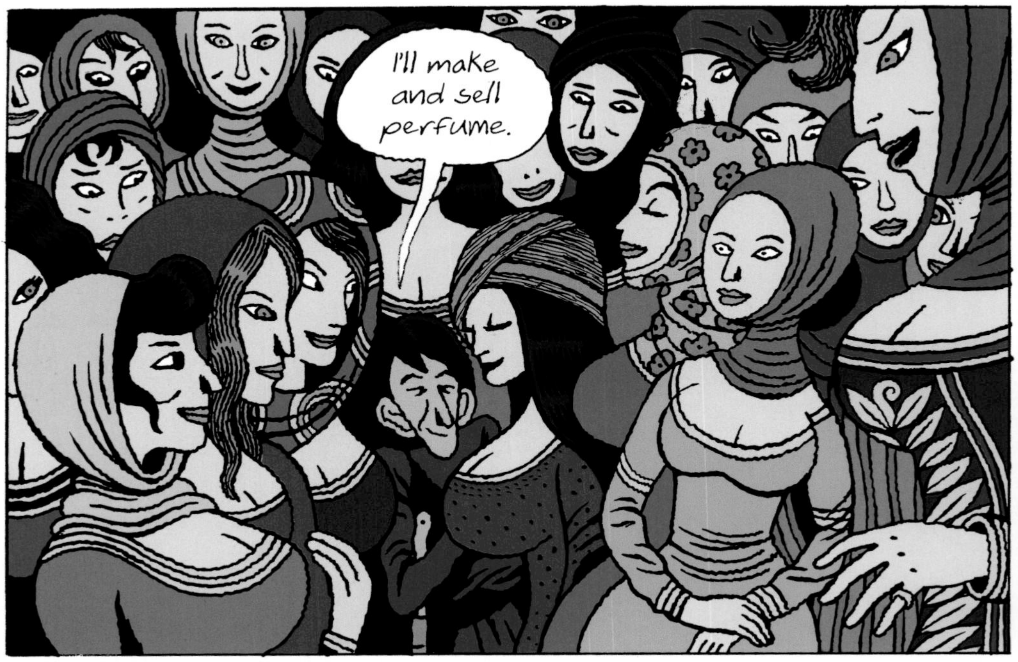
I'll make and sell perfume.
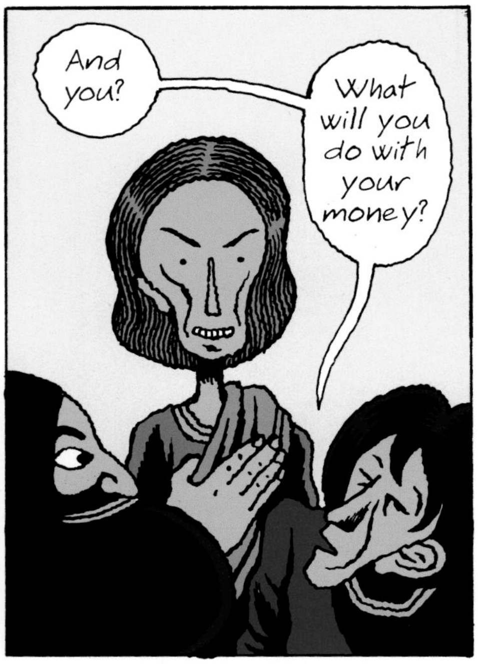
And you?
What will you do with your money?
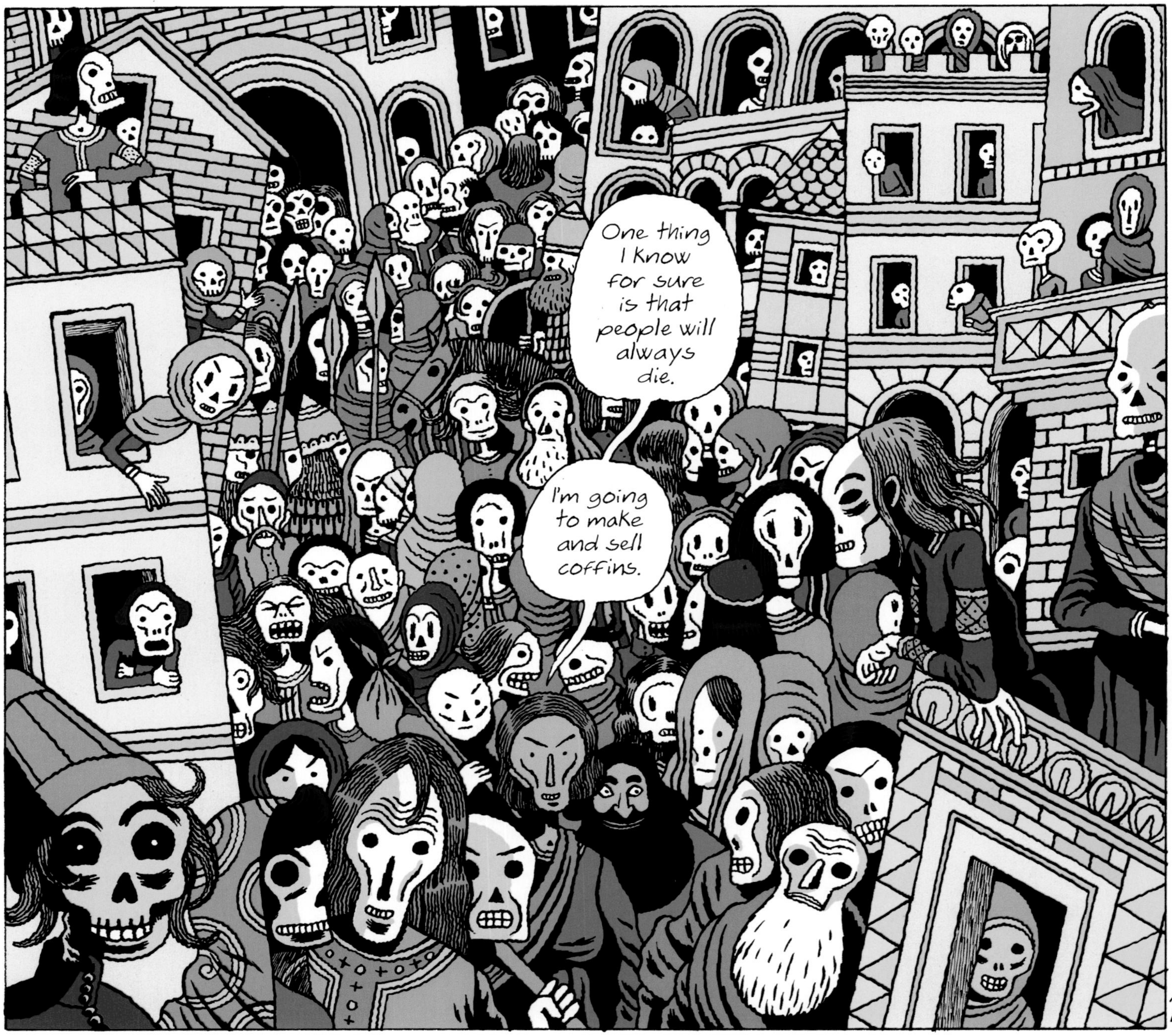
One thing I know for sure is that people will always die.
I'm going to make and sell coffins.

14

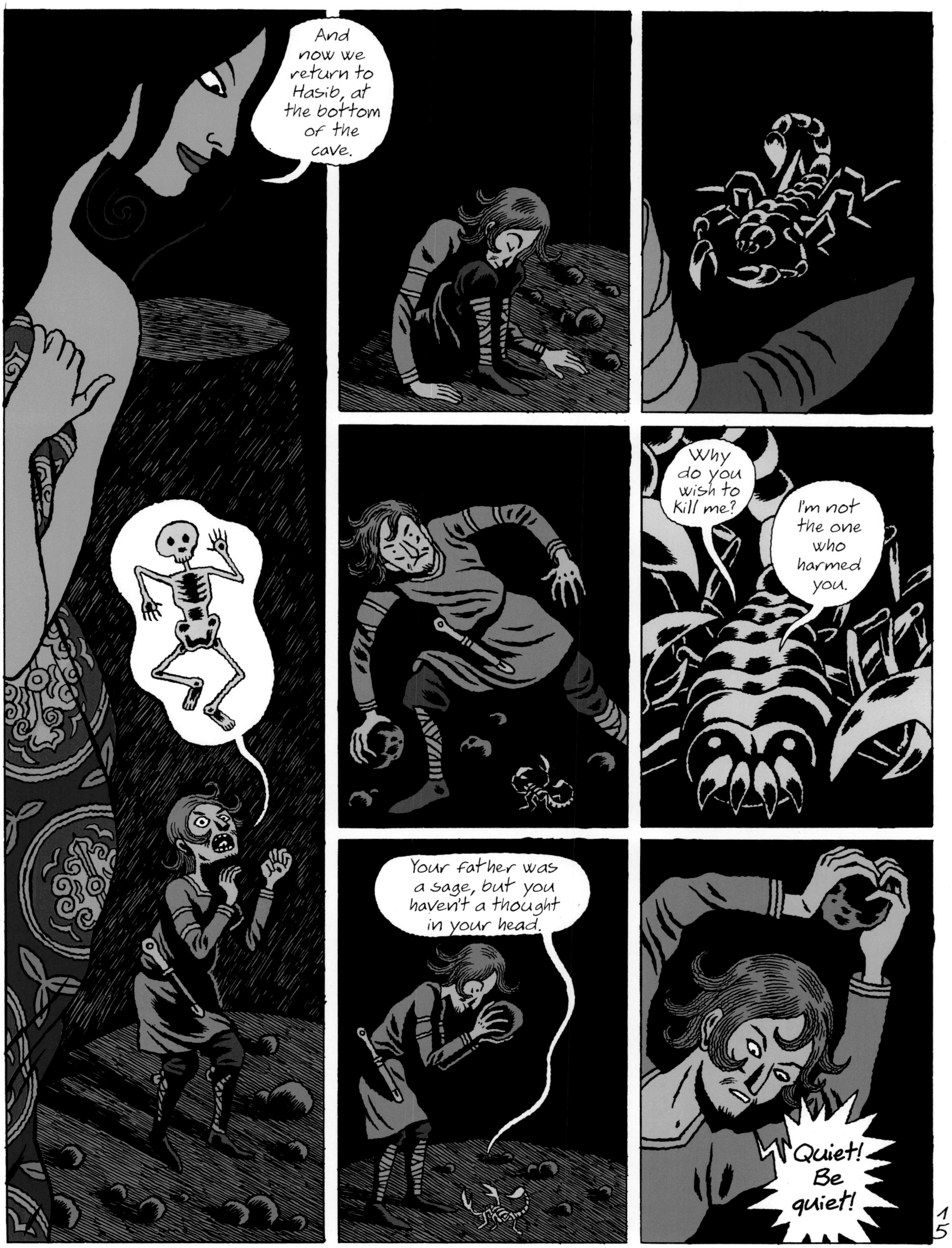
And now we return to Hasib, at the bottom of the cave.
Why do you wish to kill me?
I'm not the one who harmed you.
Your father was a sage, but you haven't a thought in your head.
Quiet! Be quiet!
15

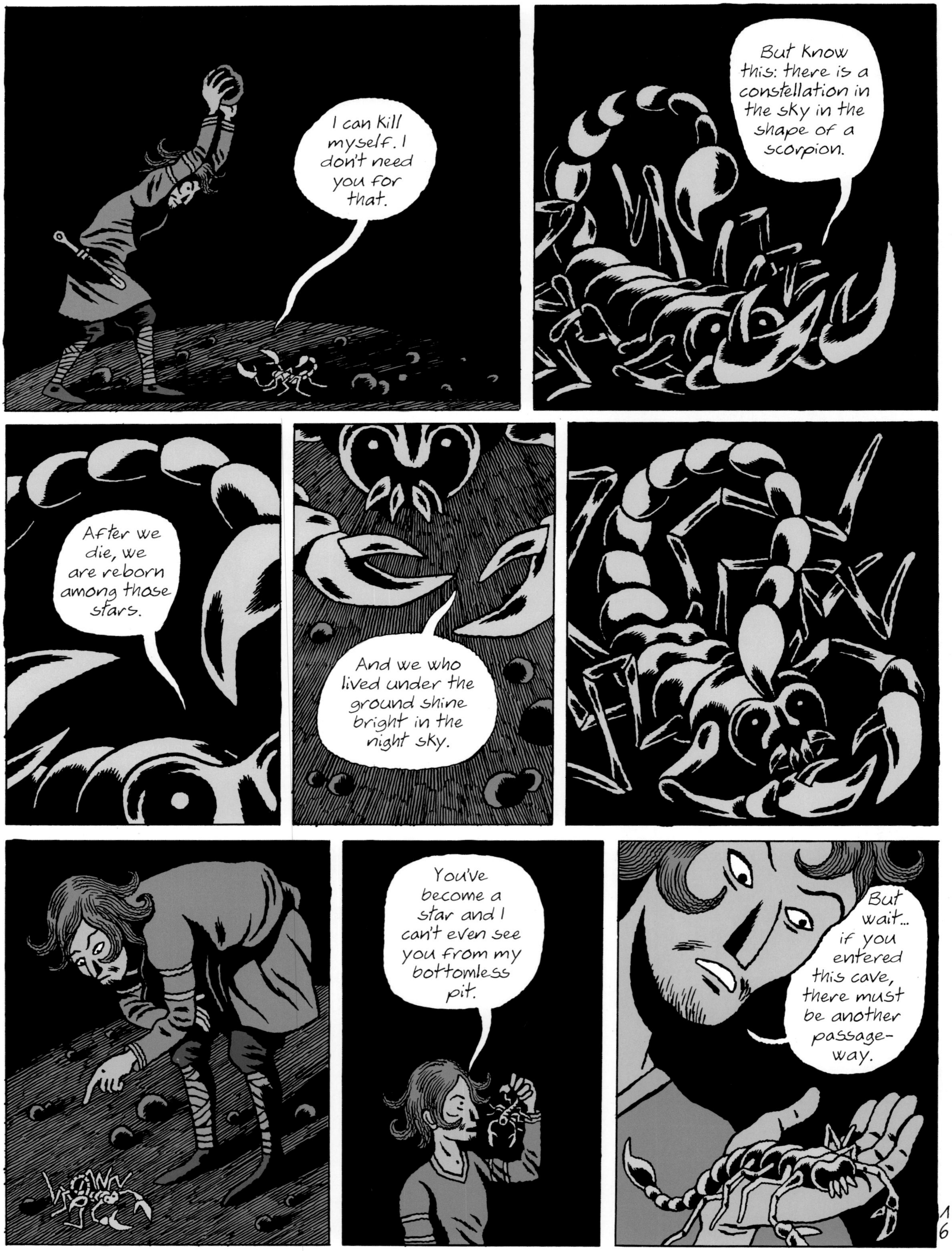

I can Kill myself. I don't need you for that.
But know this: there is a constellation in the sky in the shape of a scorpion.
After we die, we are reborn among those stars.
And we who lived under the ground shine bright in the night sky.
You've become a star and I can't even see you from my bottomless pit.
But wait... if you entered this cave, there must be another passage-way.

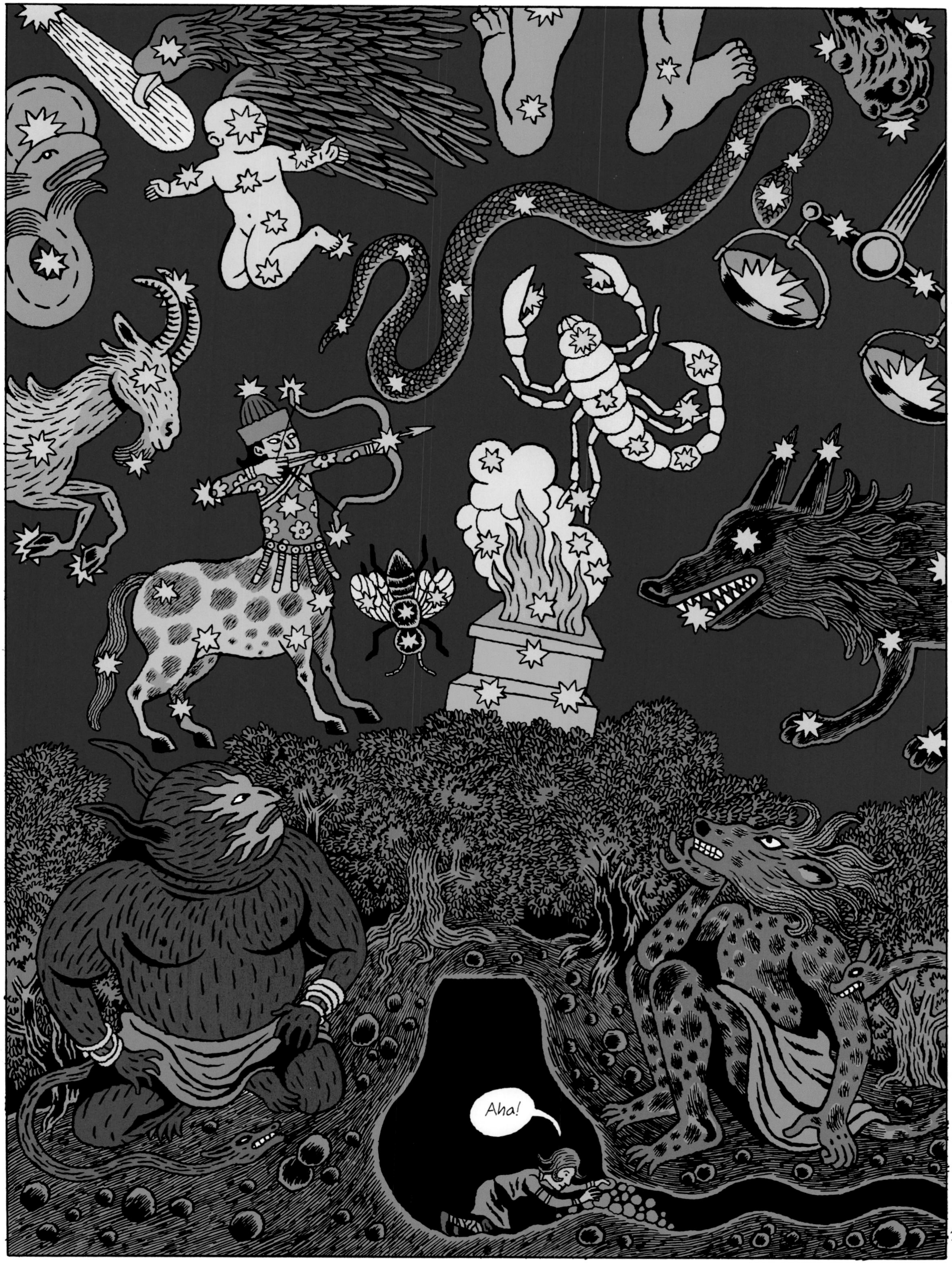
Aha!

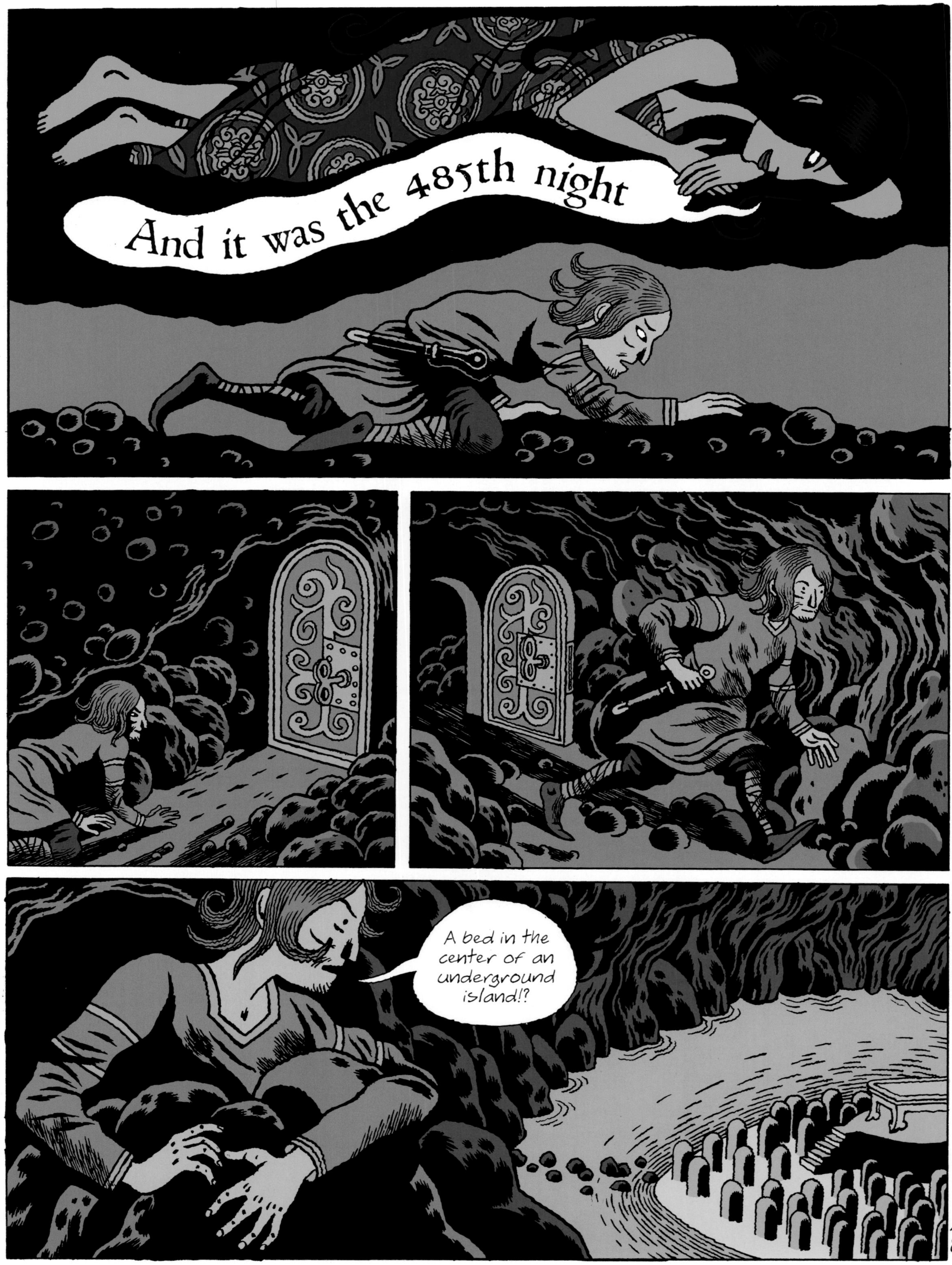
And it was the 485th night
A bed in the center of an underground island!?

18

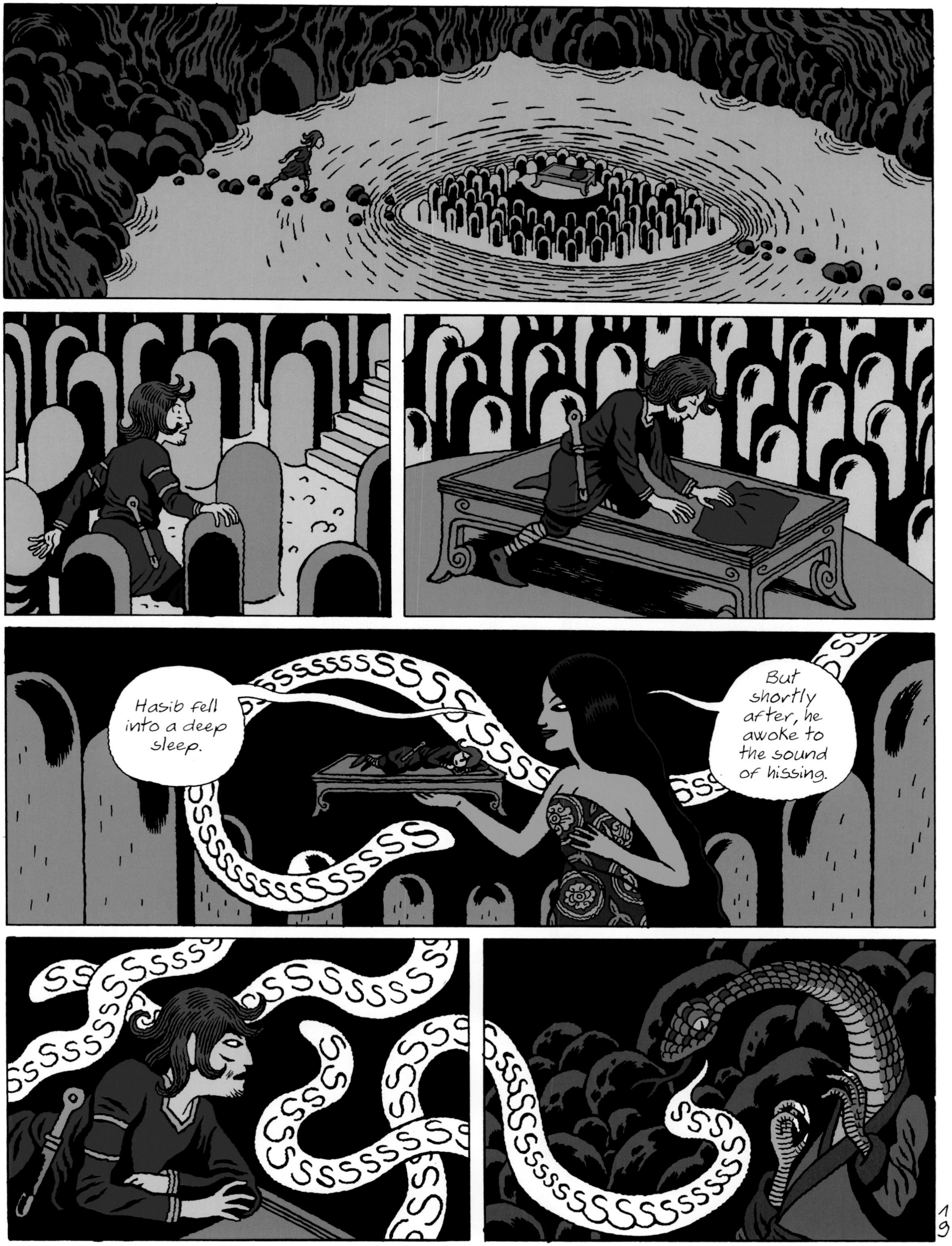
Hasib fell into a deep sleep.
But shortly after, he awoke to the sound of hissing.
19

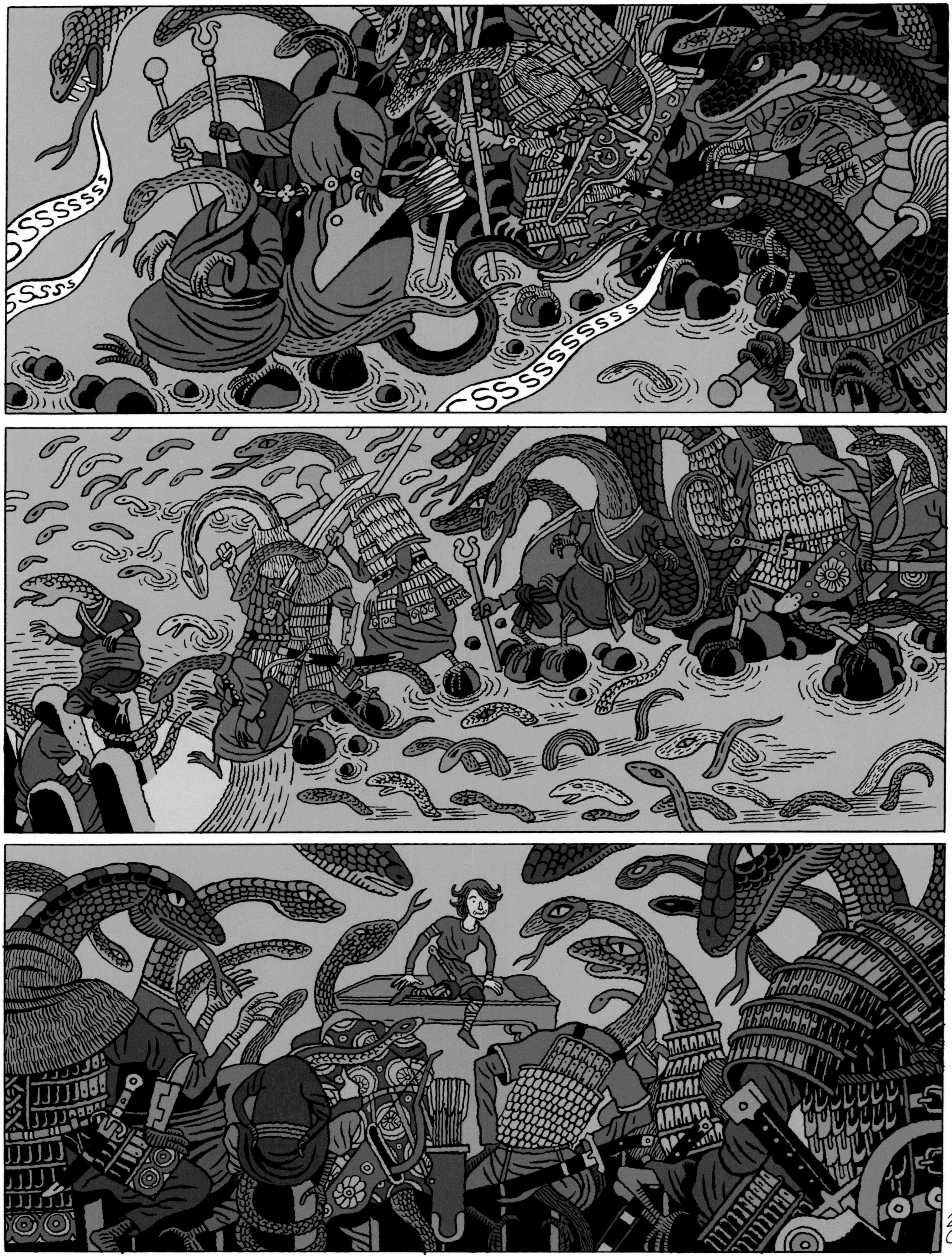
SSSSSSSSS
SSSSSs
SSSSSSSSSSSSS

20

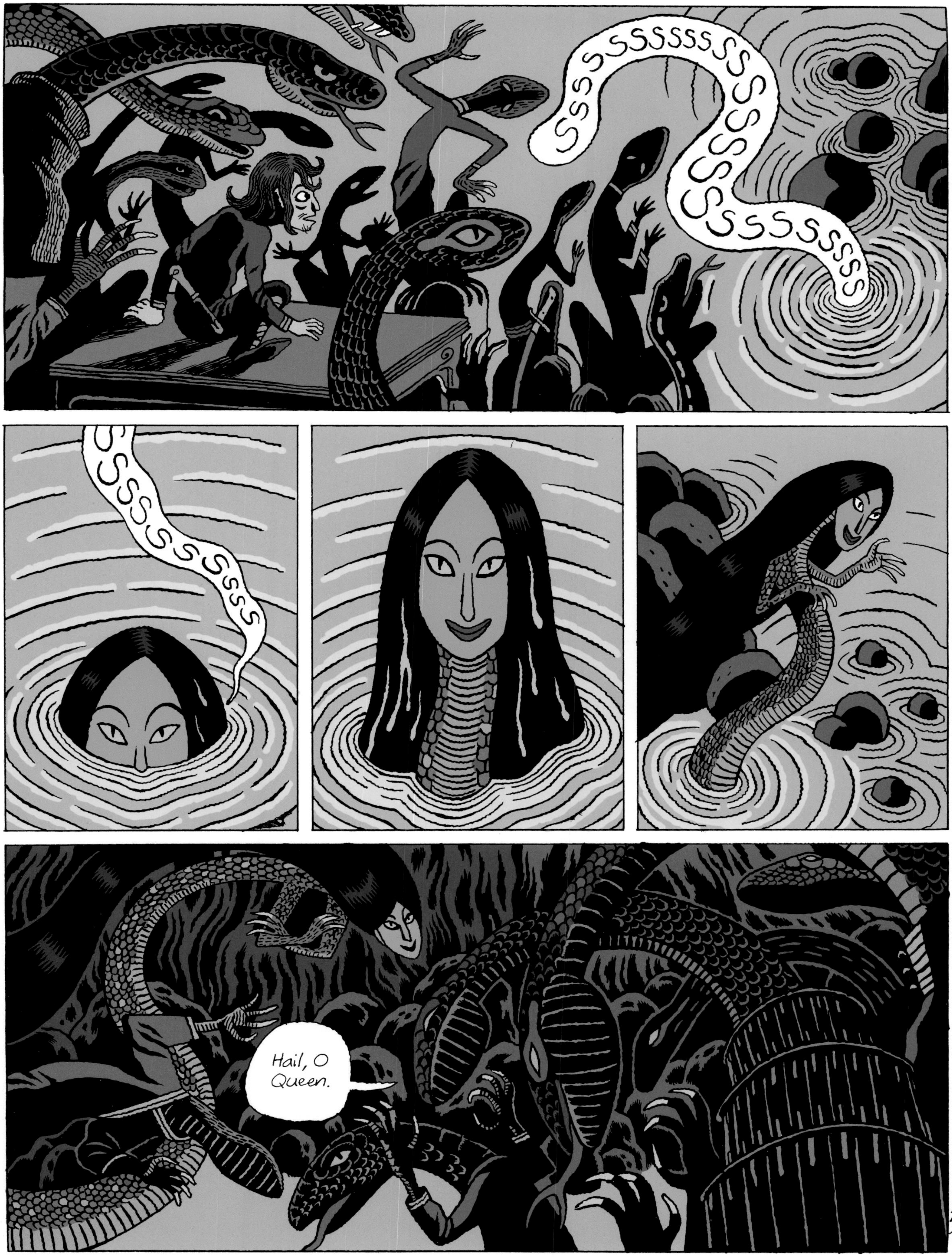
SSSSSSSSSSSSSSSSSSSSSSSSSSS
SSSSSSSSss
Hail, O Queen.
21

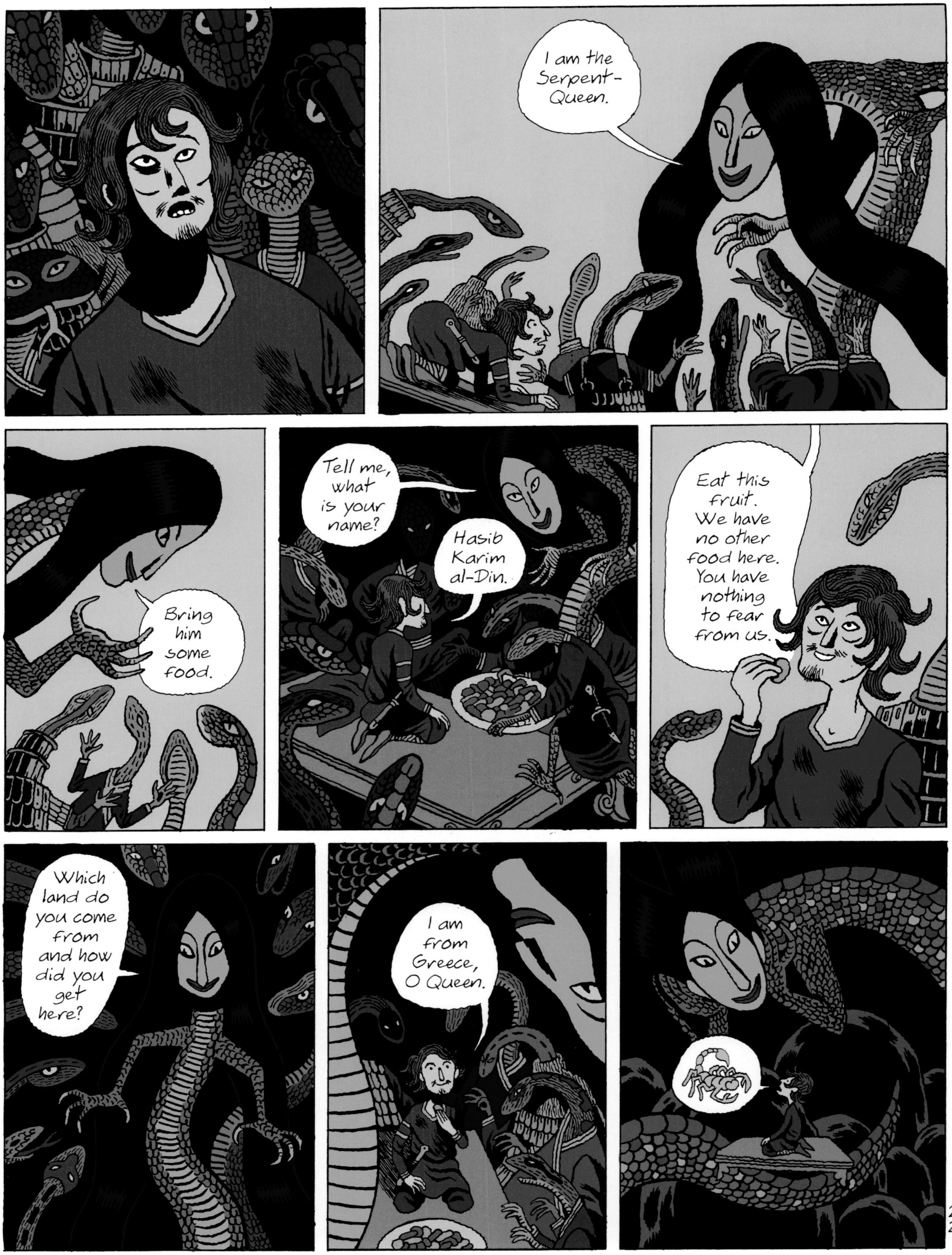
I am the Serpent-Queen.
Bring him some food.
Tell me, what is your name?
Hasib Karim al-Din.
Eat this fruit. We have no other food here. You have nothing to fear from us.
Which land do you come from and how did you get here?
I am from Greece, O Queen.
22

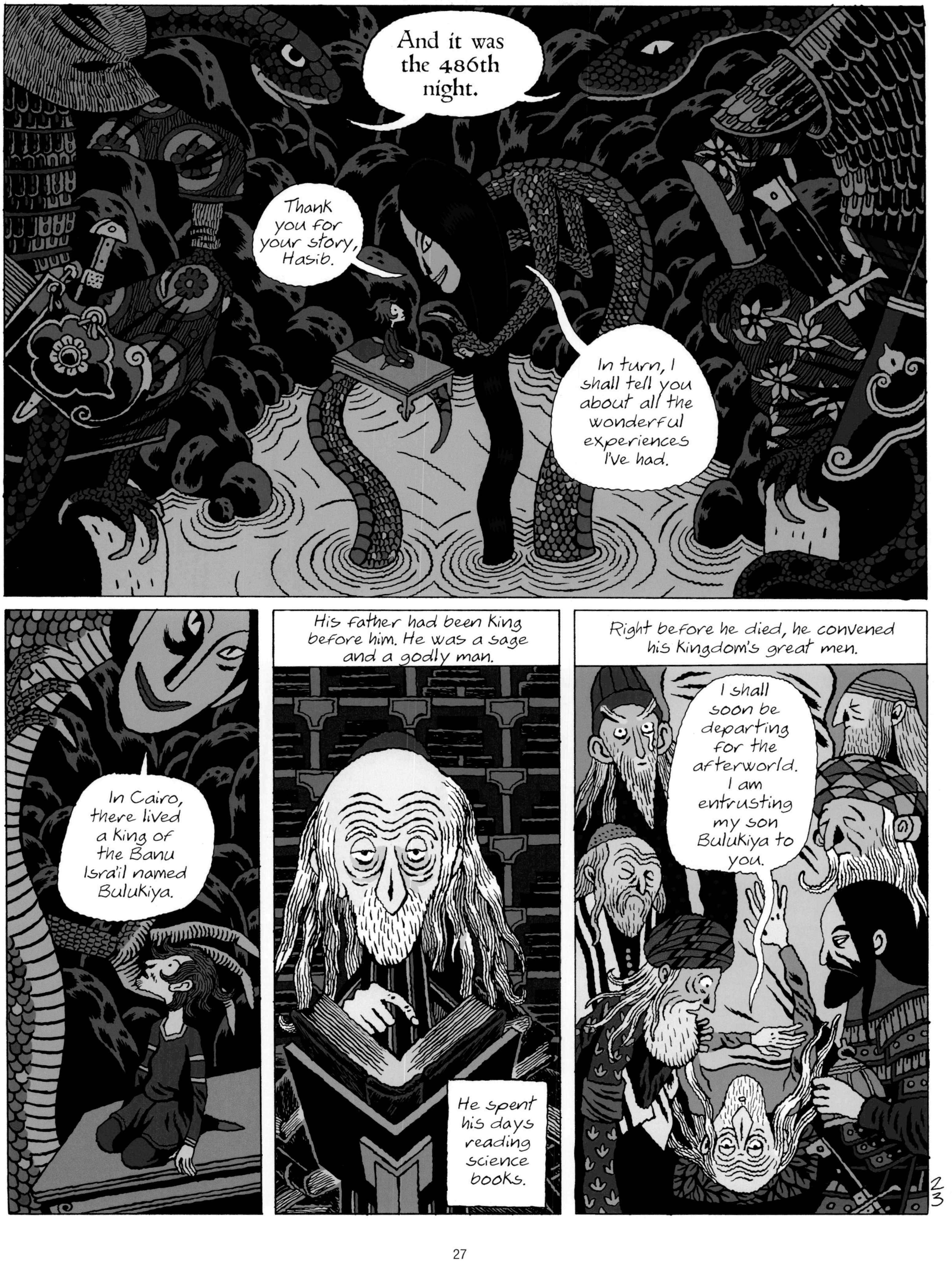
And it was the 486th night.
Thank you for your story, Hasib.
In turn, I shall tell you about all the wonderful experiences I've had.
In Cairo, there lived a King of the Banu Isra'il named Bulukiya.
His father had been King before him. He was a sage and a godly man.
He spent his days reading science books.
Right before he died, he convened his Kingdom's great men.
I shall soon be departing for the afterworld. I am entrusting my son Bulukiya to you.

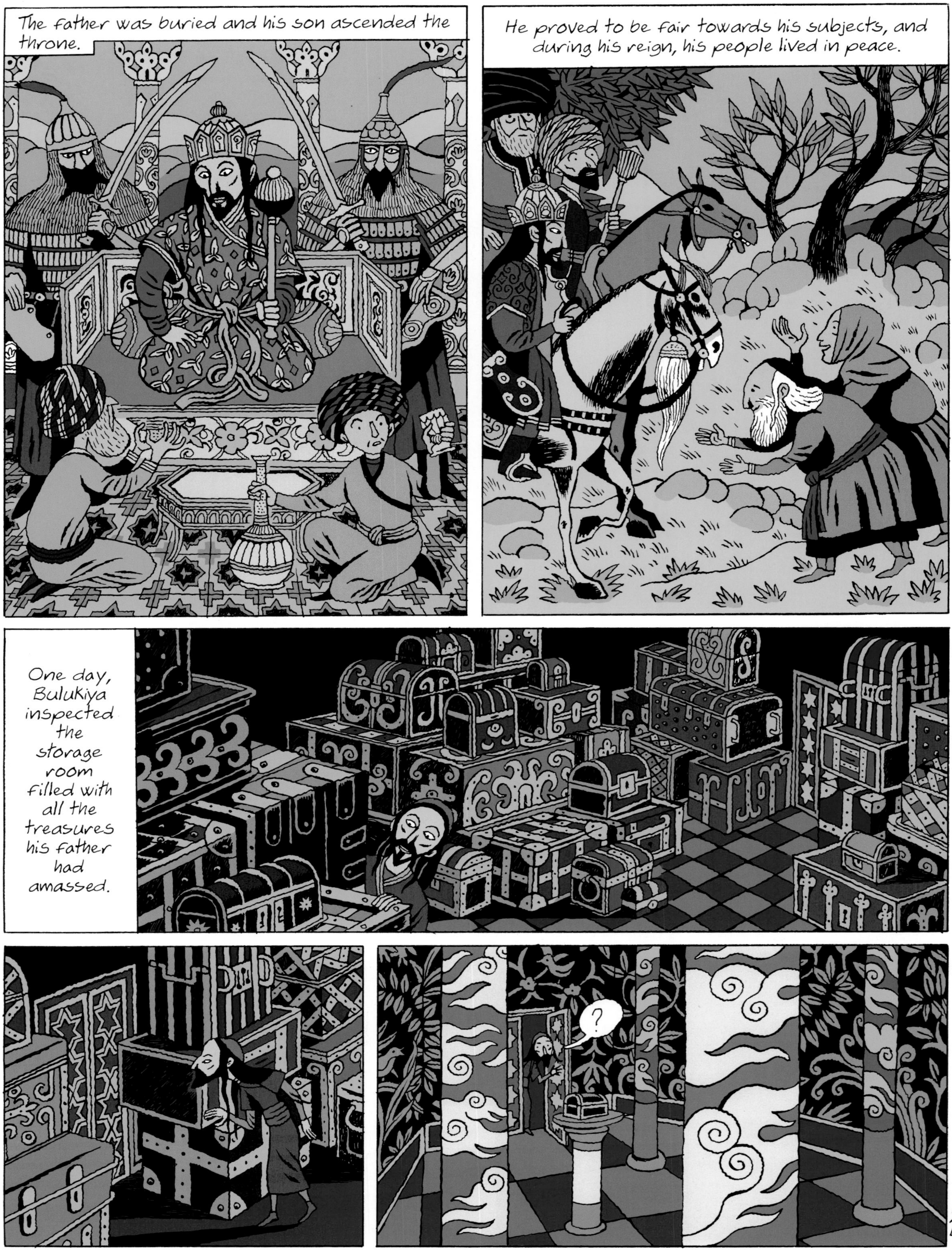
The father was buried and his son ascended the throne.
He proved to be fair towards his subjects, and during his reign, his people lived in peace.
One day, Bulukiya inspected the storage room filled with all the treasures his father had amassed.
?
24

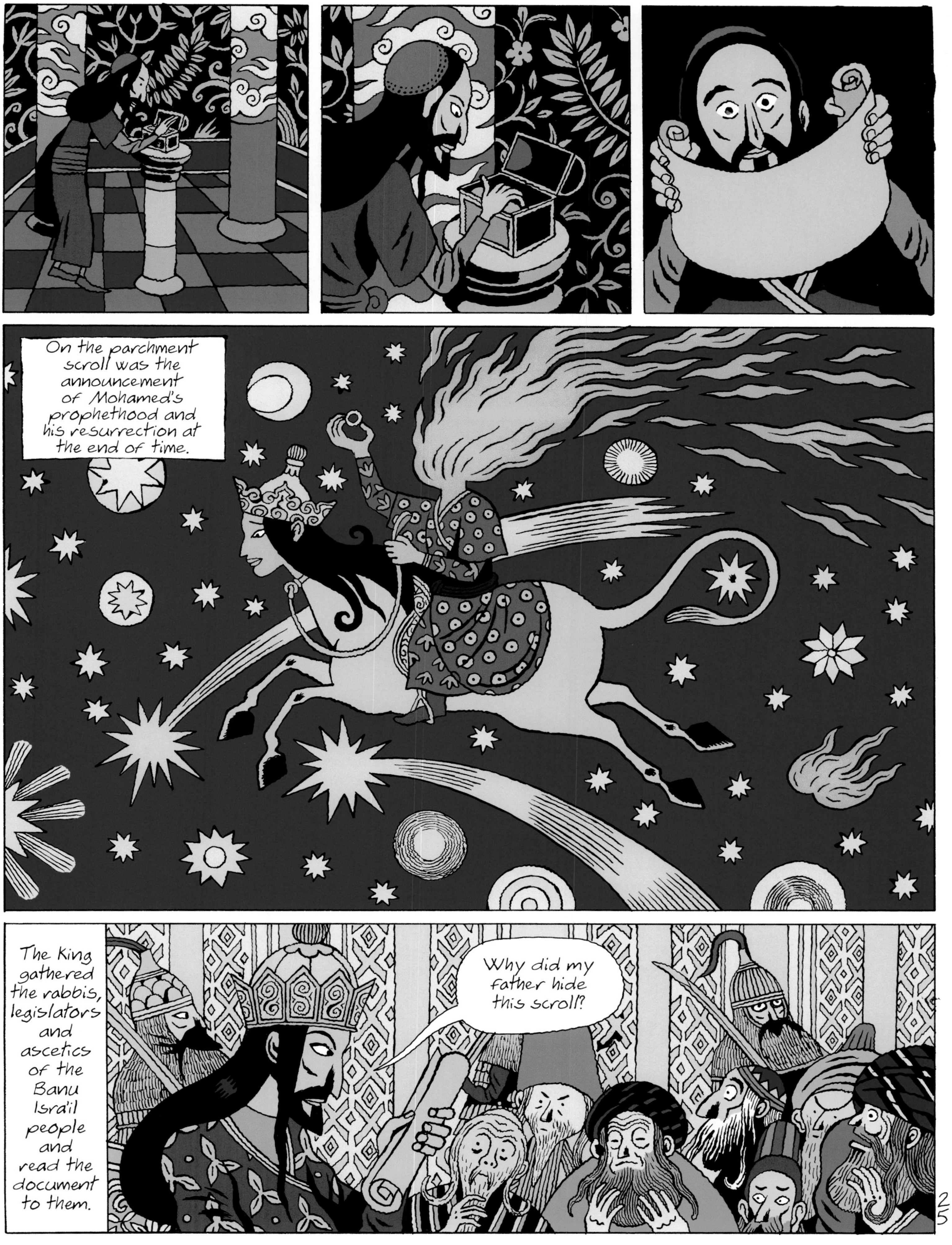
On the parchment scroll was the announcement of Mohamed's prophethood and his resurrection at the end of time.
The King gathered the rabbis, legislators and ascetics of the Banu Isra'il people and read the document to them.
Why did my father hide this scroll?
25

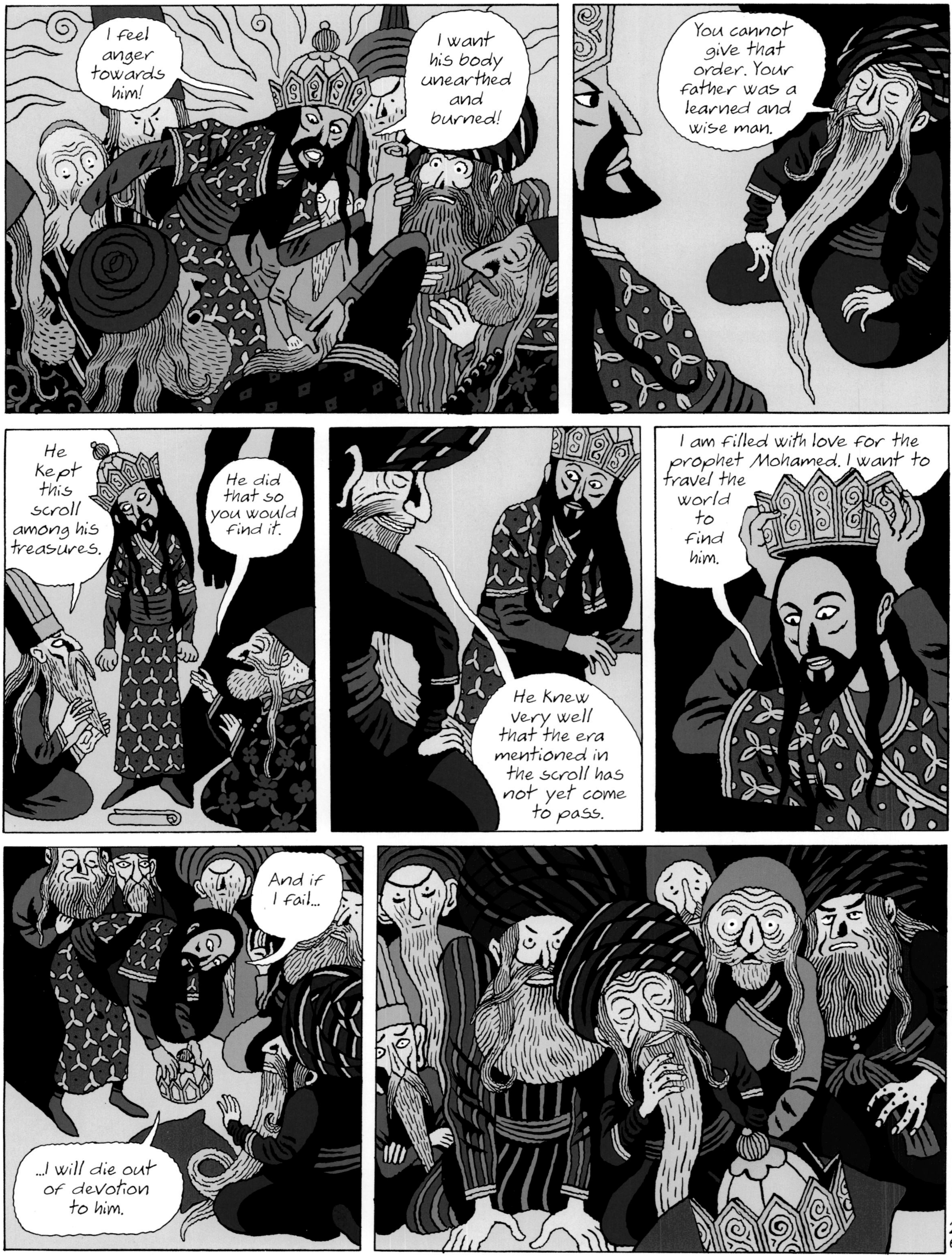
I feel anger towards him!
I want his body unearthed and burned!
You cannot give that order. Your father was a learned and wise man.
He kept this scroll among his treasures.
He did that so you would find it.
He knew very well that the era mentioned in the scroll has not yet come to pass.
I am filled with love for the prophet Mohamed. I want to travel the world to find him.
And if I fail...
...I will die out of devotion to him.
26

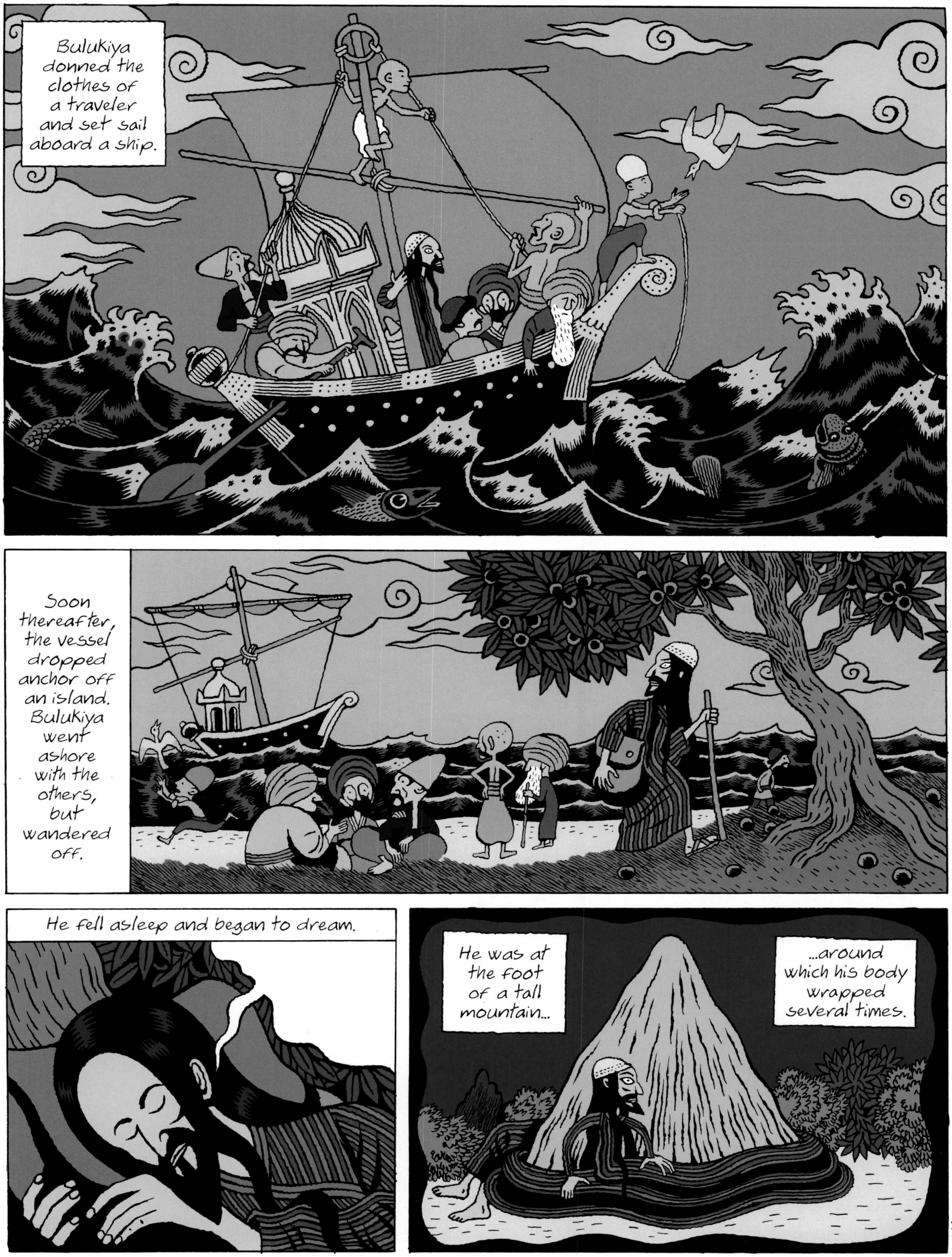

Bulukiya donned the clothes of a traveler and set sail aboard a ship.
Soon thereafter, the vessel dropped anchor off an island. Bulukiya went ashore with the others, but wandered off.
He fell asleep and began to dream.
He was at the foot of a tall mountain...
...around which his body wrapped several times.
27

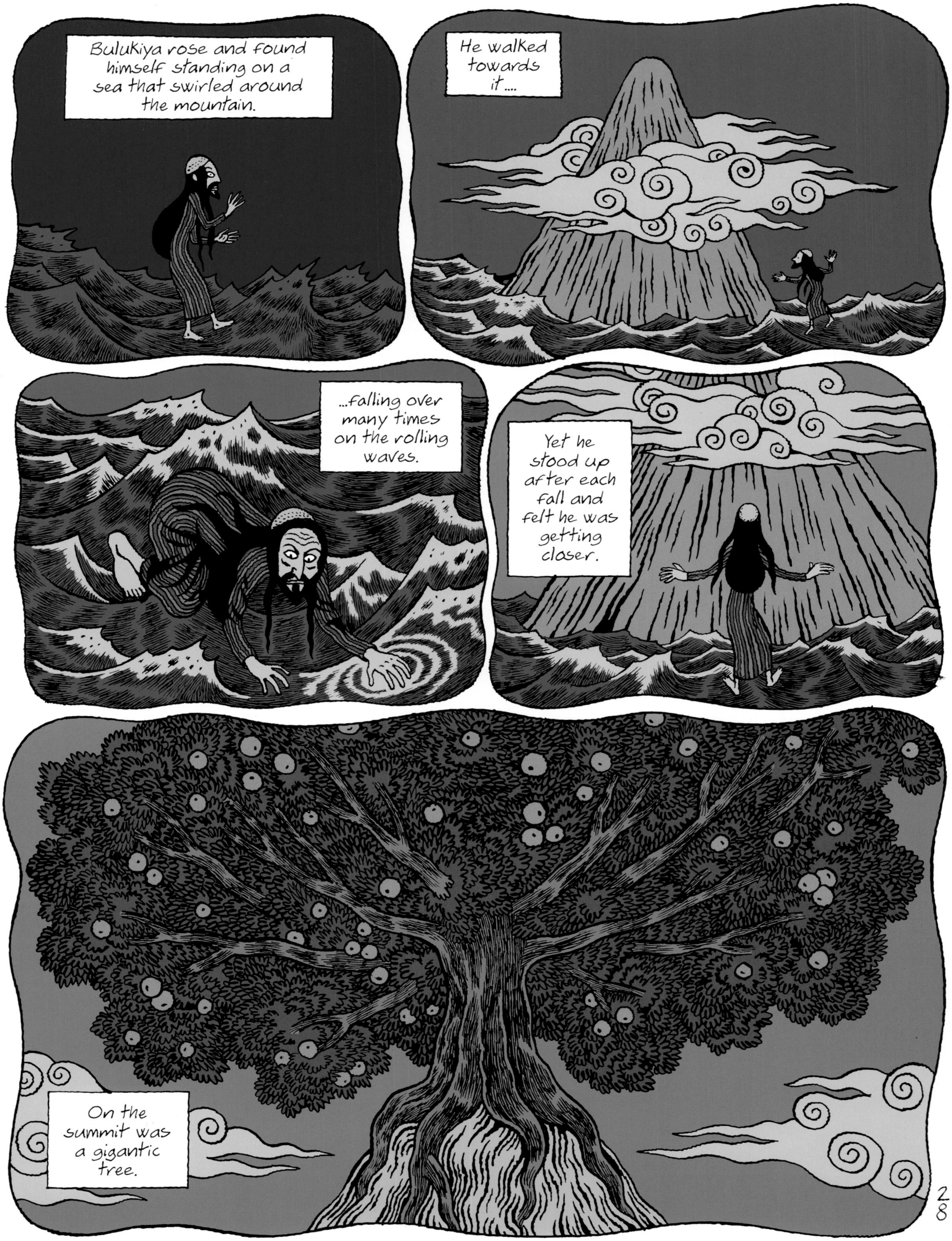
Bulukiya rose and found himself standing on a sea that swirled around the mountain.
He walked towards it....
...falling over many times on the rolling waves.
Yet he stood up after each fall and felt he was getting closer.
On the summit was a gigantic tree.
28

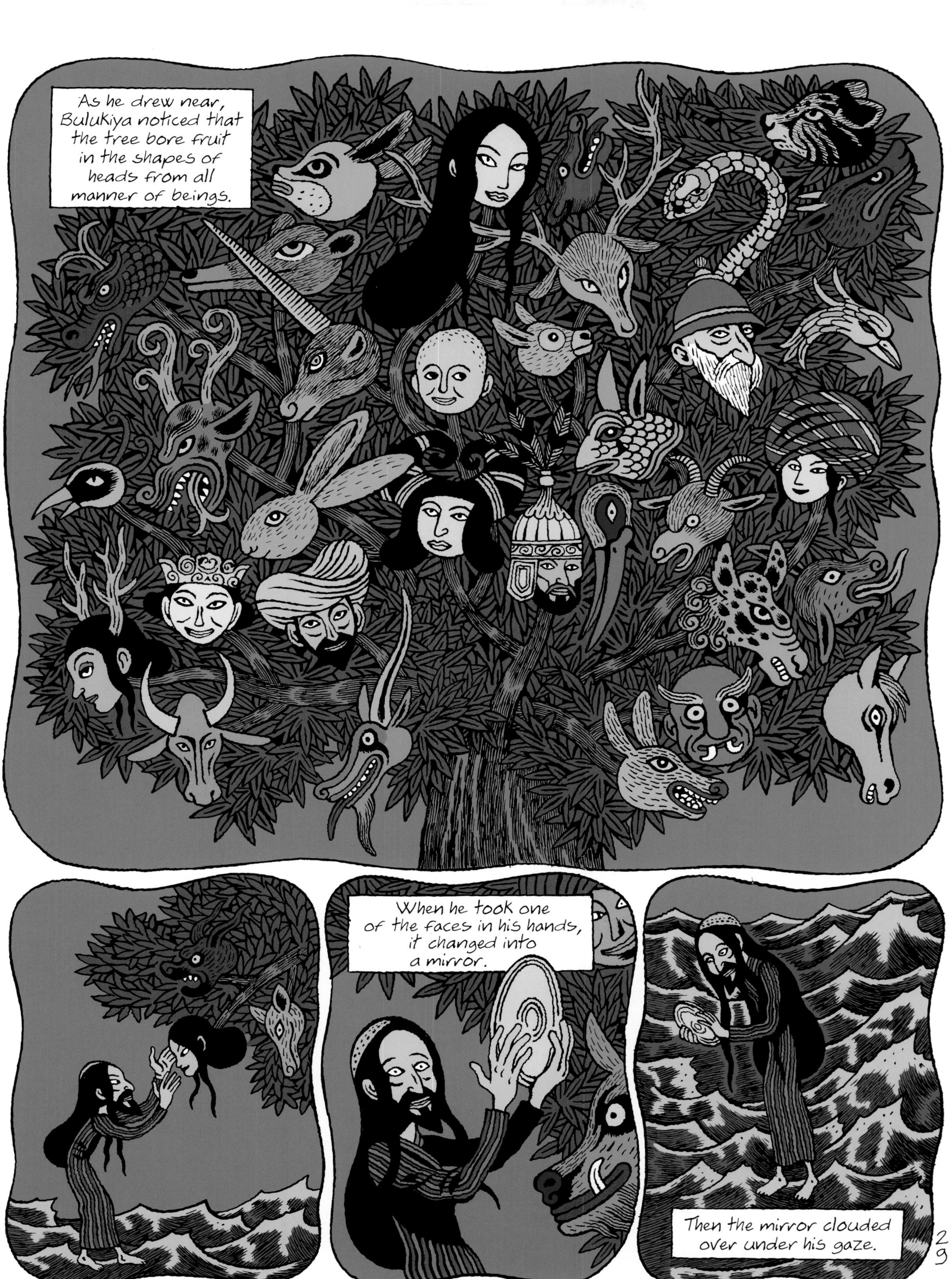
As he drew near, Bulukiya noticed that the tree bore fruit in the shapes of heads from all manner of beings.
When he took one of the faces in his hands, it changed into a mirror.
Then the mirror clouded over under his gaze.
29

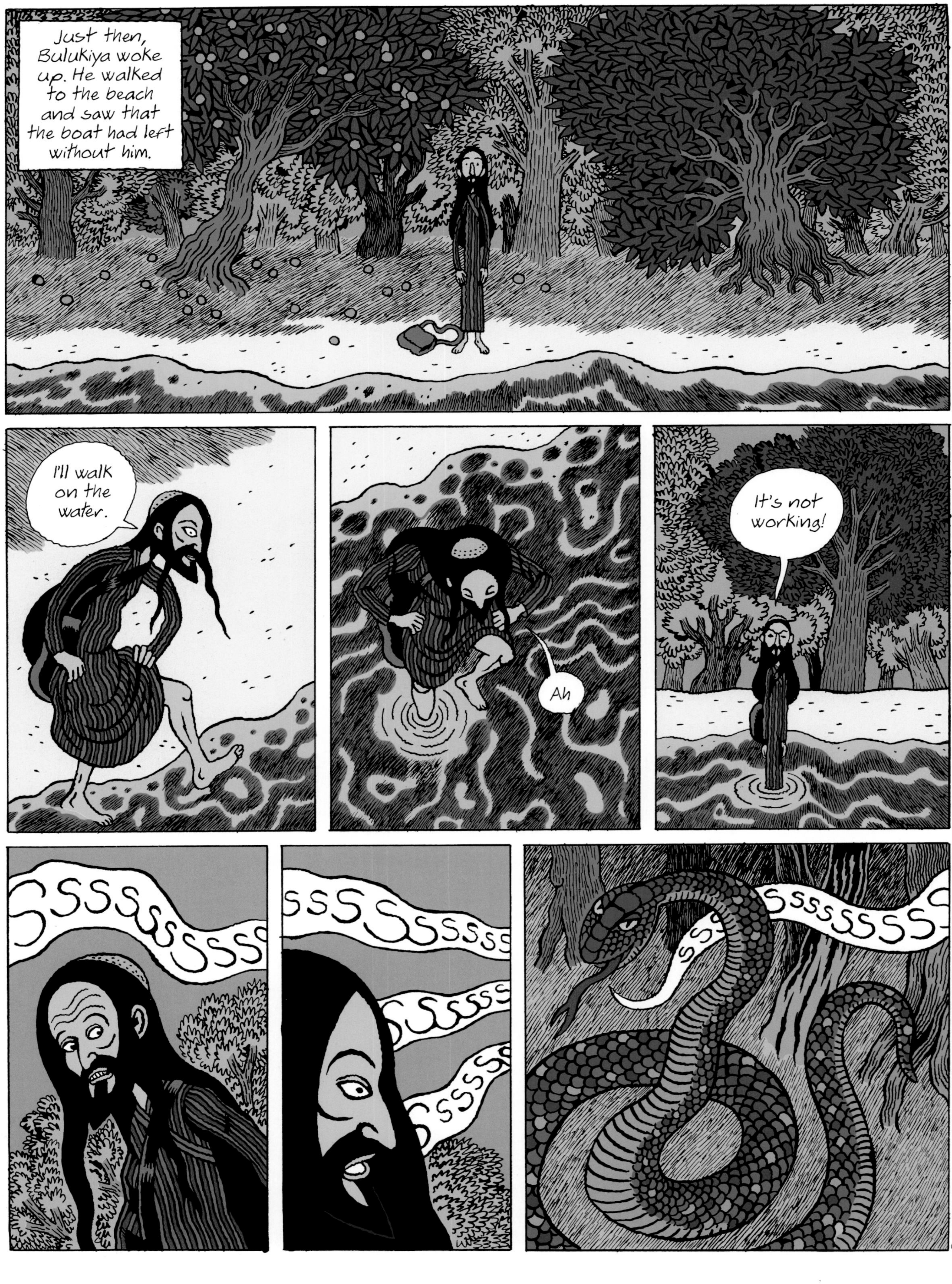
Just then, Bulukiya woke up. He walked to the beach and saw that the boat had left without him.
I'll walk on the water.
Ah
It's not working!
SSSSSSSSSS
SSSSSSSSS
SSSSS
SSSSS
SSSSSSSSSSS

30

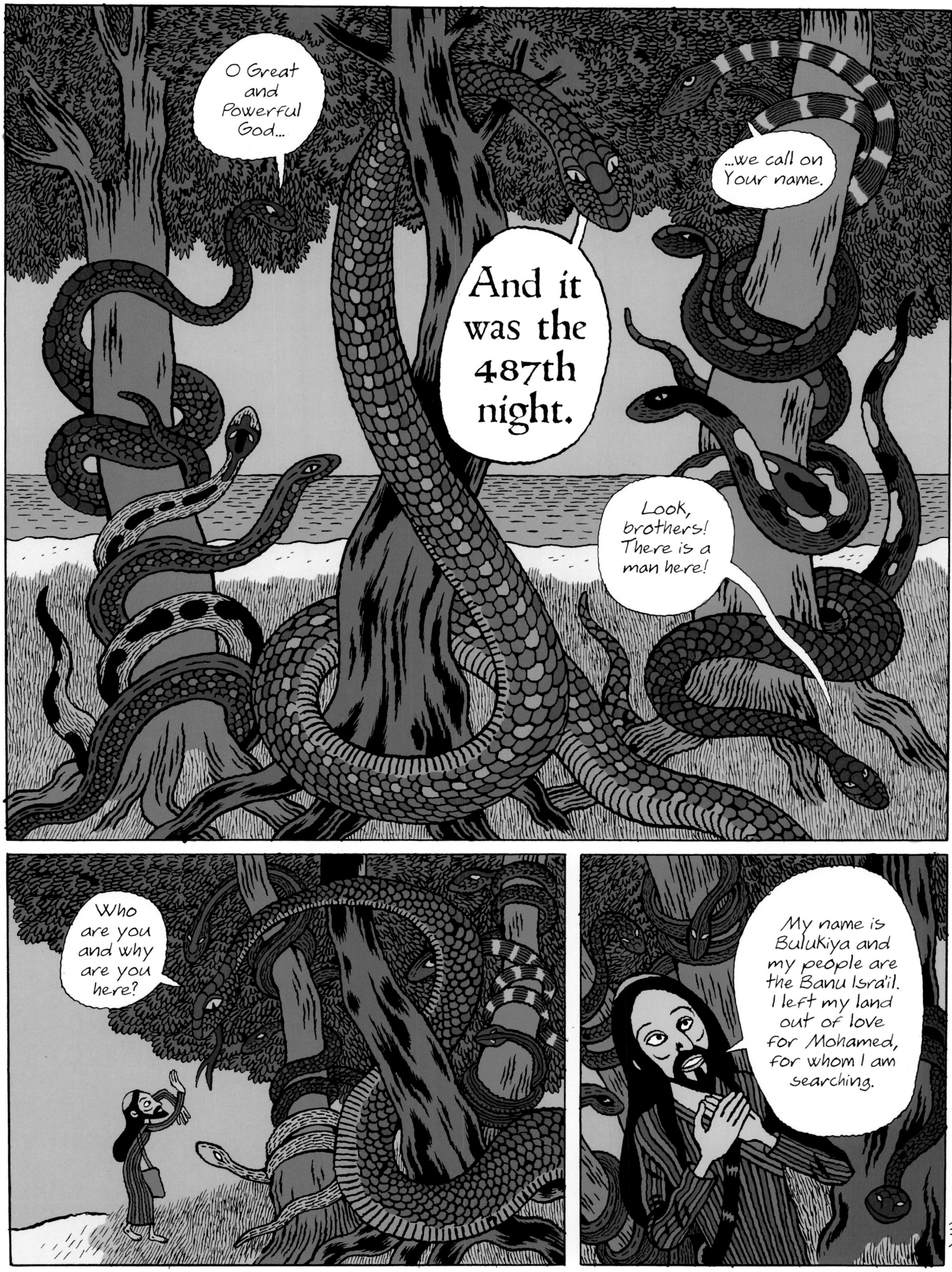
O Great and Powerful God...
...we call on Your name.
And it was the 487th night.
Look, brothers! There is a man here!
Who are you and why are you here?
My name is Bulukiya and my people are the Banu Isra'il. I left my land out of love for Mohamed, for whom I am searching.
31

I am the Serpent-Queen.

We call on the name of Mohamed for it is engraved on the door of the hell we've come from.

God created us to chastise the ungodly.

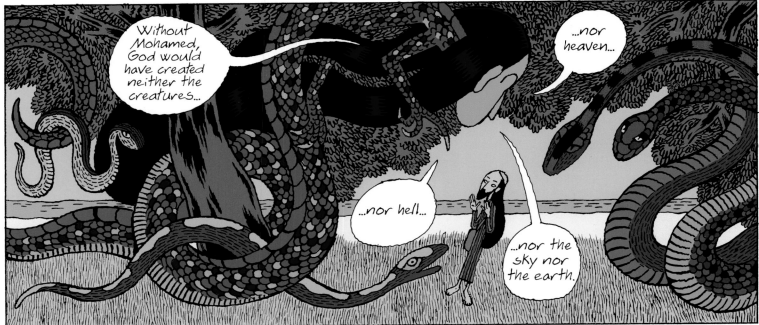

Without Mohamed, God would have created neither the creatures...

...nor heaven...

...nor hell...

...nor the sky nor the earth.

If you should encounter Mohamed on your journey, greet him for me.

I am a prisoner of this island. The ship I came on left me here!

32

36

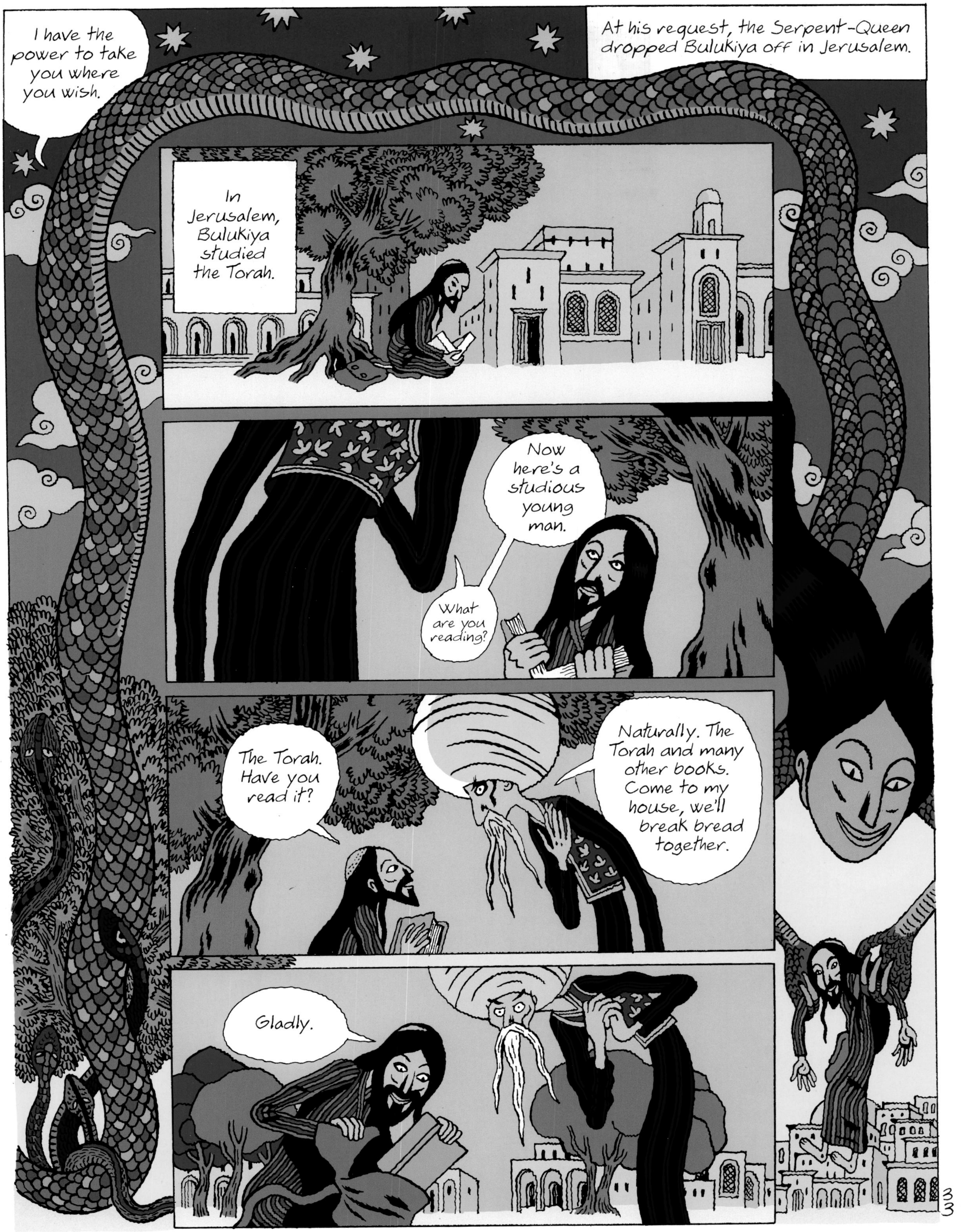
I have the power to take you where you wish.
At his request, the Serpent-Queen dropped Bulukiya off in Jerusalem.
In Jerusalem, Bulukiya studied the Torah.
Now here's a studious young man.
What are you reading?
The Torah. Have you read it?
Naturally. The Torah and many other books. Come to my house, we'll break bread together.
Gladly.
33

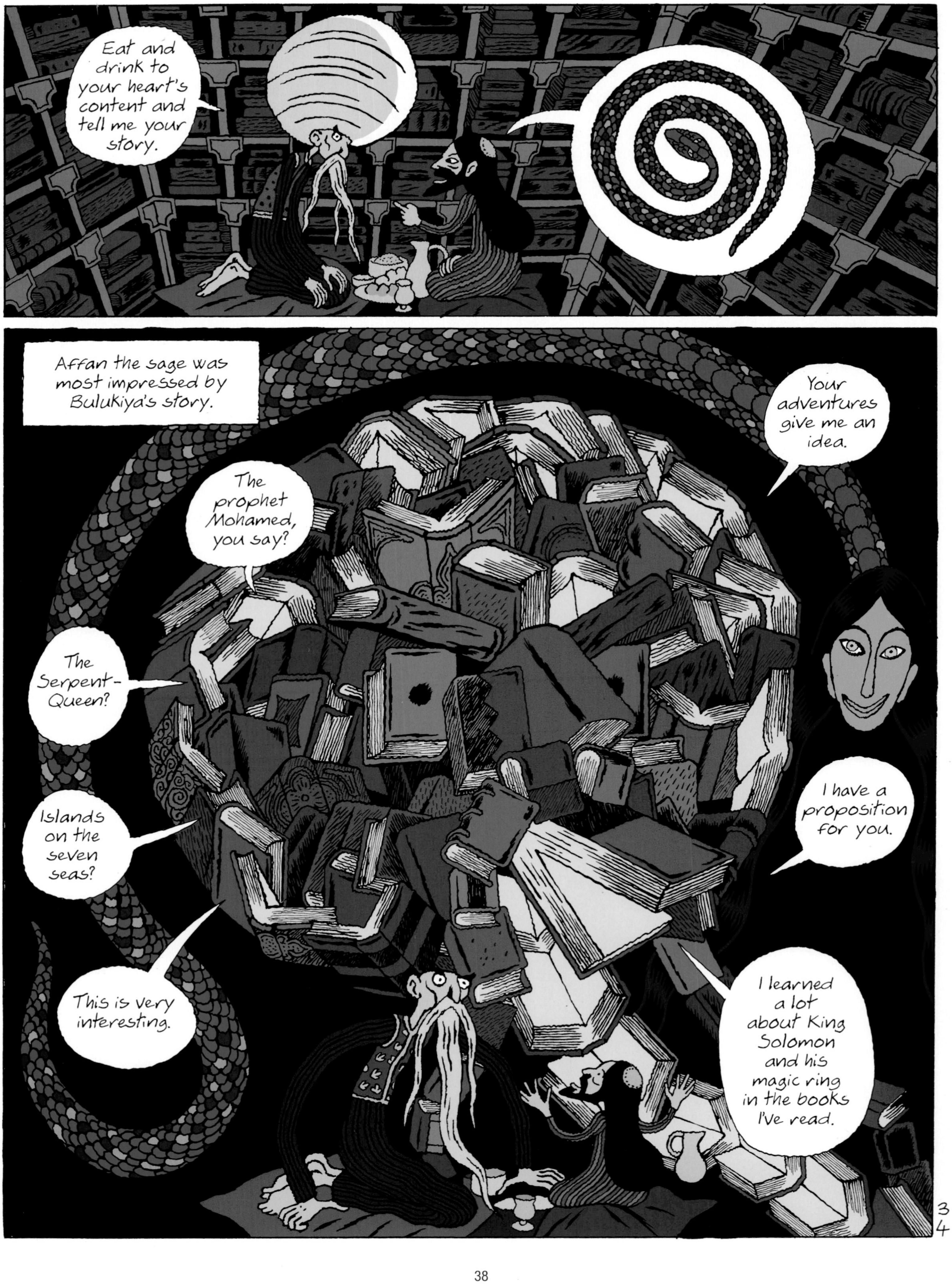
Eat and drink to your heart's content and tell me your story.
Affan the sage was most impressed by Bulukiya's story.
Your adventures give me an idea.
The prophet Mohamed, you say?
The Serpent-Queen?
Islands on the seven seas?
This is very interesting.
I have a proposition for you.
I learned a lot about King Solomon and his magic ring in the books I've read.
34

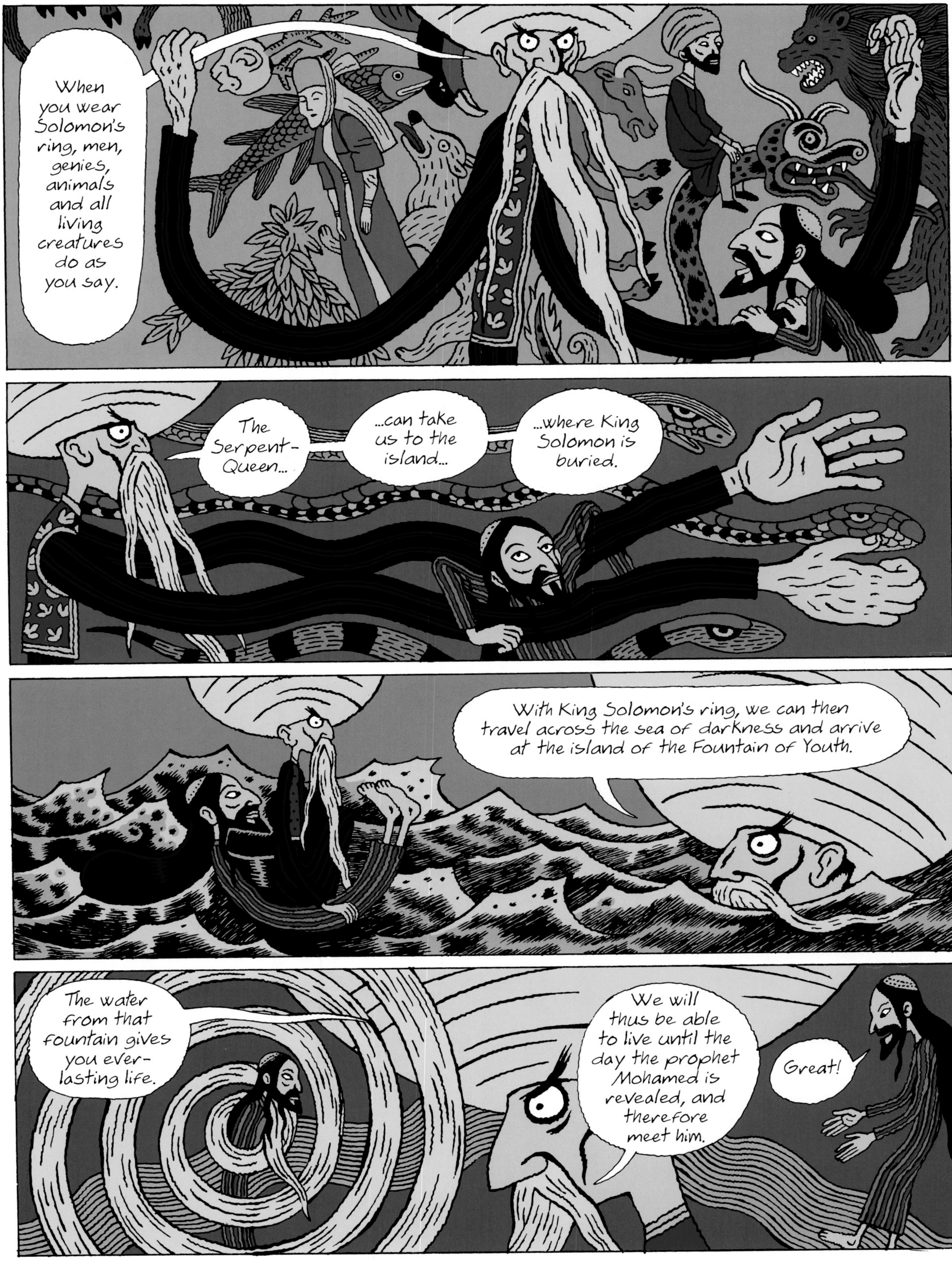
When you wear Solomon's ring, men, genies, animals and all living creatures do as you say.
The Serpent-Queen...
...can take us to the island...
...where King Solomon is buried.
With King Solomon's ring, we can then travel across the sea of darkness and arrive at the island of the Fountain of Youth.
The water from that fountain gives you ever-lasting life.
We will thus be able to live until the day the prophet Mohamed is revealed, and therefore meet him.
Great!
35

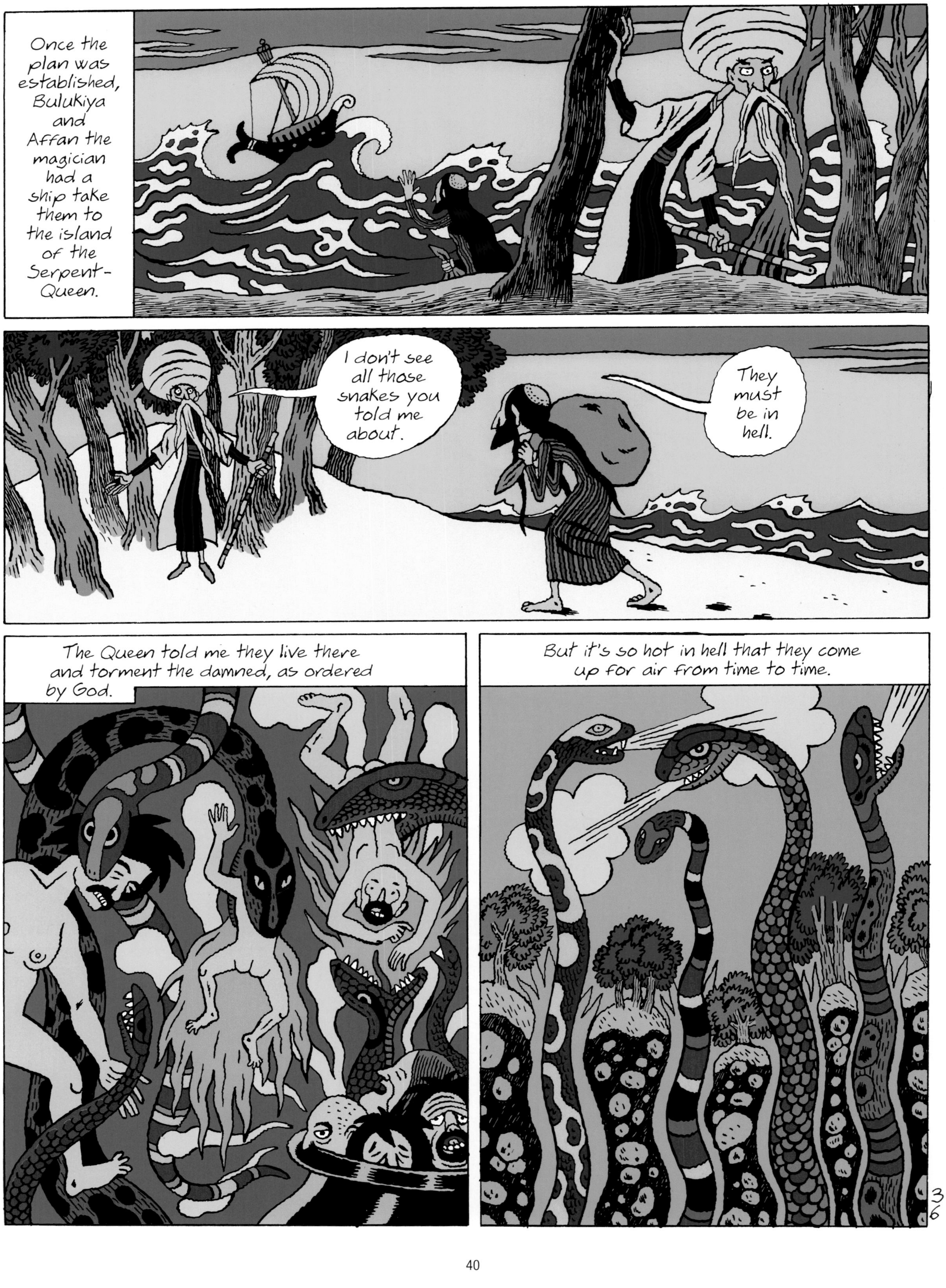
Once the plan was established, Bulukiya and Affan the magician had a ship take them to the island of the Serpent-Queen.
I don't see all those snakes you told me about.
They must be in hell.
The Queen told me they live there and torment the damned, as ordered by God.
But it's so hot in hell that they come up for air from time to time.
36

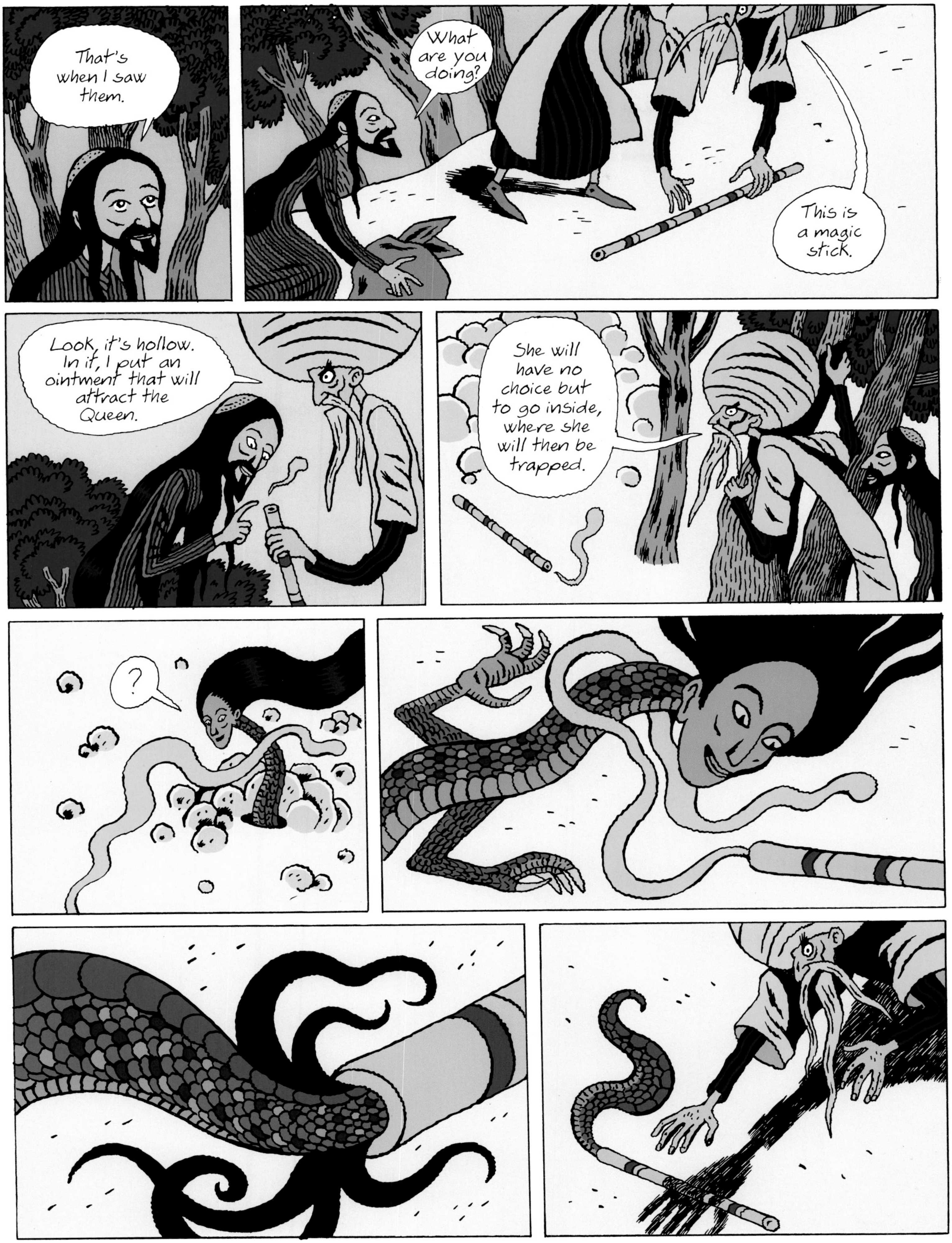

That's when I saw them.
What are you doing?
This is a magic stick.
Look, it's hollow. In it, I put an ointment that will attract the Queen.
She will have no choice but to go inside, where she will then be trapped.
?

37

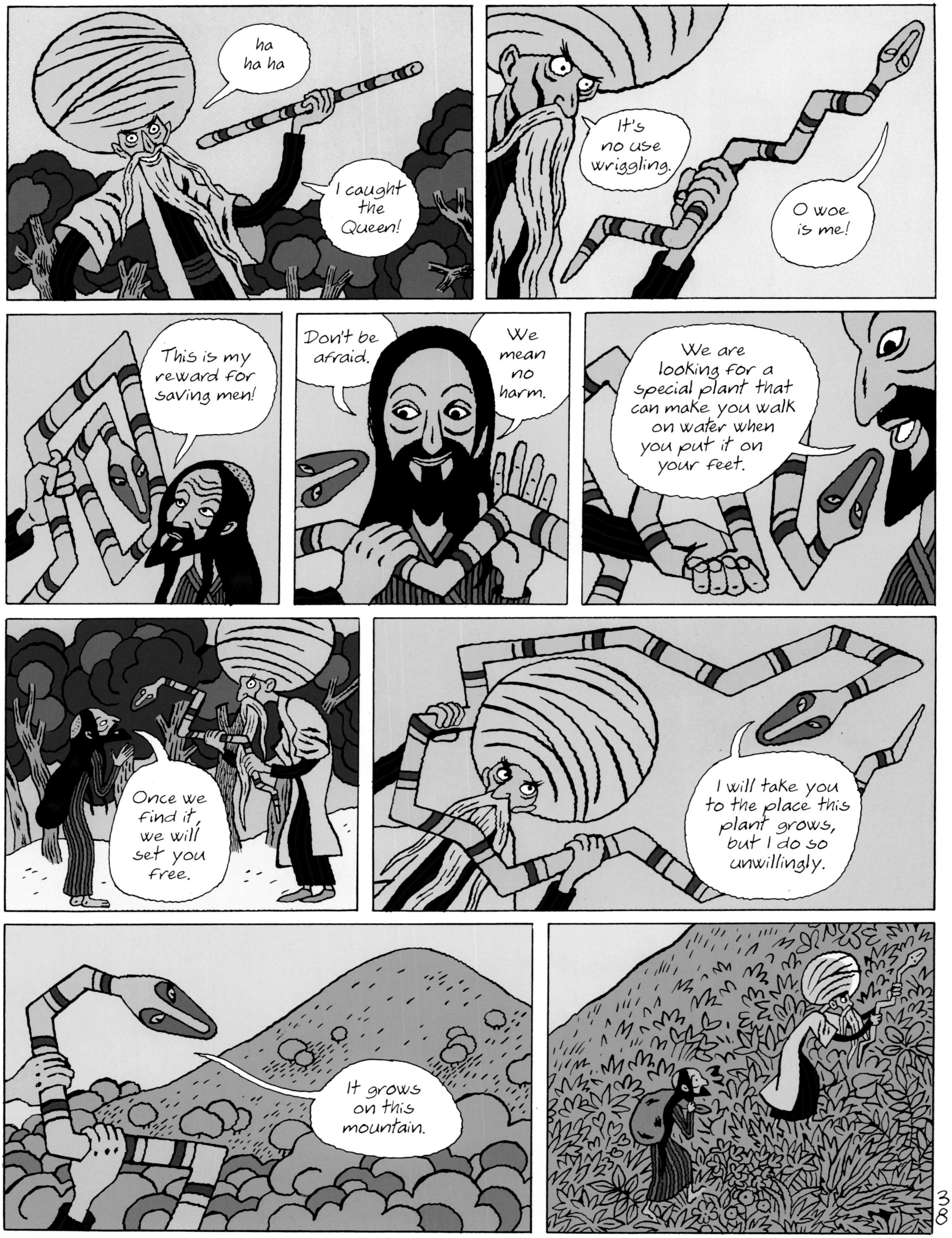
ha ha ha
I caught the Queen!
It's no use wriggling.
O woe is me!
This is my reward for saving men!
Don't be afraid.
We mean no harm.
We are looking for a special plant that can make you walk on water when you put it on your feet.
Once we find it, we will set you free.
I will take you to the place this plant grows, but I do so unwillingly.
It grows on this mountain.
38

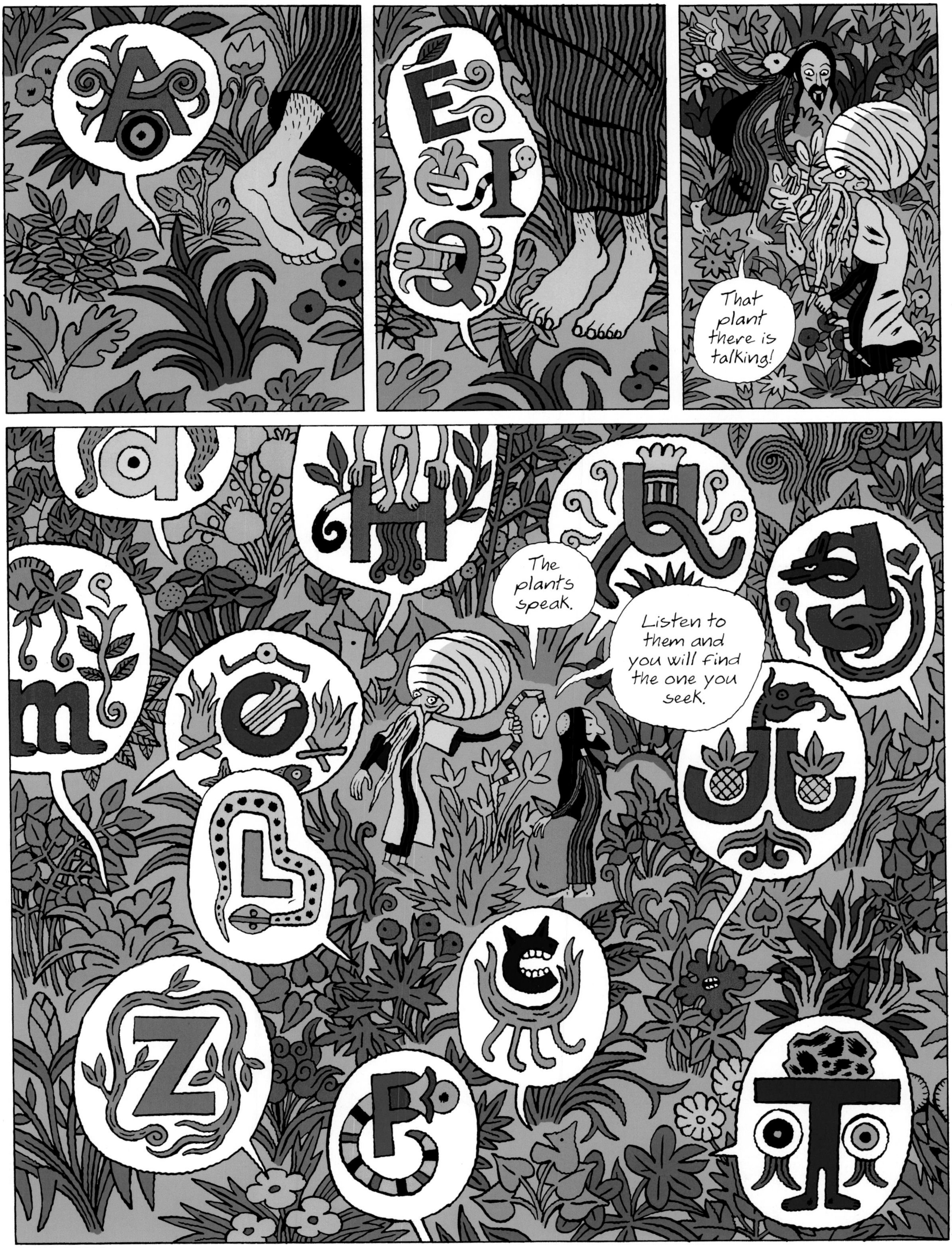
That plant there is talking!
The plants speak.
Listen to them and you will find the one you seek.

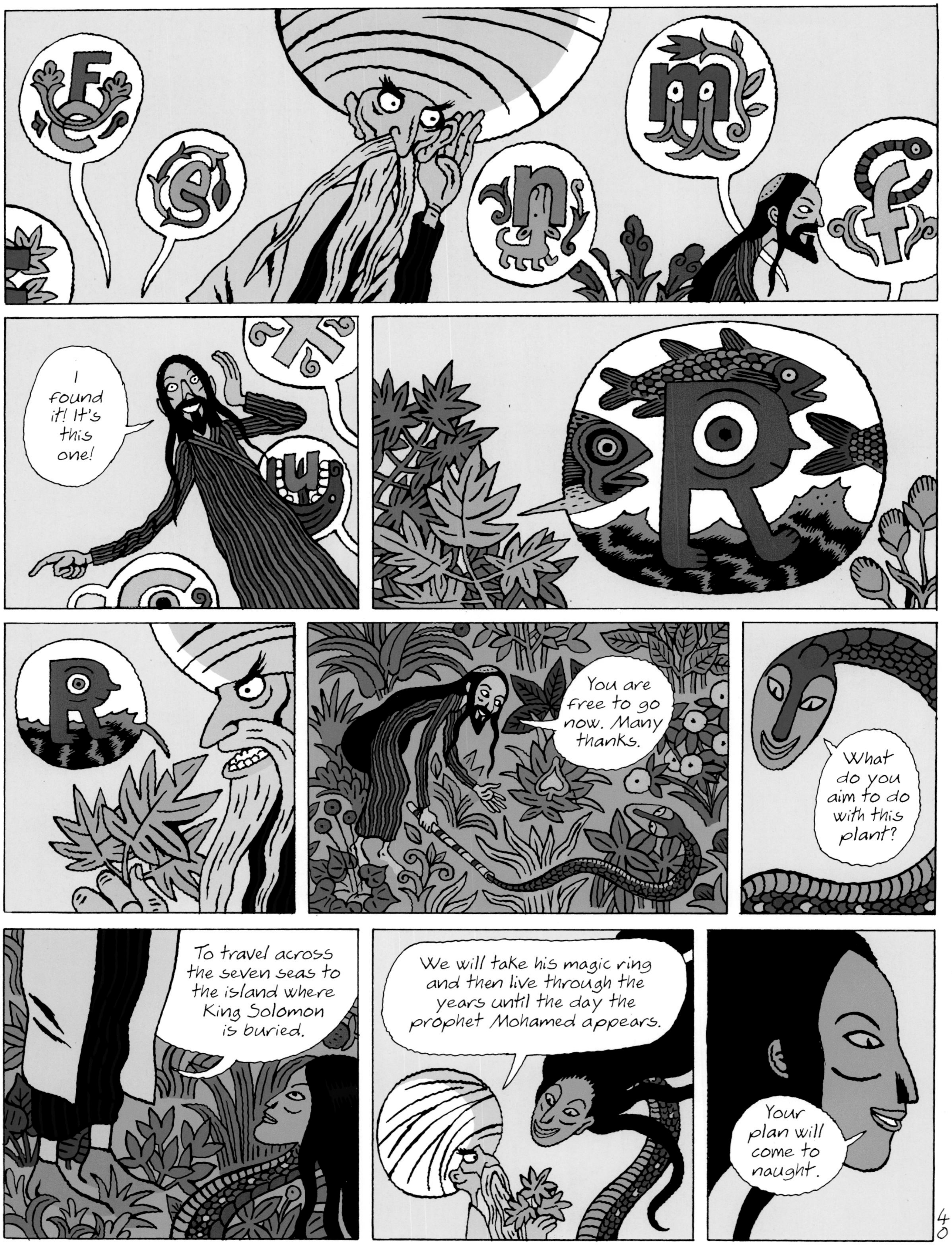
I found it! It's this one!
You are free to go now. Many thanks.
What do you aim to do with this plant?
To travel across the seven seas to the island where King Solomon is buried.
We will take his magic ring and then live through the years until the day the prophet Mohamed appears.
Your plan will come to naught.
40

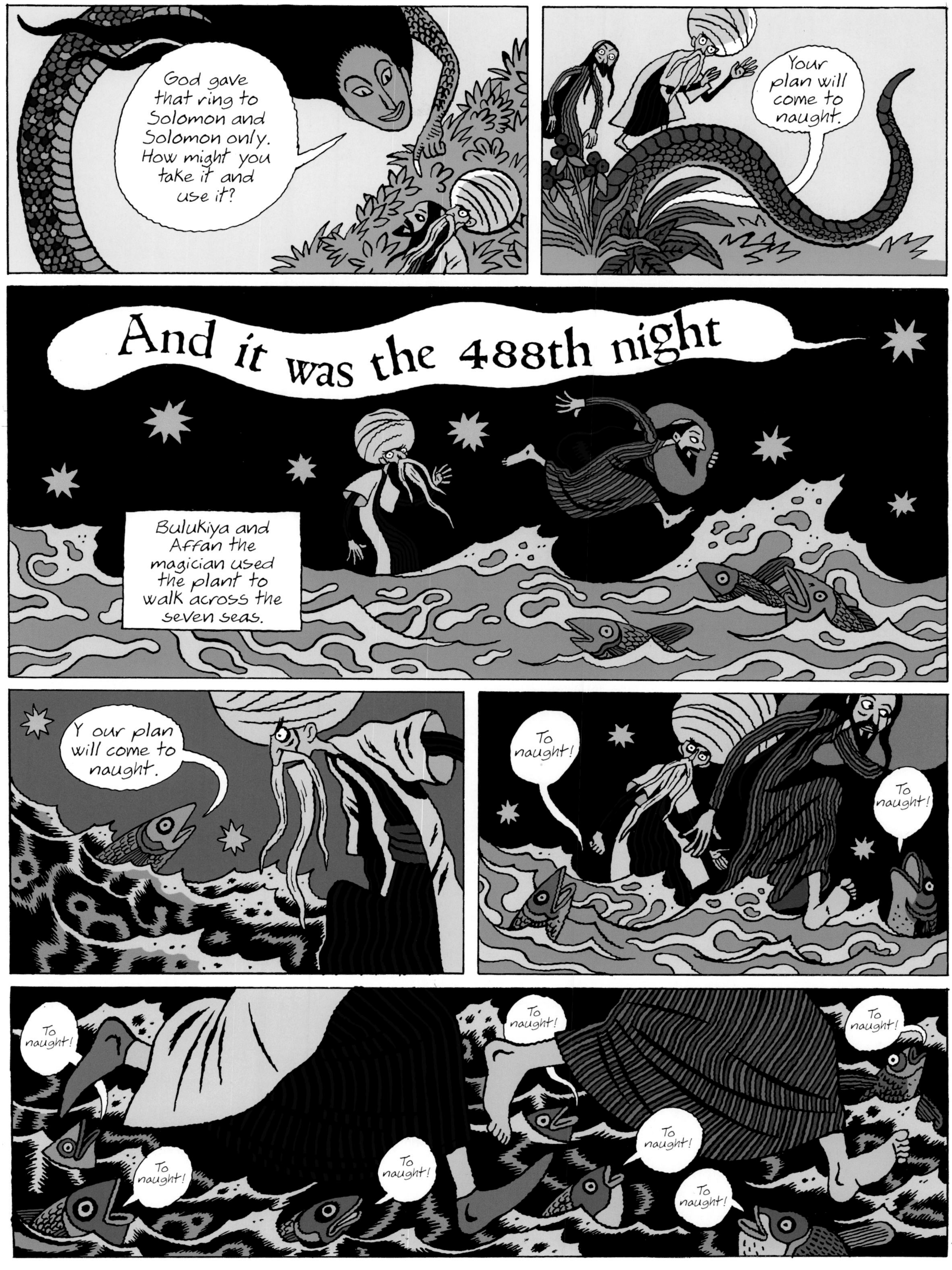
God gave that ring to Solomon and Solomon only. How might you take it and use it?
Your plan will come to naught.
And it was the 488th night
Bulukiya and Affan the magician used the plant to walk across the seven seas.
Y our plan will come to naught.
To naught!
To naught!
To naught!
To naught!
To naught!
To naught!
To naught!
To naught!
To naught!

4
1

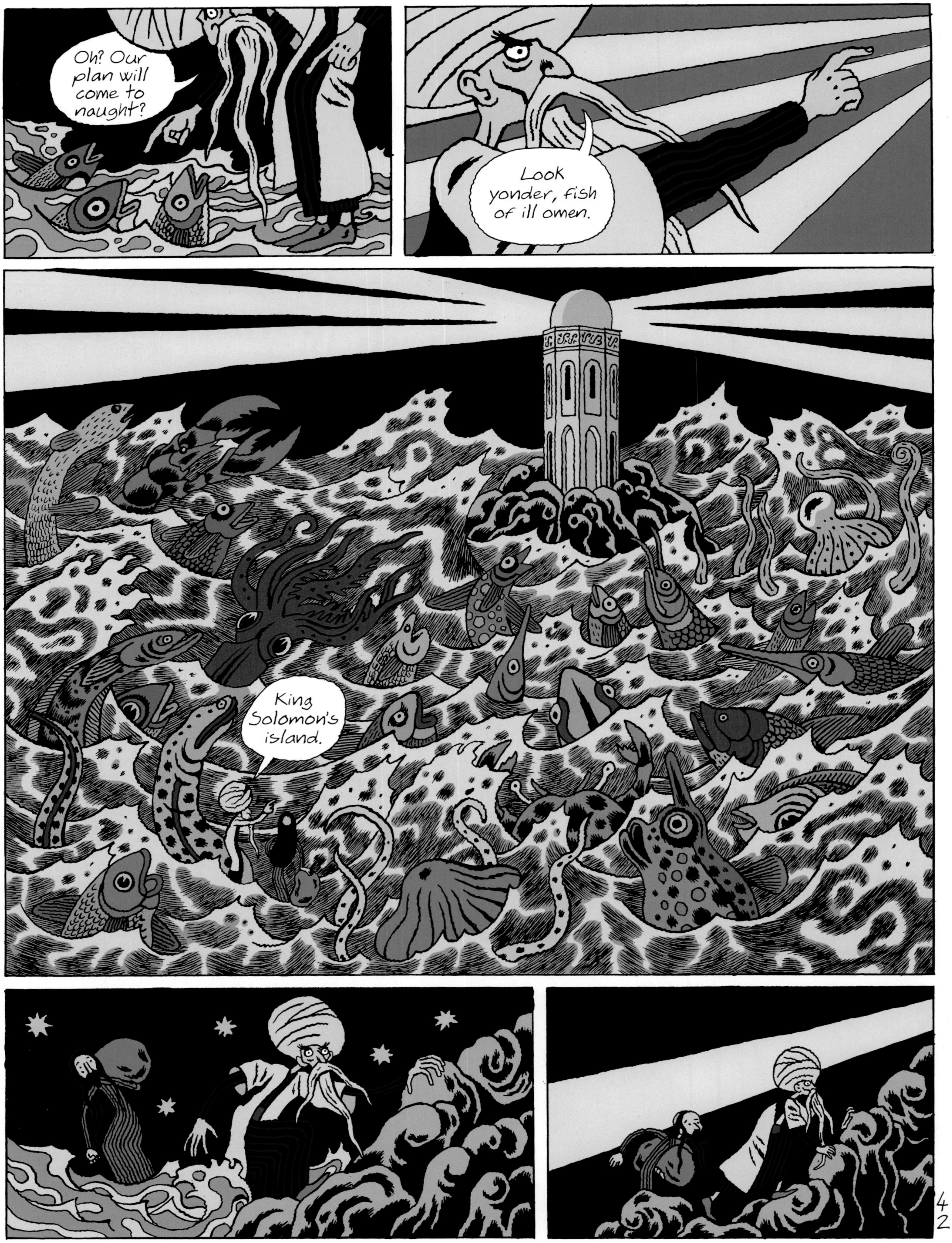

Oh? Our plan will come to naught?
Look yonder, fish of ill omen.
King Solomon's island.
42

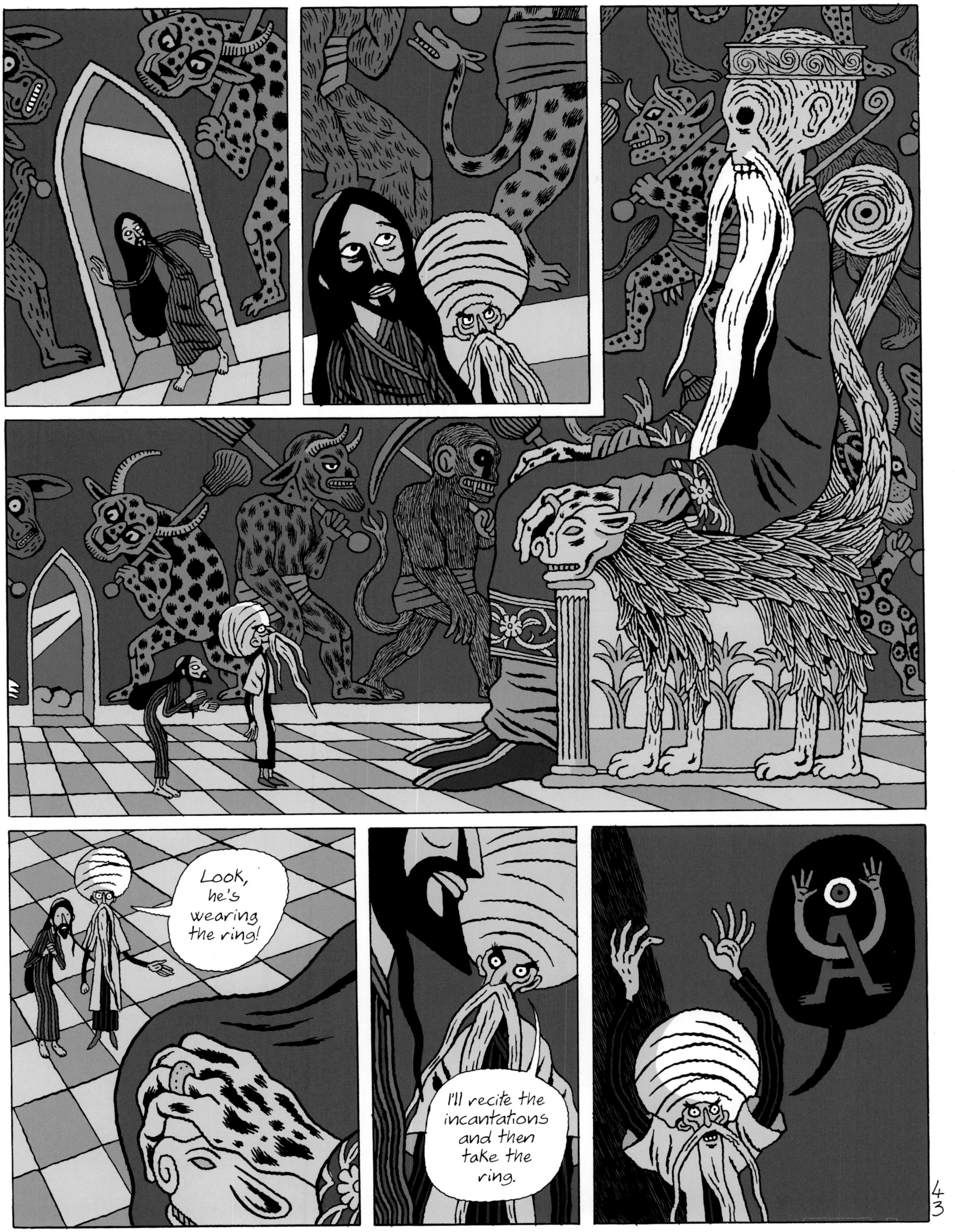
Look, he's wearing the ring!
I'll recite the incantations and then take the ring.
43

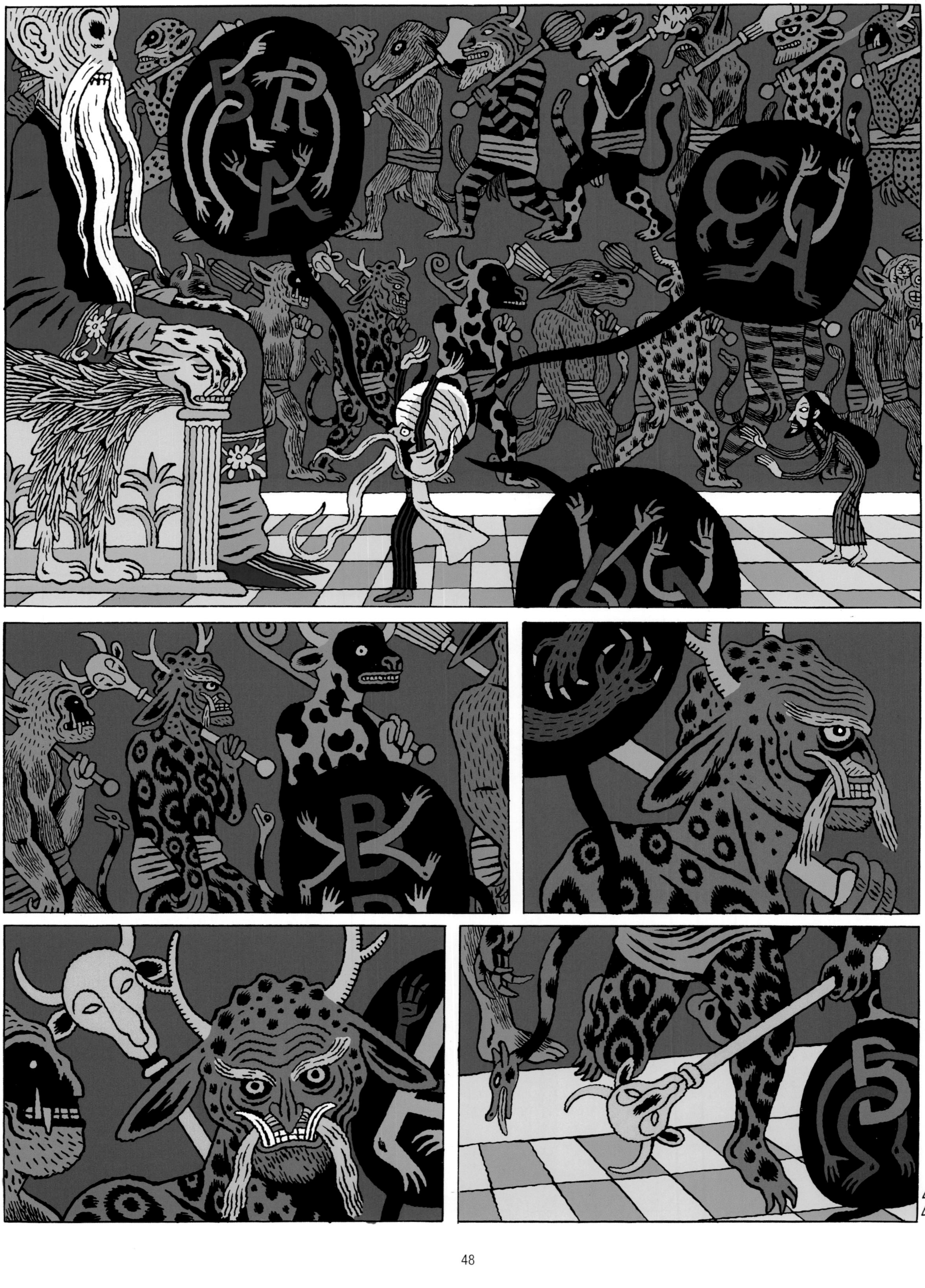

44

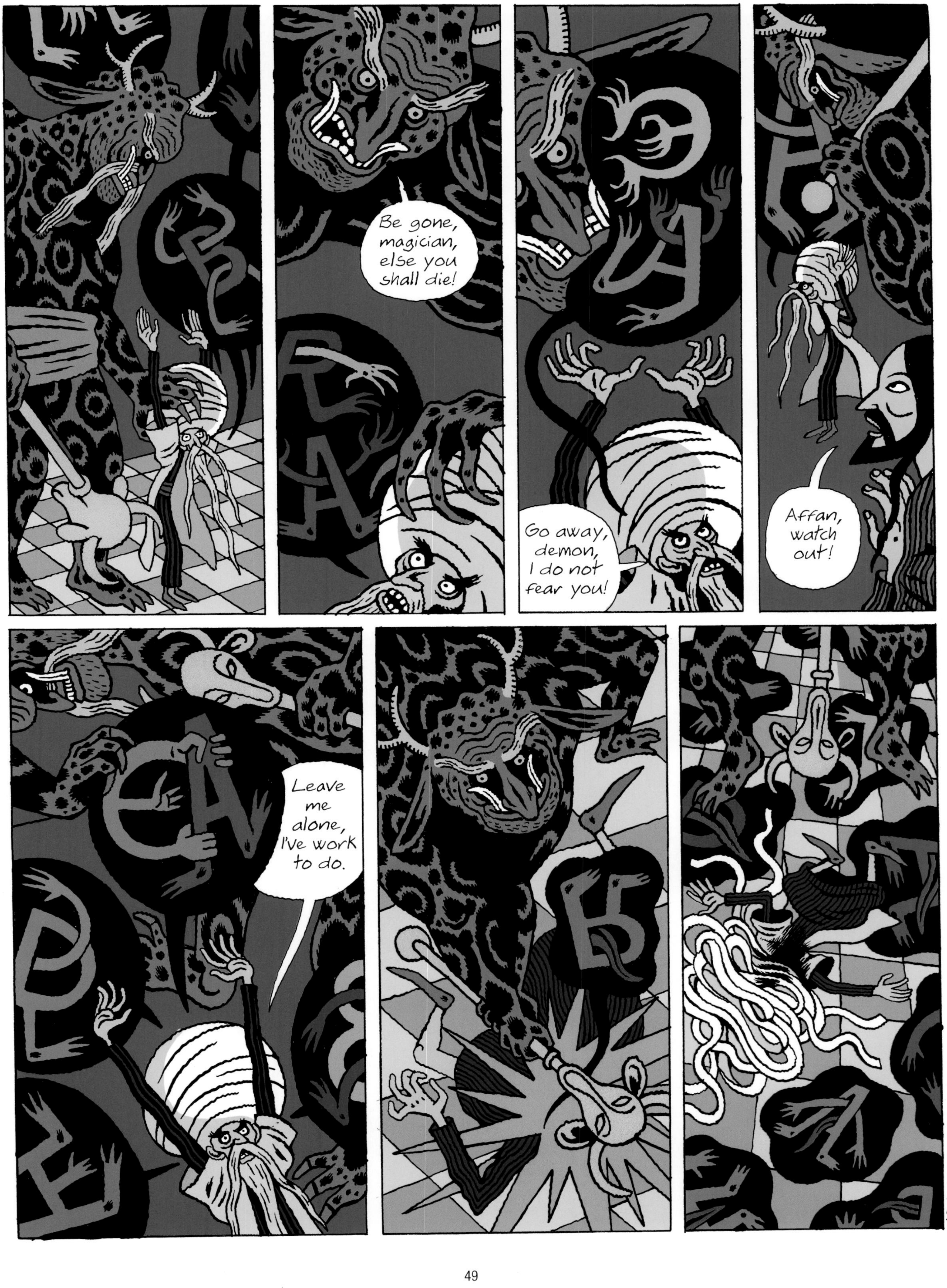
Be gone, magician, else you shall die!
Go away, demon, I do not fear you!
Affan, watch out!
Leave me alone, I've work to do.

45

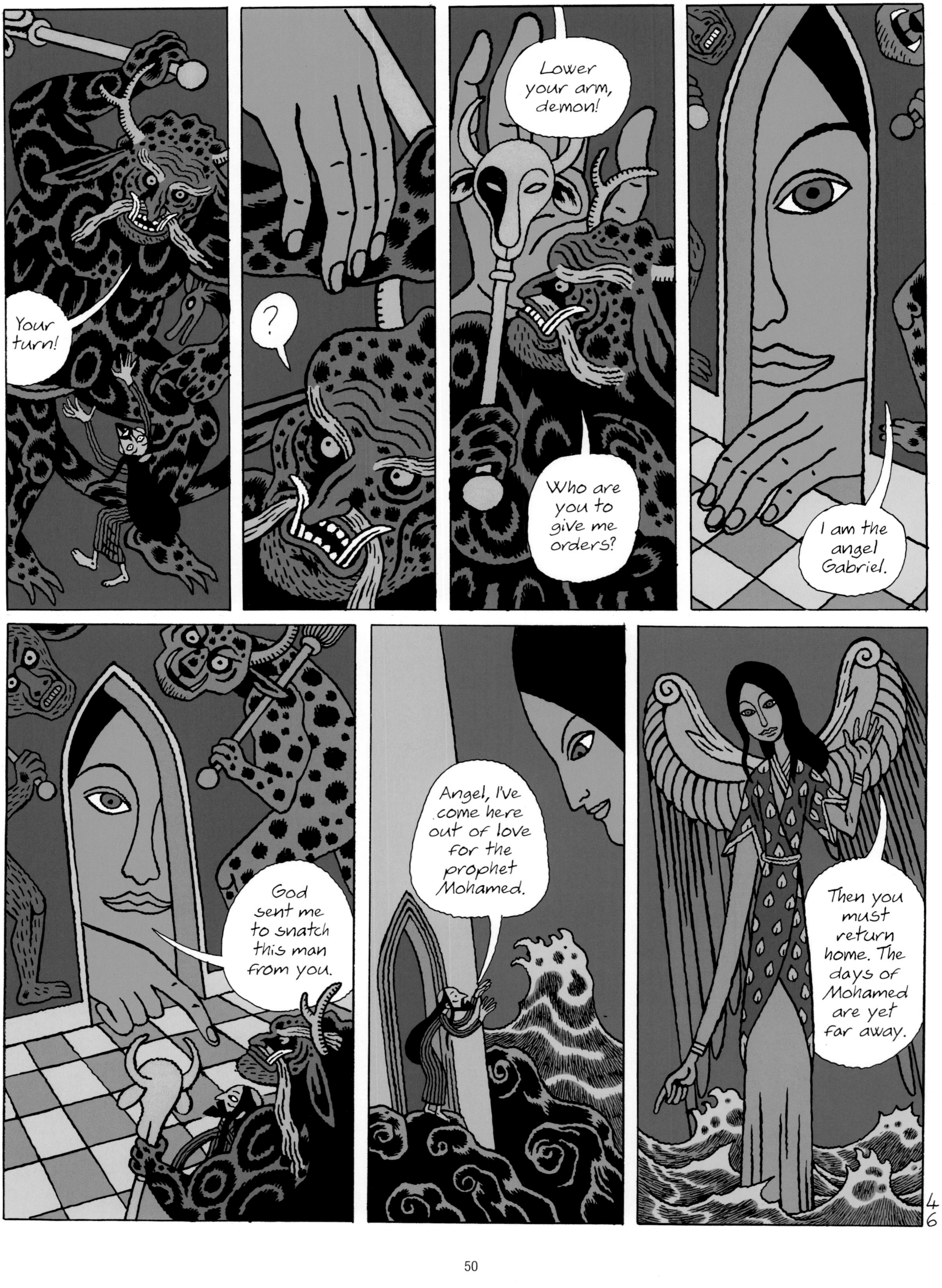

Your turn!
?
Lower your arm, demon!
Who are you to give me orders?
I am the angel Gabriel.
God sent me to snatch this man from you.
Angel, I've come here out of love for the prophet Mohamed.
Then you must return home. The days of Mohamed are yet far away.
46

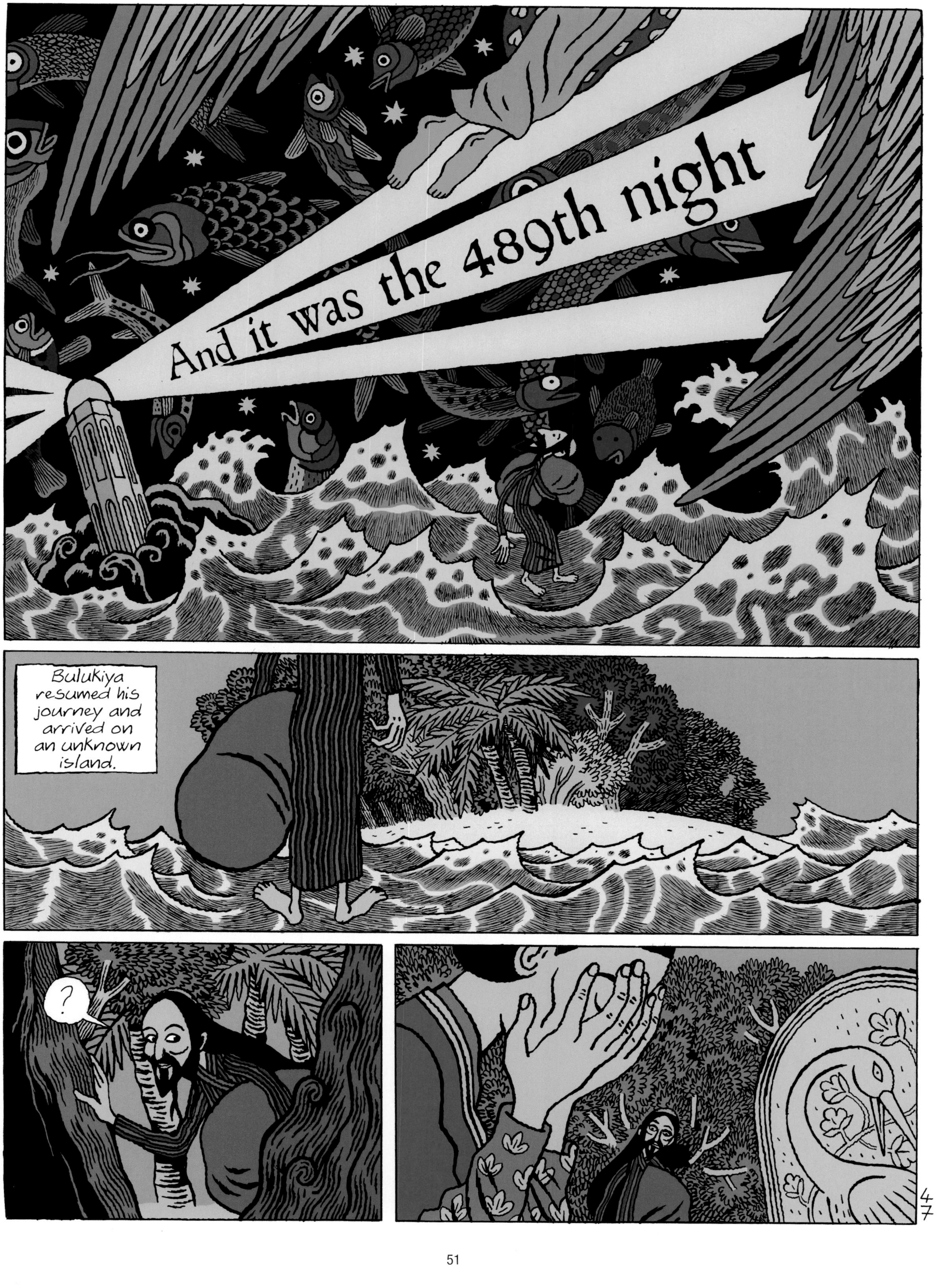
And it was the 489th night
Bulukiya resumed his journey and arrived on an unknown island.
?
47

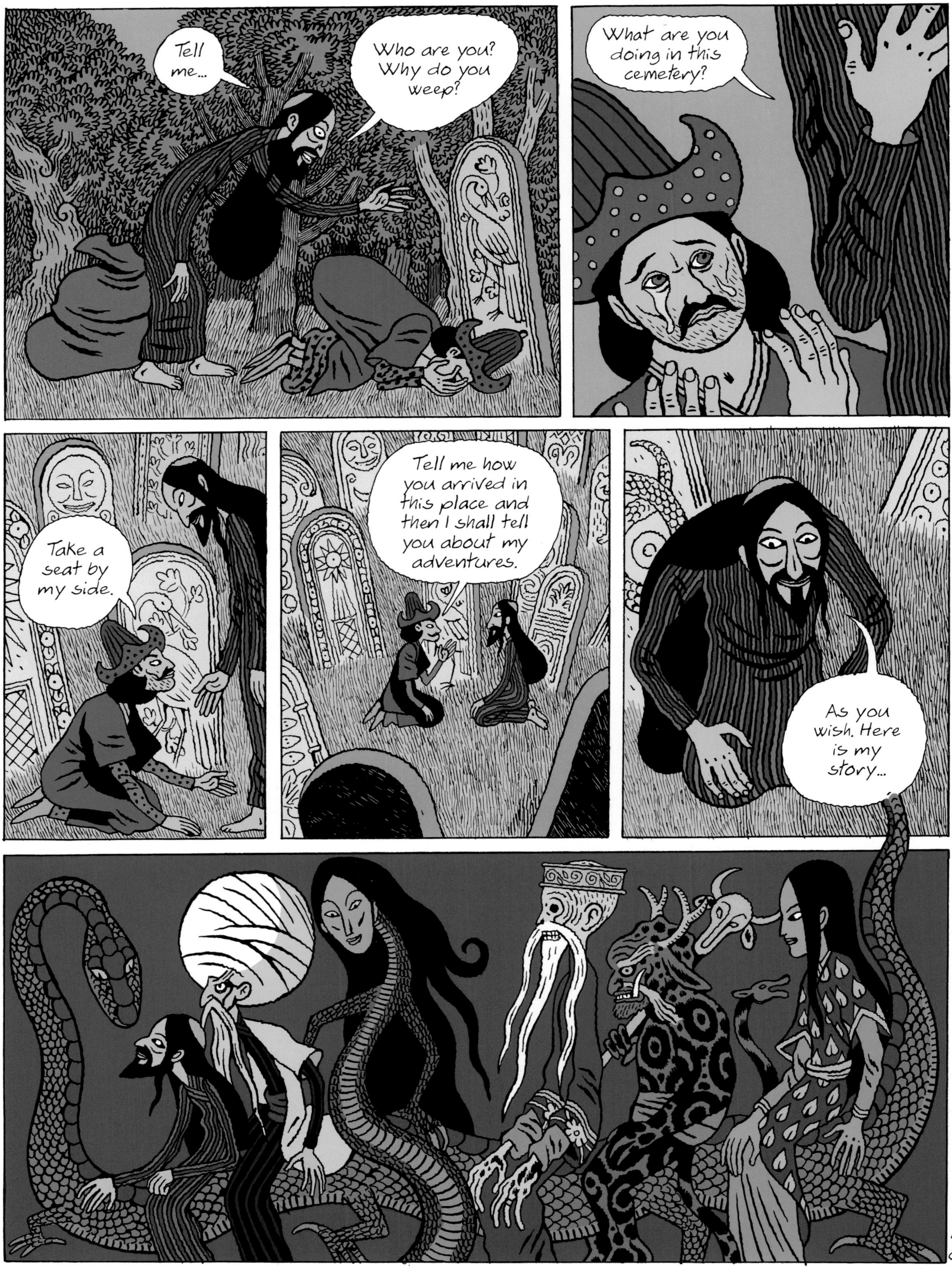
Tell me...
Who are you? Why do you weep?
What are you doing in this cemetery?
Take a seat by my side.
Tell me how you arrived in this place and then I shall tell you about my adventures.
As you wish. Here is my story...
48

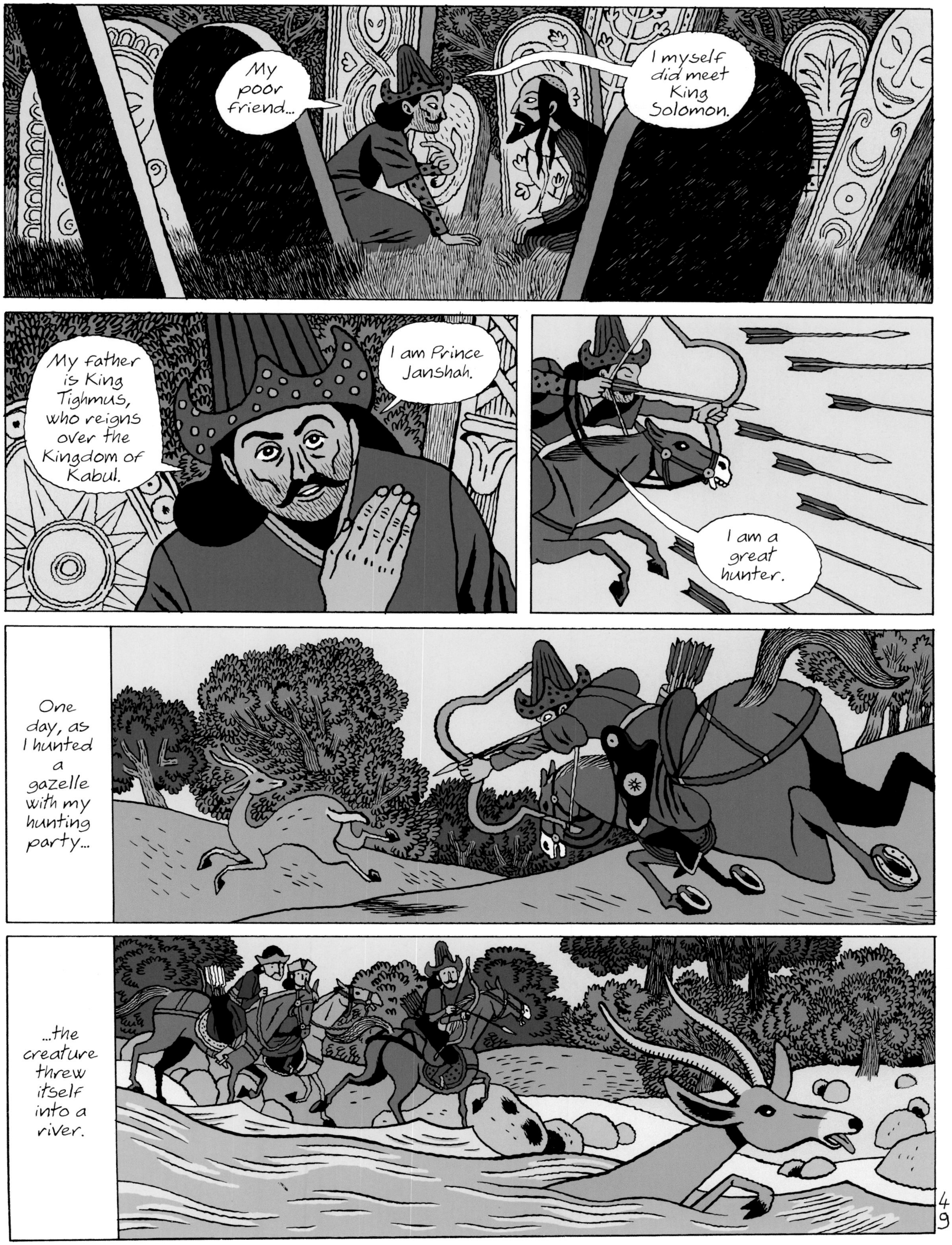
My poor friend...
I myself did meet King Solomon.
My father is King Tighmus, who reigns over the Kingdom of Kabul.
I am Prince Janshah.
I am a great hunter.
One day, as I hunted a gazelle with my hunting party...
...the creature threw itself into a river.
49

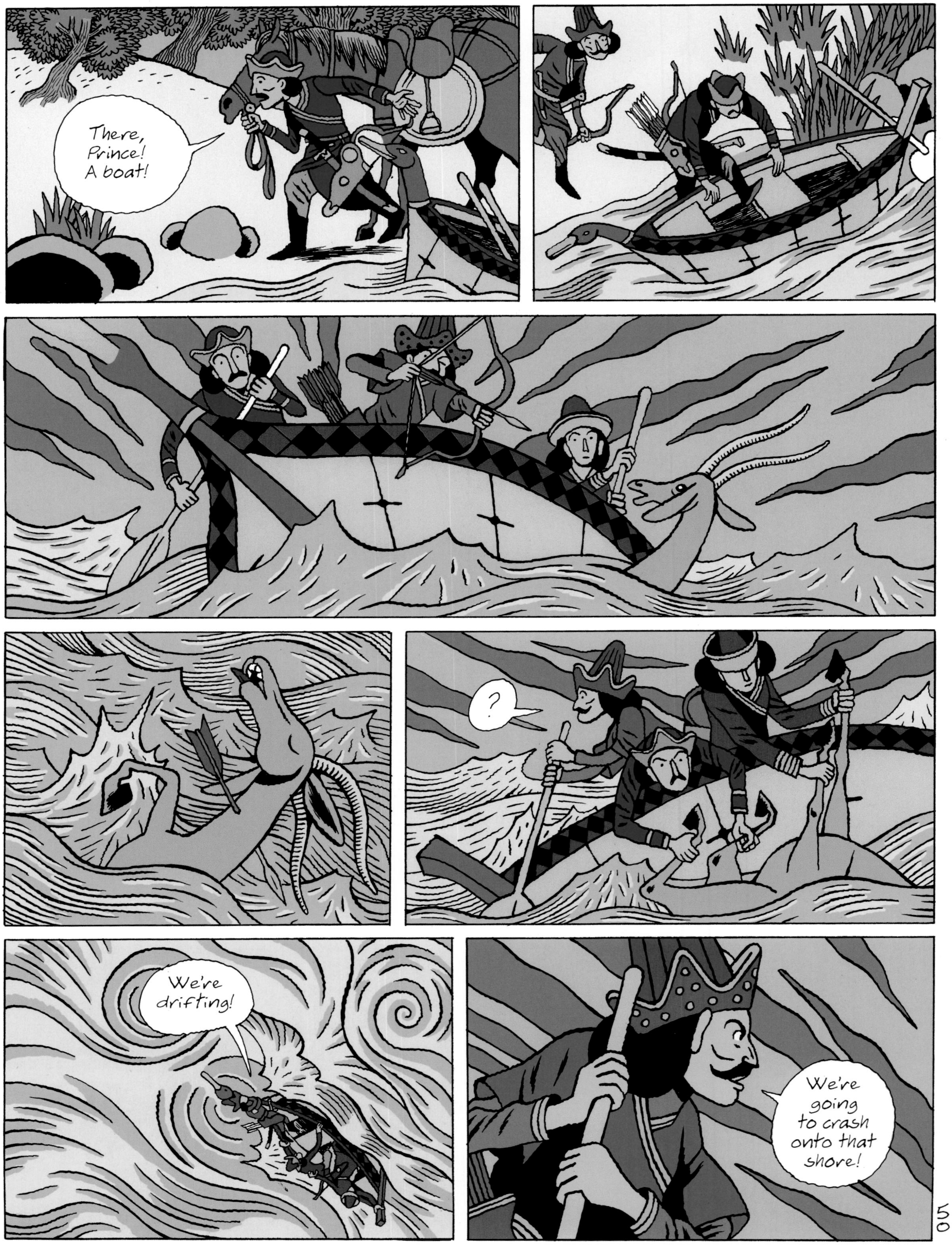
There, Prince! A boat!
?
We're drifting!
We're going to crash onto that shore!
50

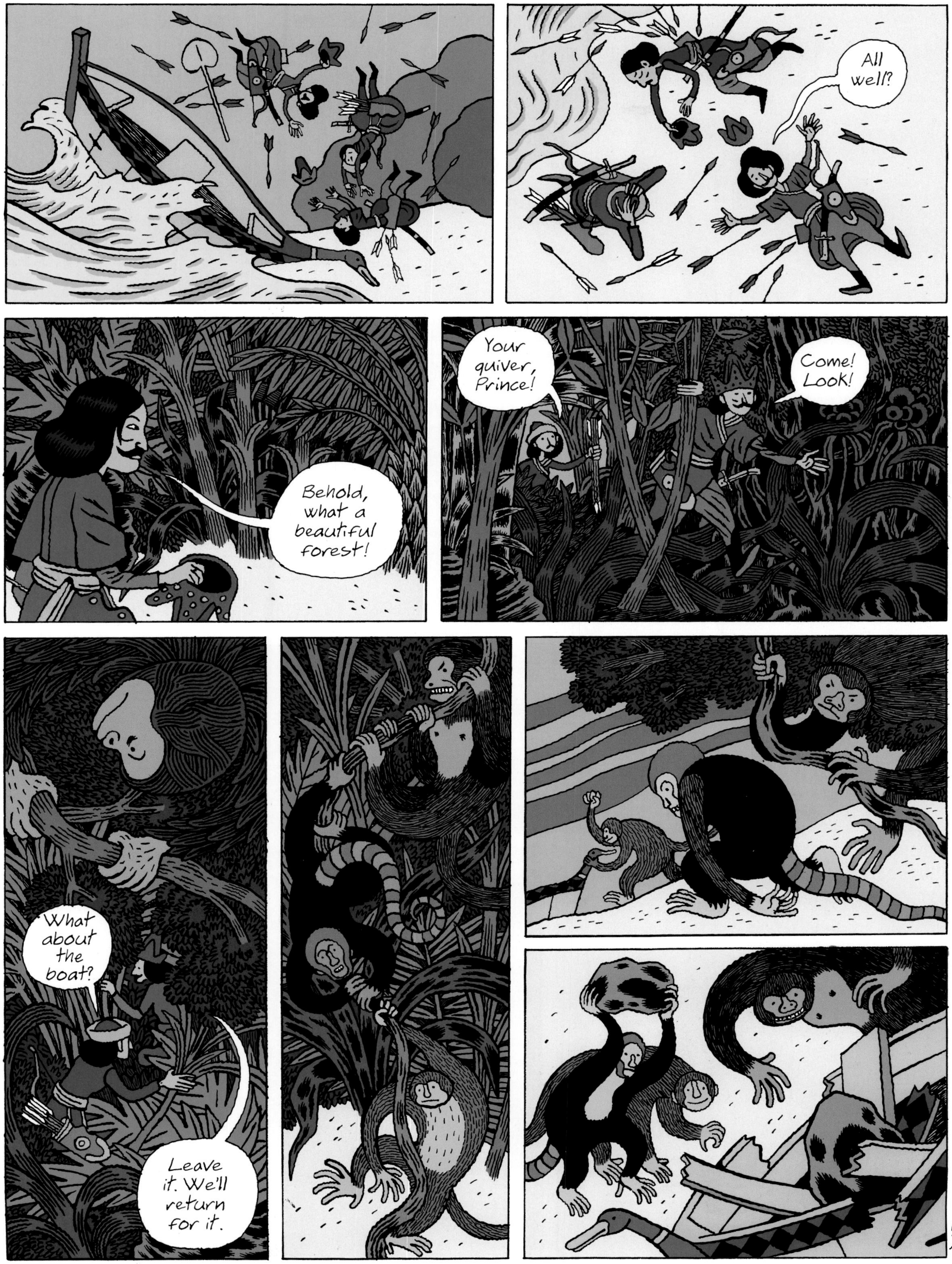

All well?
Behold, what a beautiful forest!
Your quiver, Prince!
Come! Look!
What about the boat?
Leave it. We'll return for it.
51

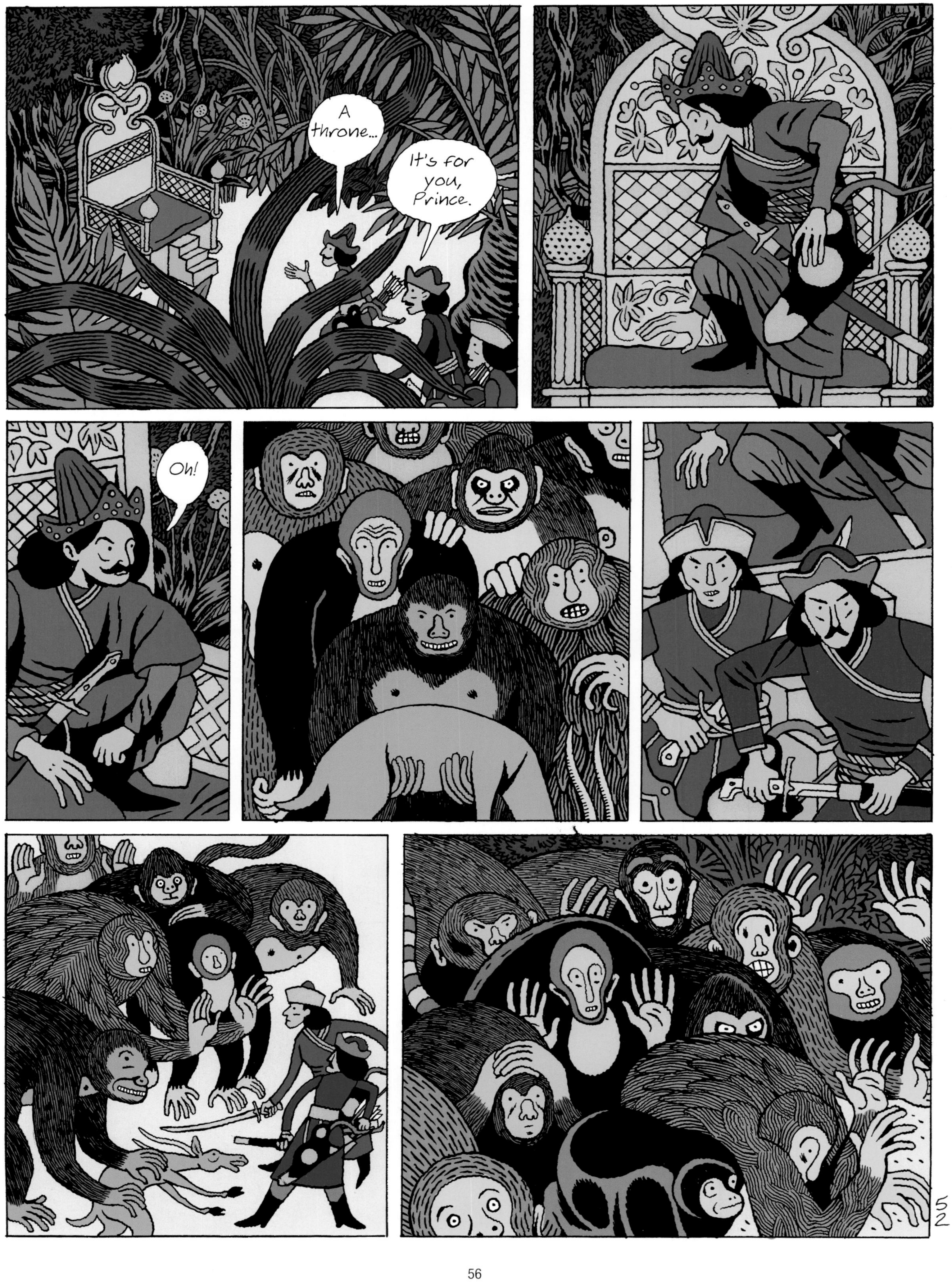
A throne...
It's for you, Prince.
Oh!
52

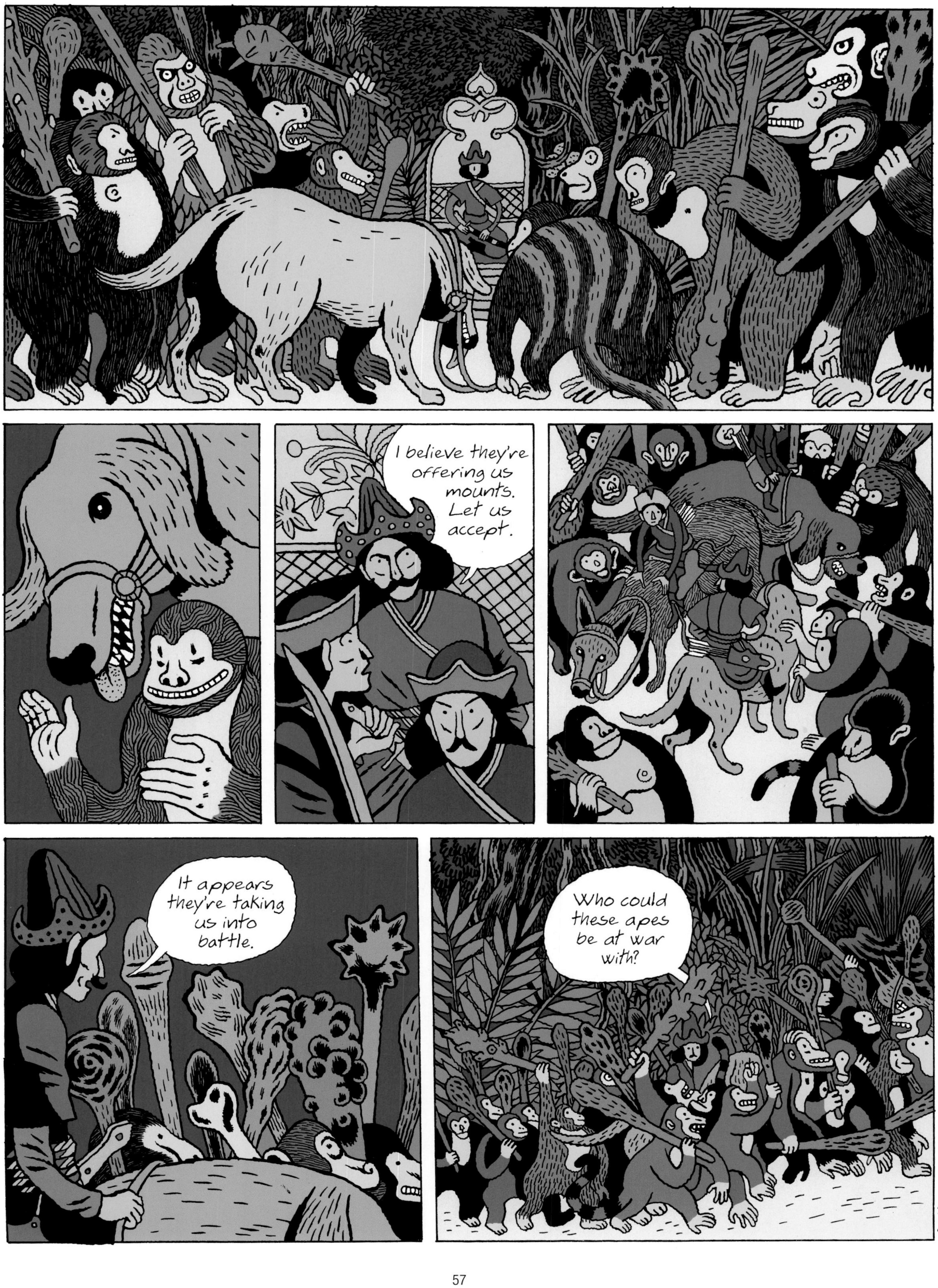
I believe they're offering us mounts. Let us accept.
It appears they're taking us into battle.
Who could these apes be at war with?

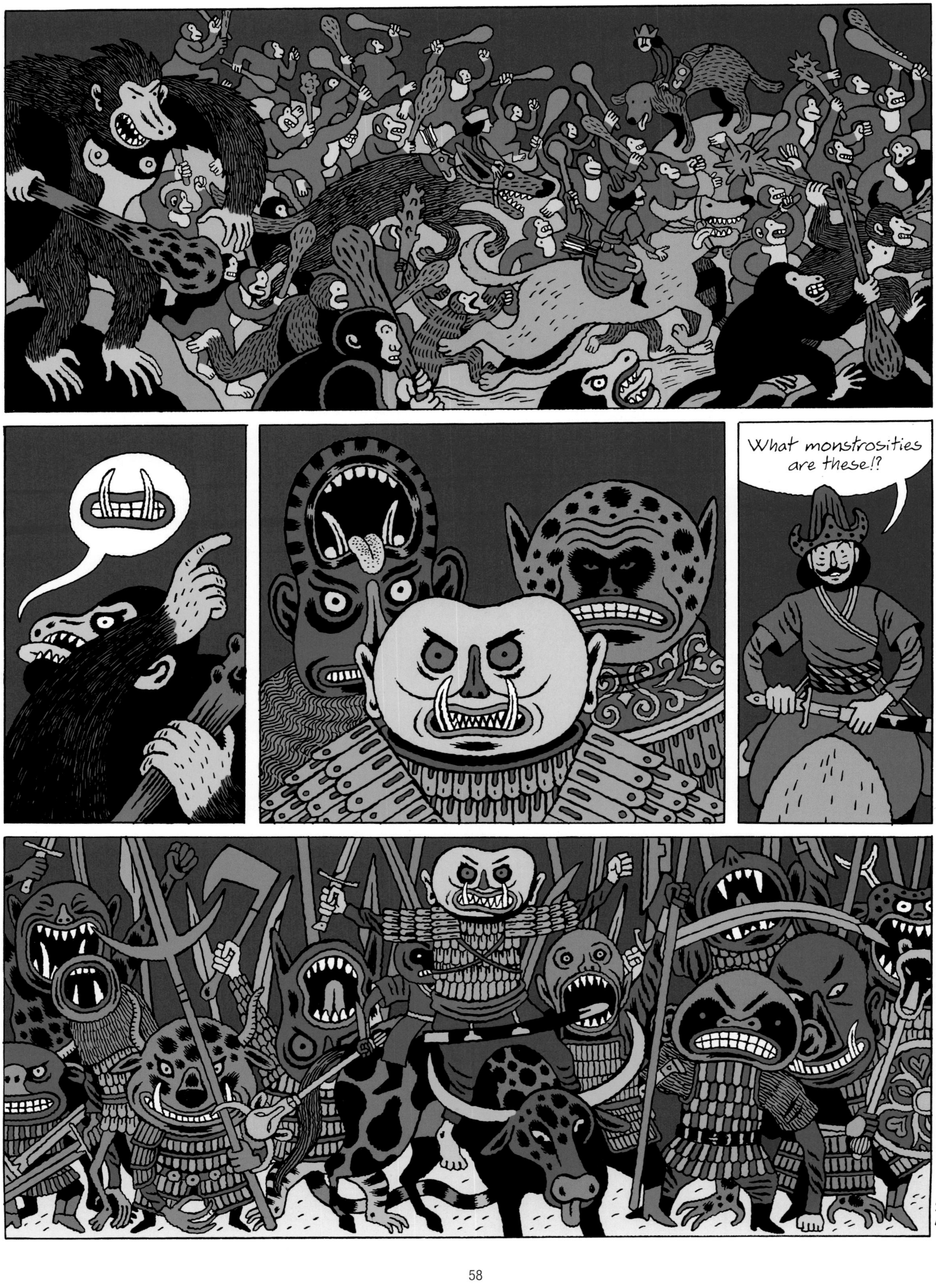
What monstrosities are these!?
54

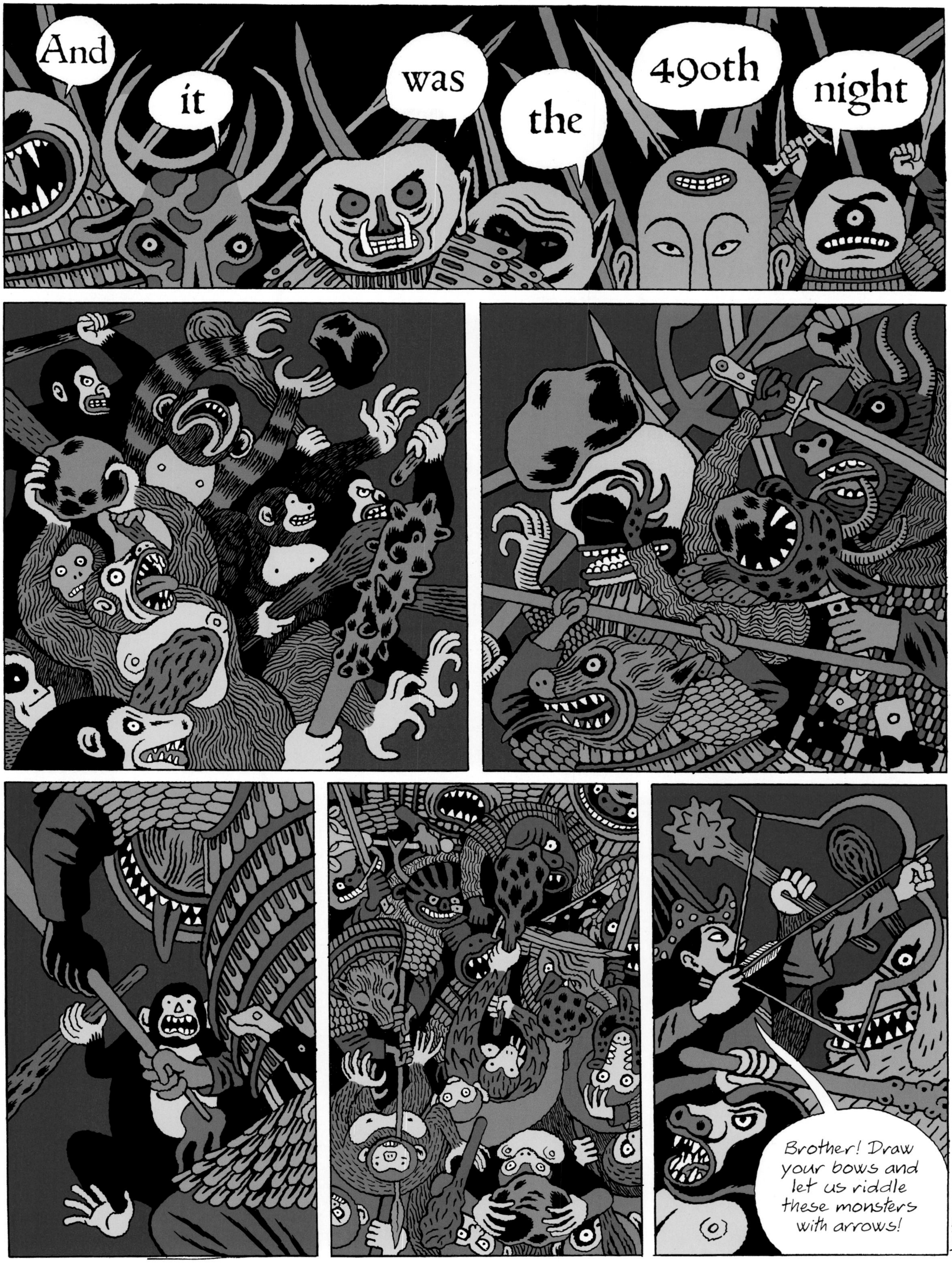
And
it
was
the
490th
night
Brother! Draw your bows and let us riddle these monsters with arrows!

5
5

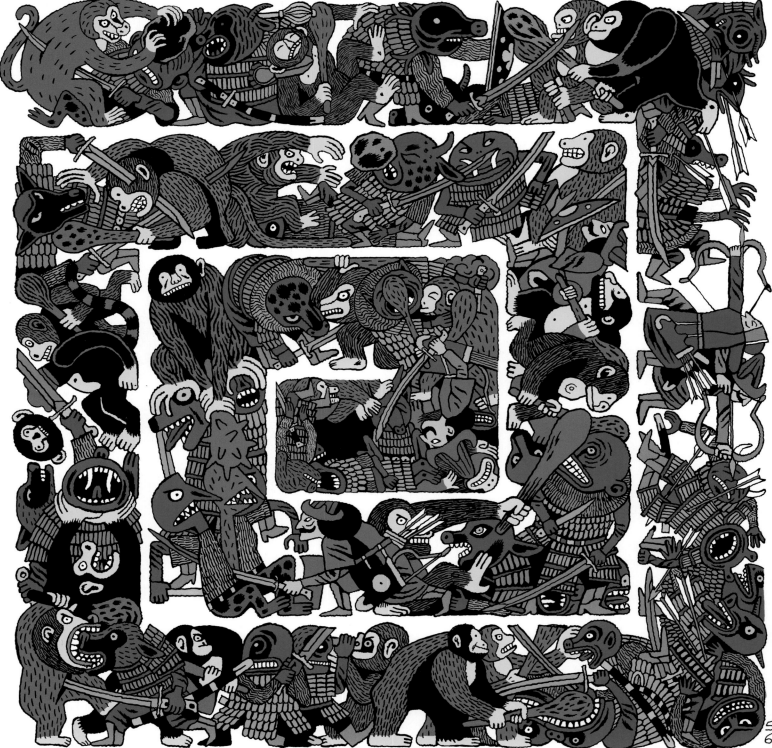

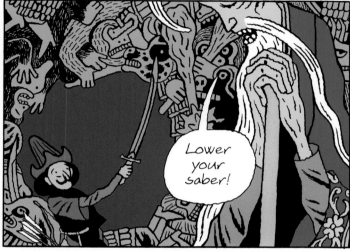

Lower your saber!

I will not harm you.

I have come from the thick of this battle to tell you your destiny.

The river on which you sailed is the river that goes around the world. The monkey people chose you to fight the ogres.

If you wish to return to the Kingdom of Kabul, you must go east.

57

61

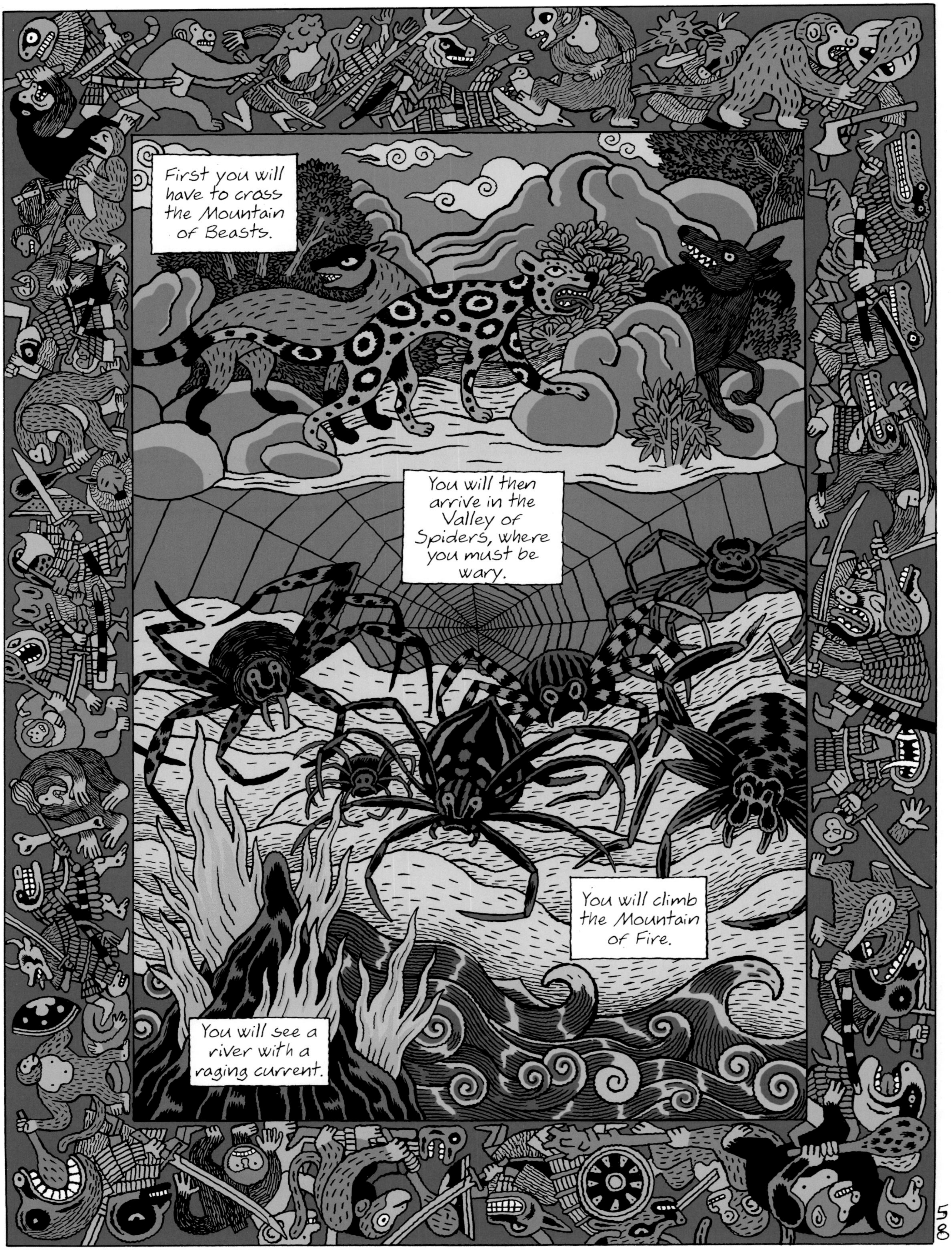
First you will have to cross the Mountain of Beasts.
You will then arrive in the Valley of Spiders, where you must be wary.
You will climb the Mountain of Fire.
You will see a river with a raging current.
58

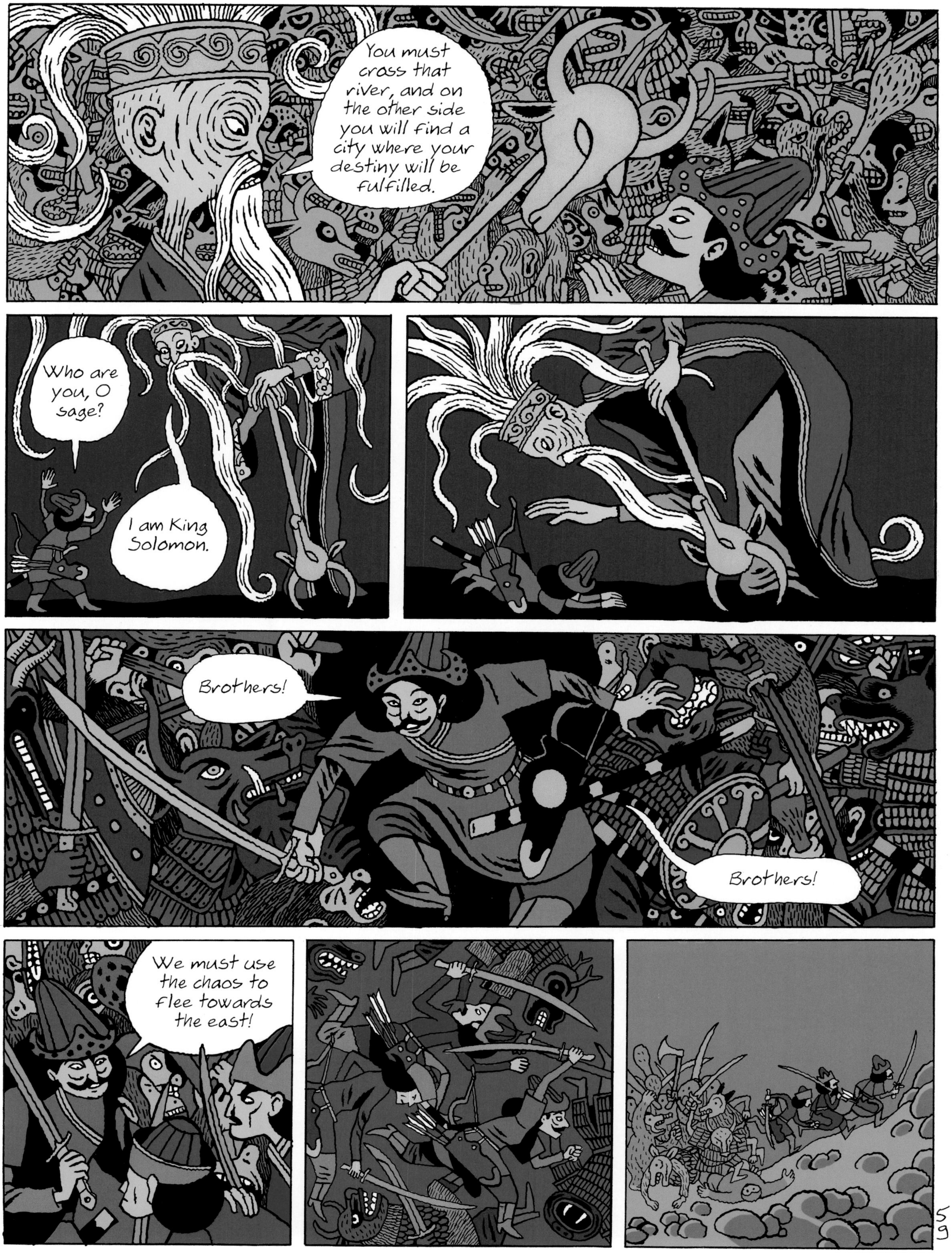
You must cross that river, and on the other side you will find a city where your destiny will be fulfilled.
Who are you, O sage?
I am King Solomon.
Brothers!
Brothers!
We must use the chaos to flee towards the east!
59

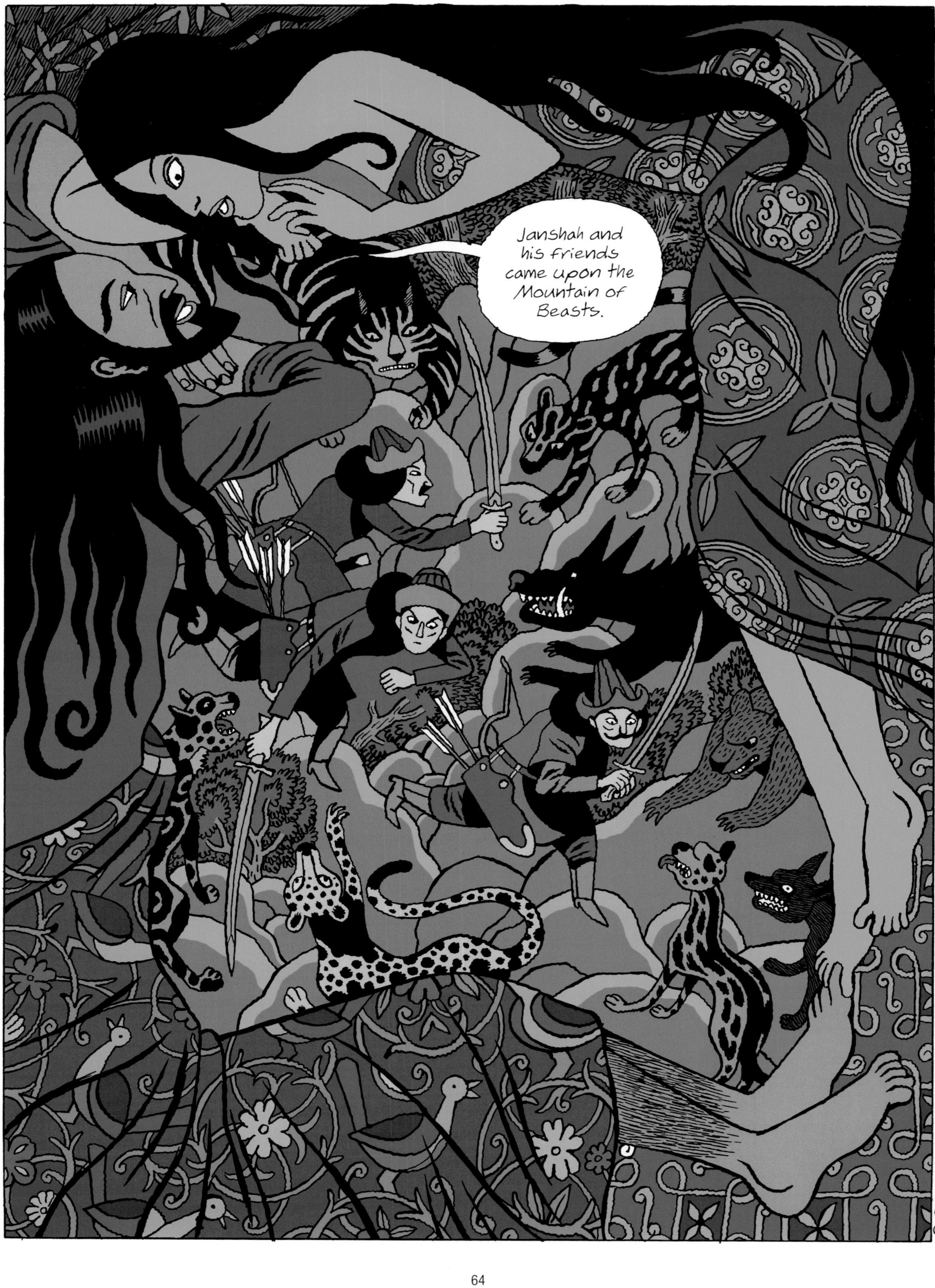
Janshah and his friends came upon the Mountain of Beasts.

60

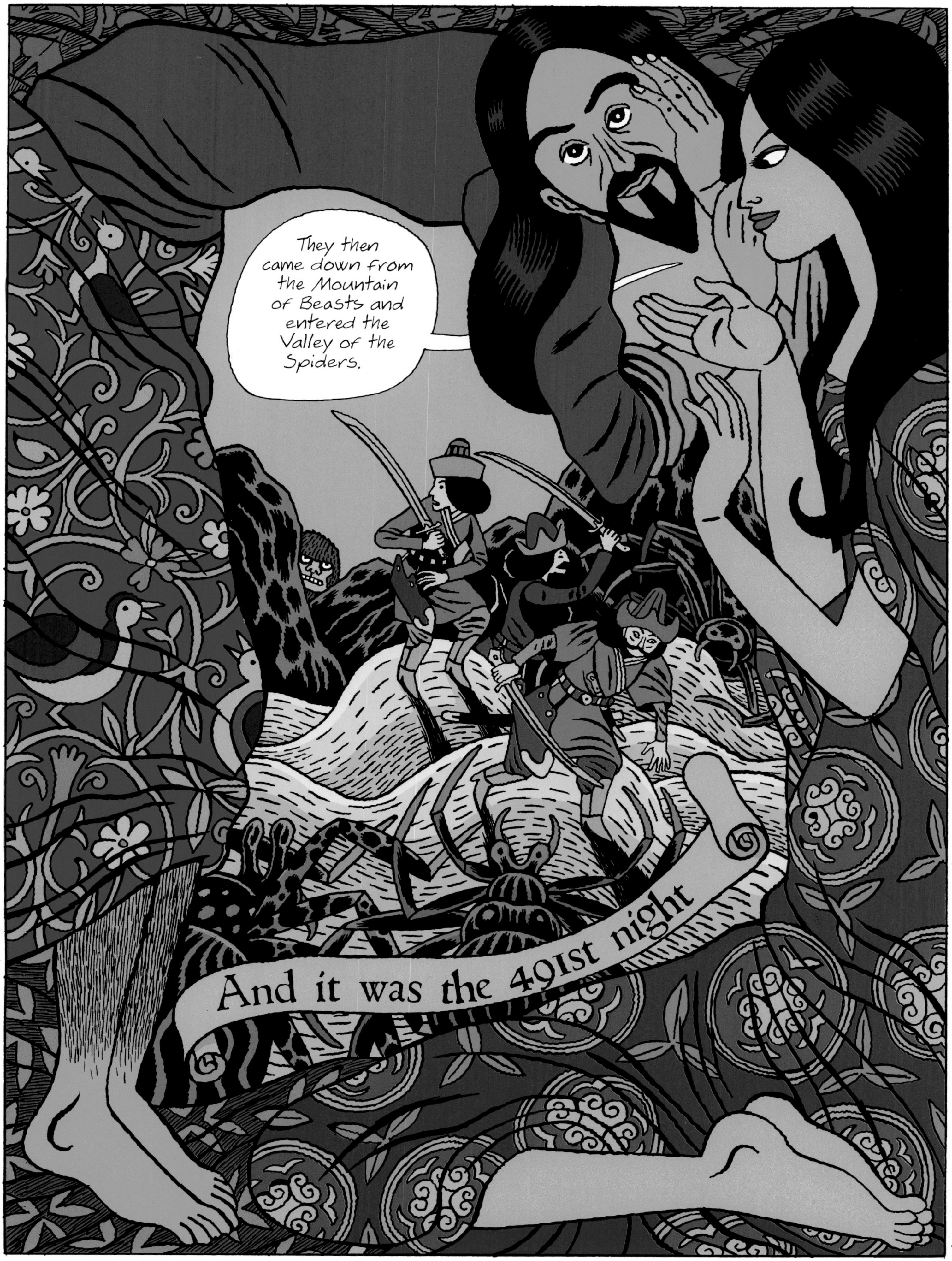
They then came down from the Mountain of Beasts and entered the Valley of the Spiders.
And it was the 491st night

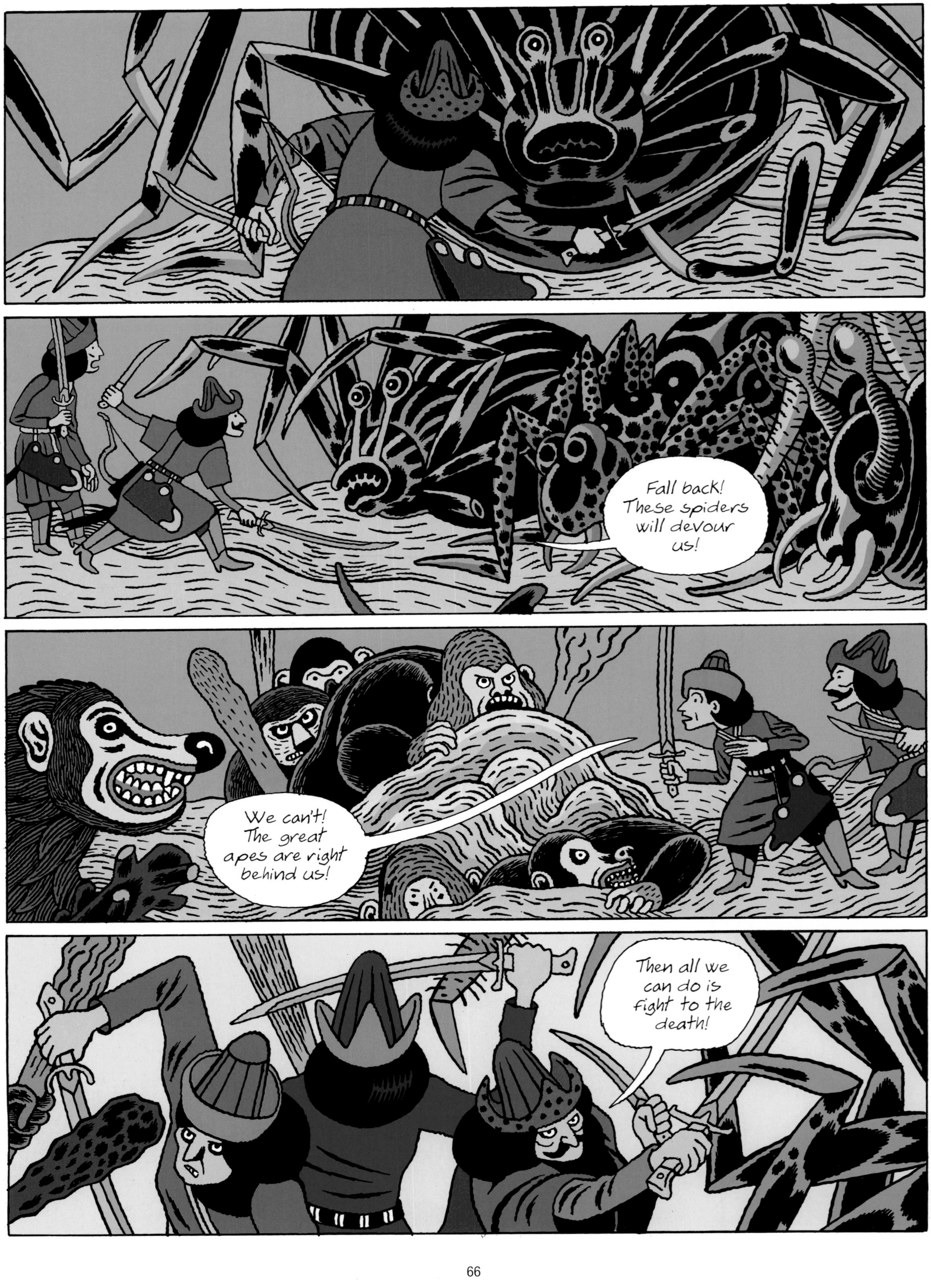
Fall back! These spiders will devour us!
We can't! The great apes are right behind us!
Then all we can do is fight to the death!

64

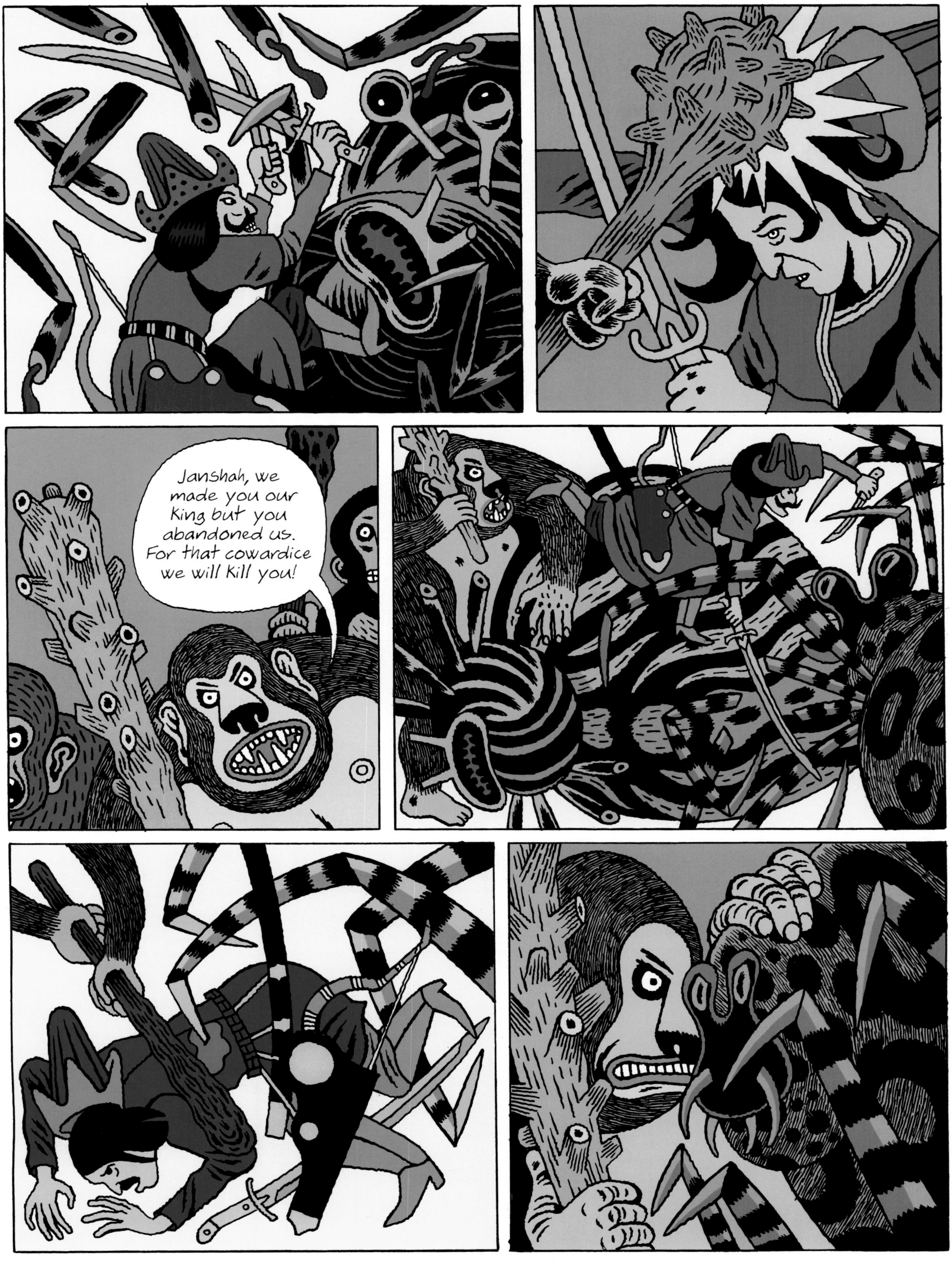
Janshah, we made you our King but you abandoned us. For that cowardice we will Kill you!

65

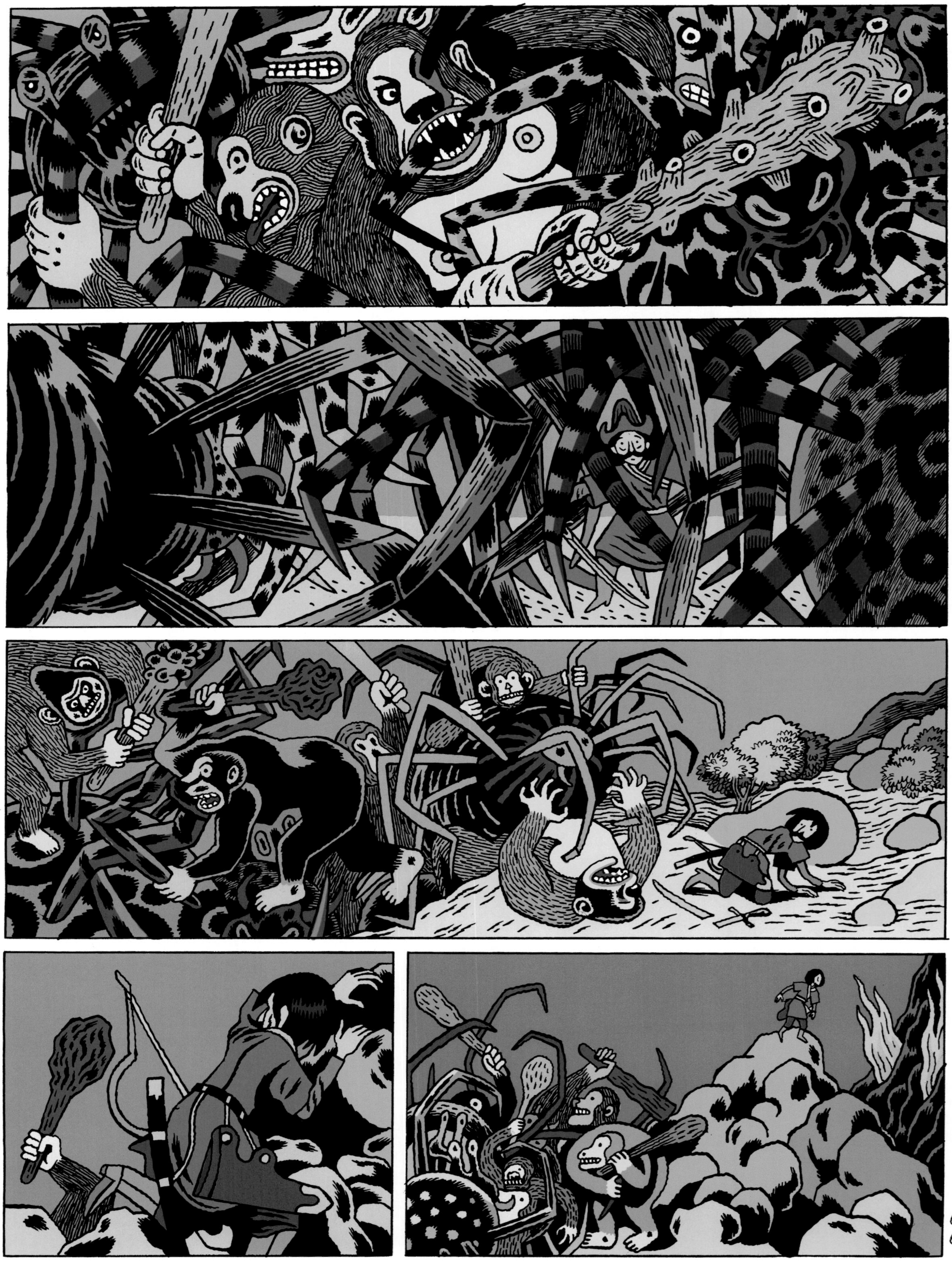

66

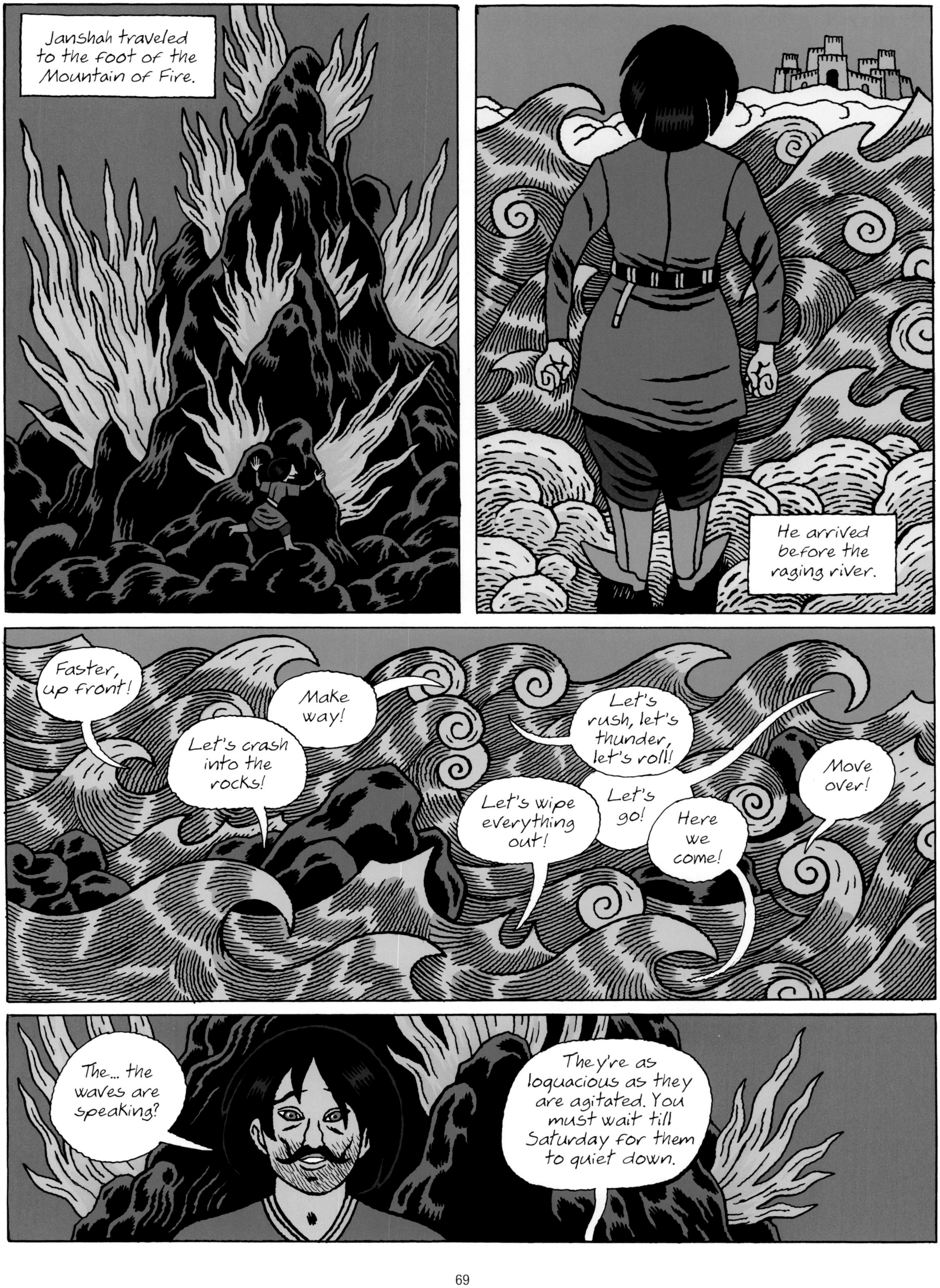
Janshah traveled to the foot of the Mountain of Fire.
He arrived before the raging river.
Faster, up front!
Make way!
Let's crash into the rocks!
Let's rush, let's thunder, let's roll!
Let's wipe everything out!
Let's go!
Here we come!
Move over!
The... the waves are speaking?
They're as loquacious as they are agitated. You must wait till Saturday for them to quiet down.

? Who are you?

A serpent! And I too wish to cross the river.

It stands between us and the land of King Solomon, whose palace you can see from here.

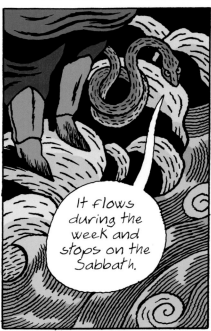

It flows during the week and stops on the Sabbath.

So let us be patient and wait.

What day are we?

The Sabbath starts tomorrow at sunset.

The next day, the river went quiet and stopped flowing.

Safe travels, human.

Thank you, serpent.

68

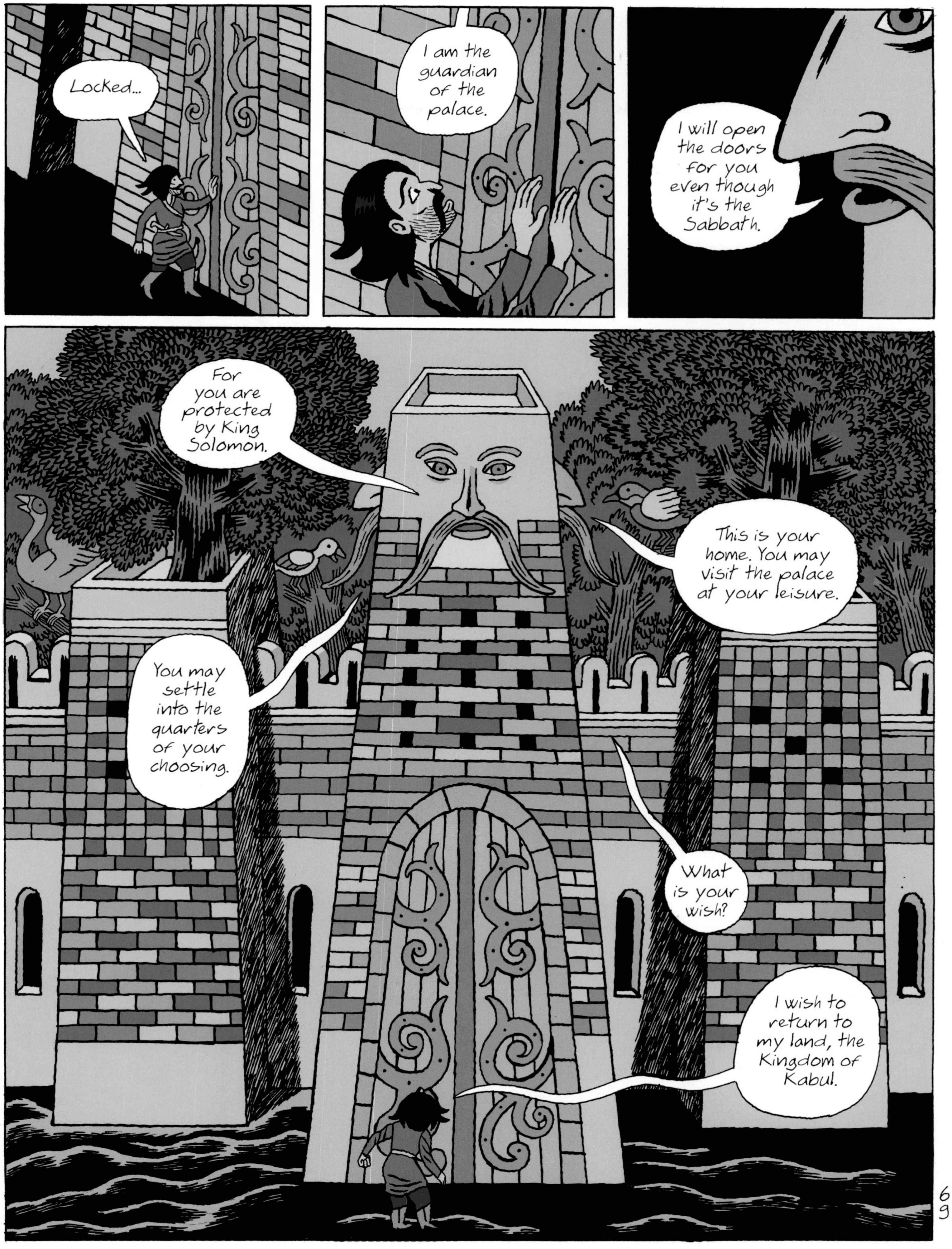
Locked...
I am the guardian of the palace.
I will open the doors for you even though it's the Sabbath.
For you are protected by King Solomon.
This is your home. You may visit the palace at your leisure.
You may settle into the quarters of your choosing.
What is your wish?
I wish to return to my land, the Kingdom of Kabul.
69

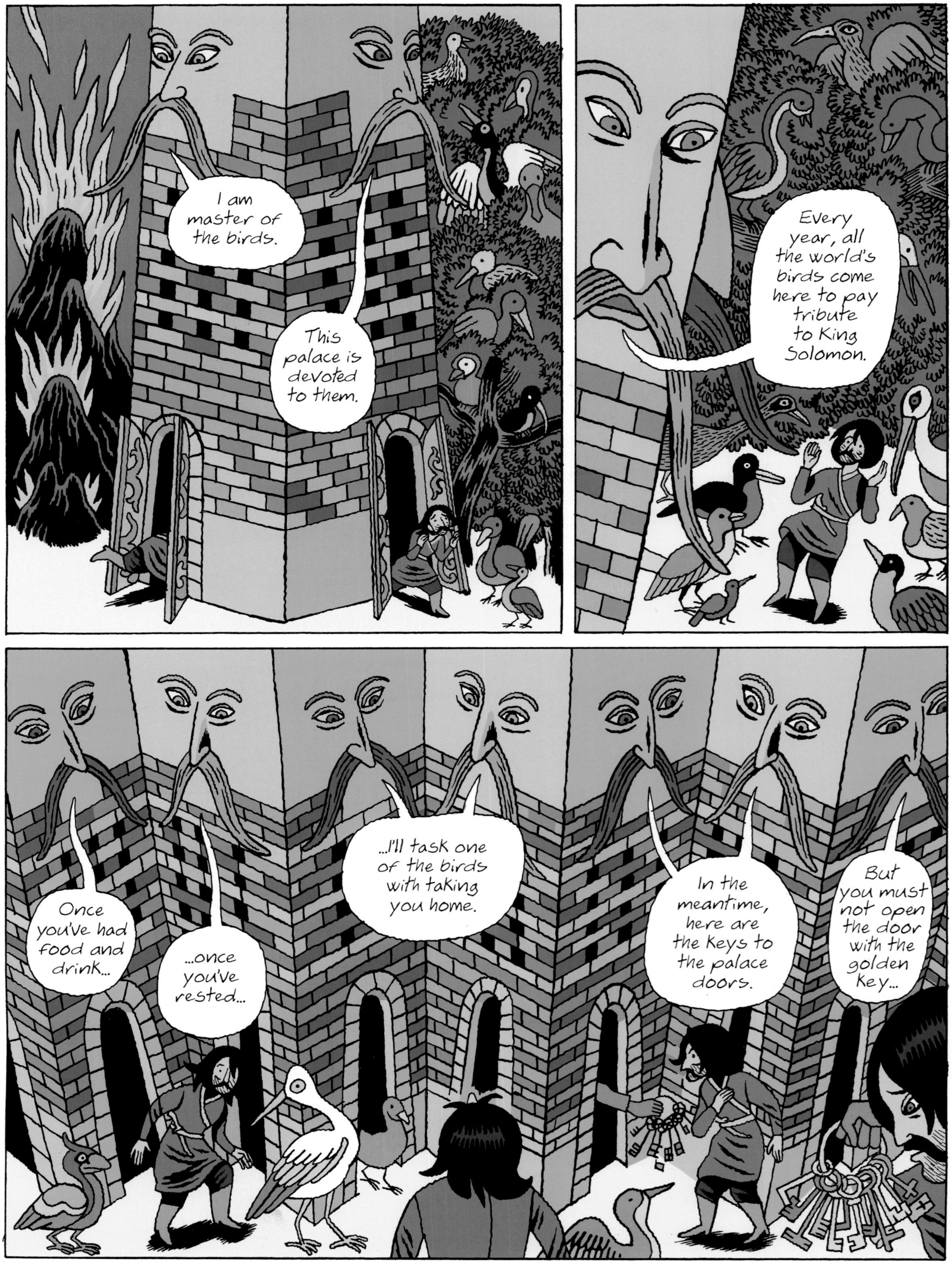
I am master of the birds.
This palace is devoted to them.
Every year, all the world's birds come here to pay tribute to King Solomon.
Once you've had food and drink...
...once you've rested...
...I'll task one of the birds with taking you home.
In the meantime, here are the keys to the palace doors.
But you must not open the door with the golden key...
70

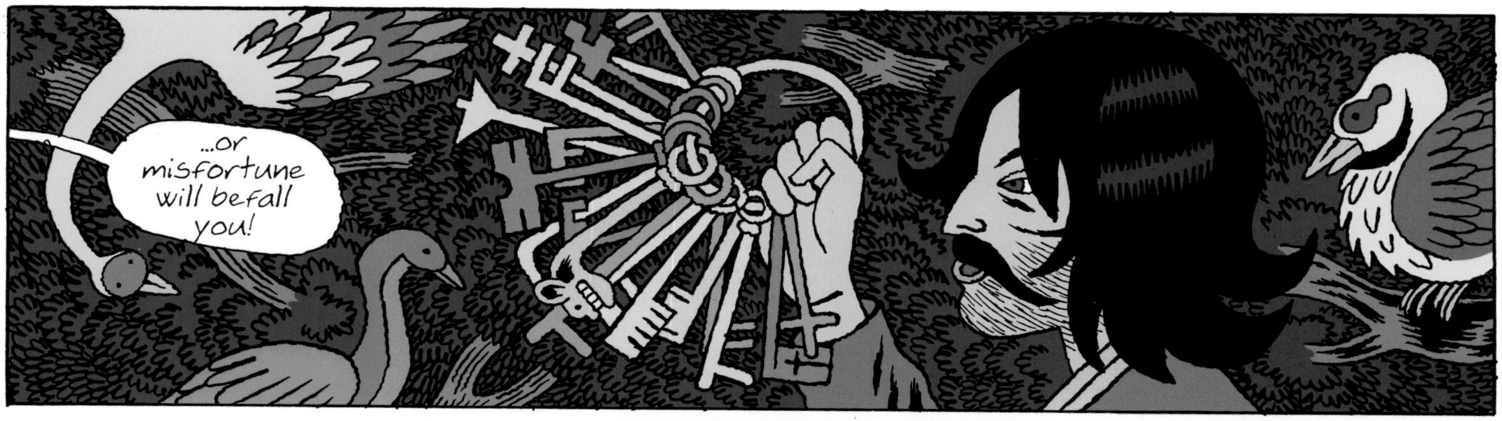
...or misfortune will befall you!

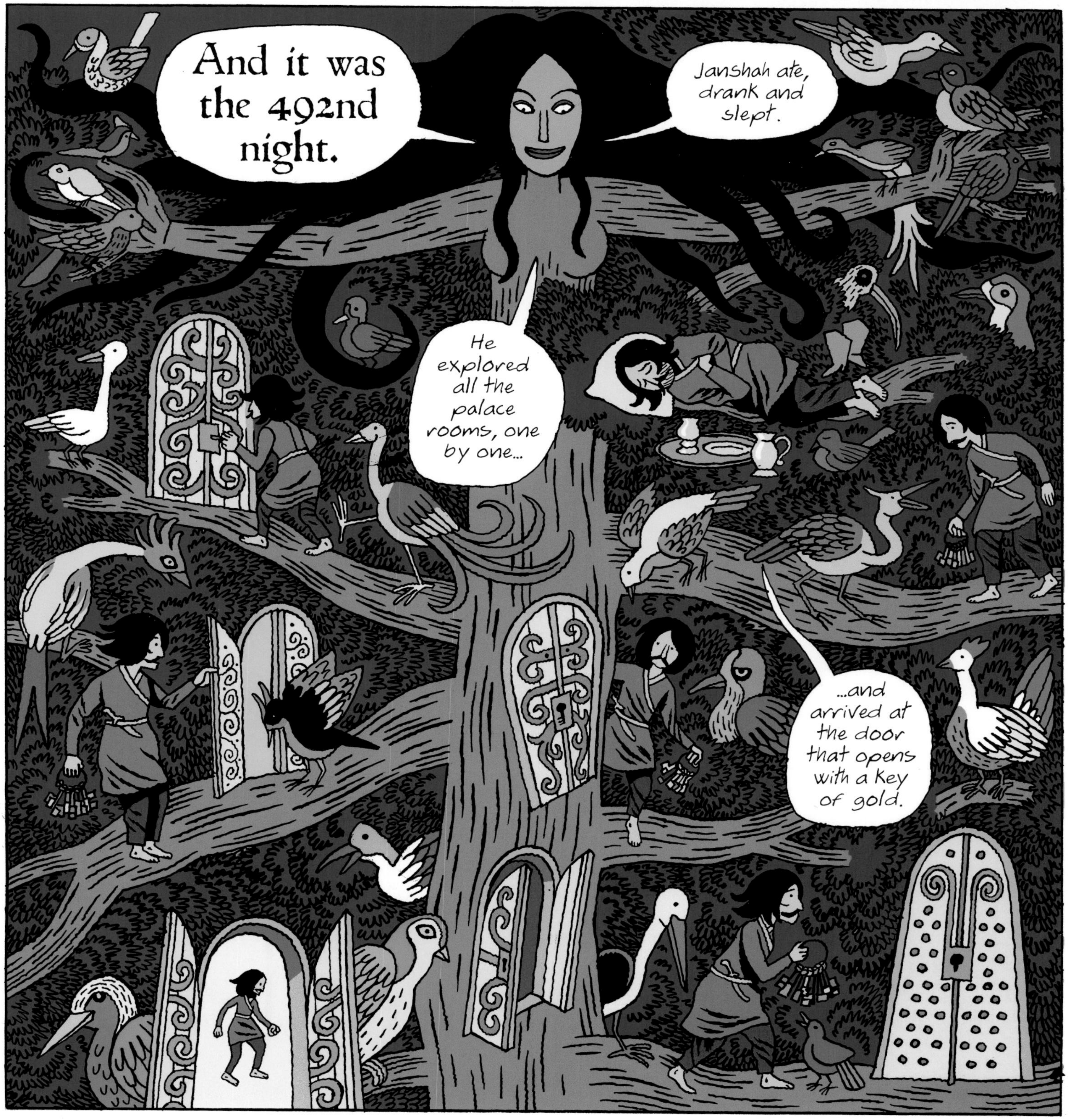
And it was the 492nd night.
Janshah ate, drank and slept.
He explored all the palace rooms, one by one...
...and arrived at the door that opens with a key of gold.

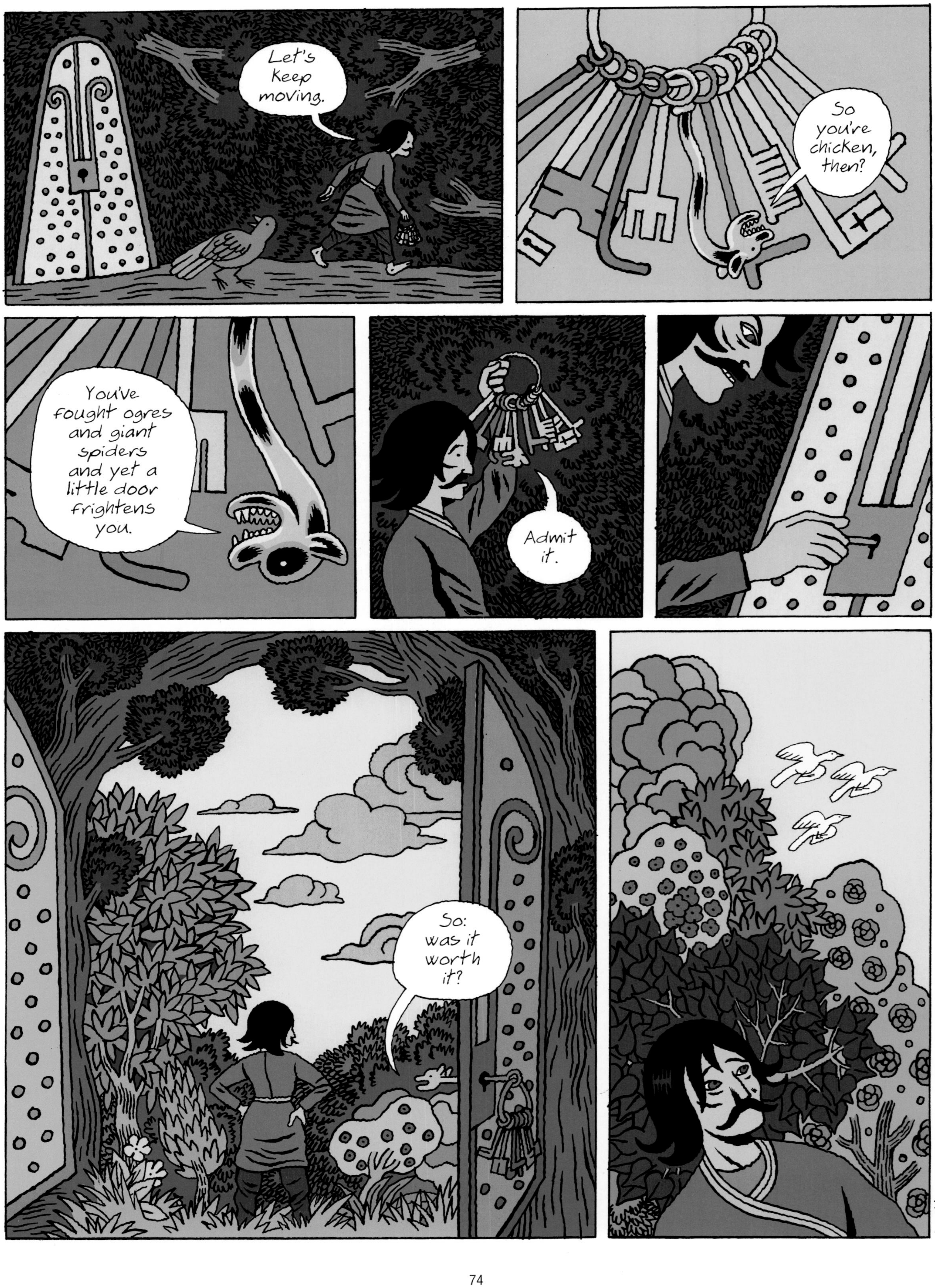
Let's keep moving.
So you're chicken, then?
You've fought ogres and giant spiders and yet a little door frightens you.
Admit it.
So: was it worth it?
7
2

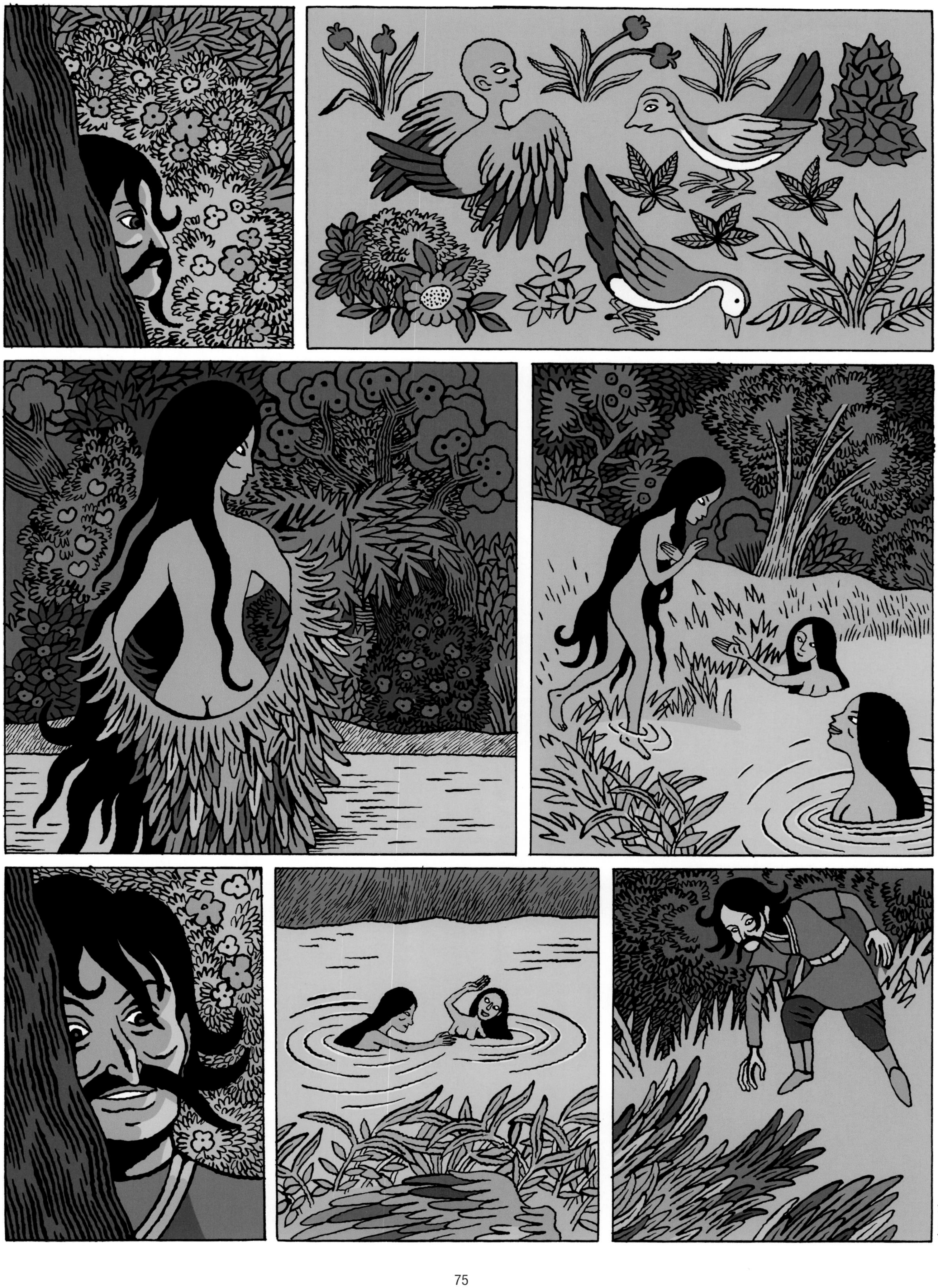

73

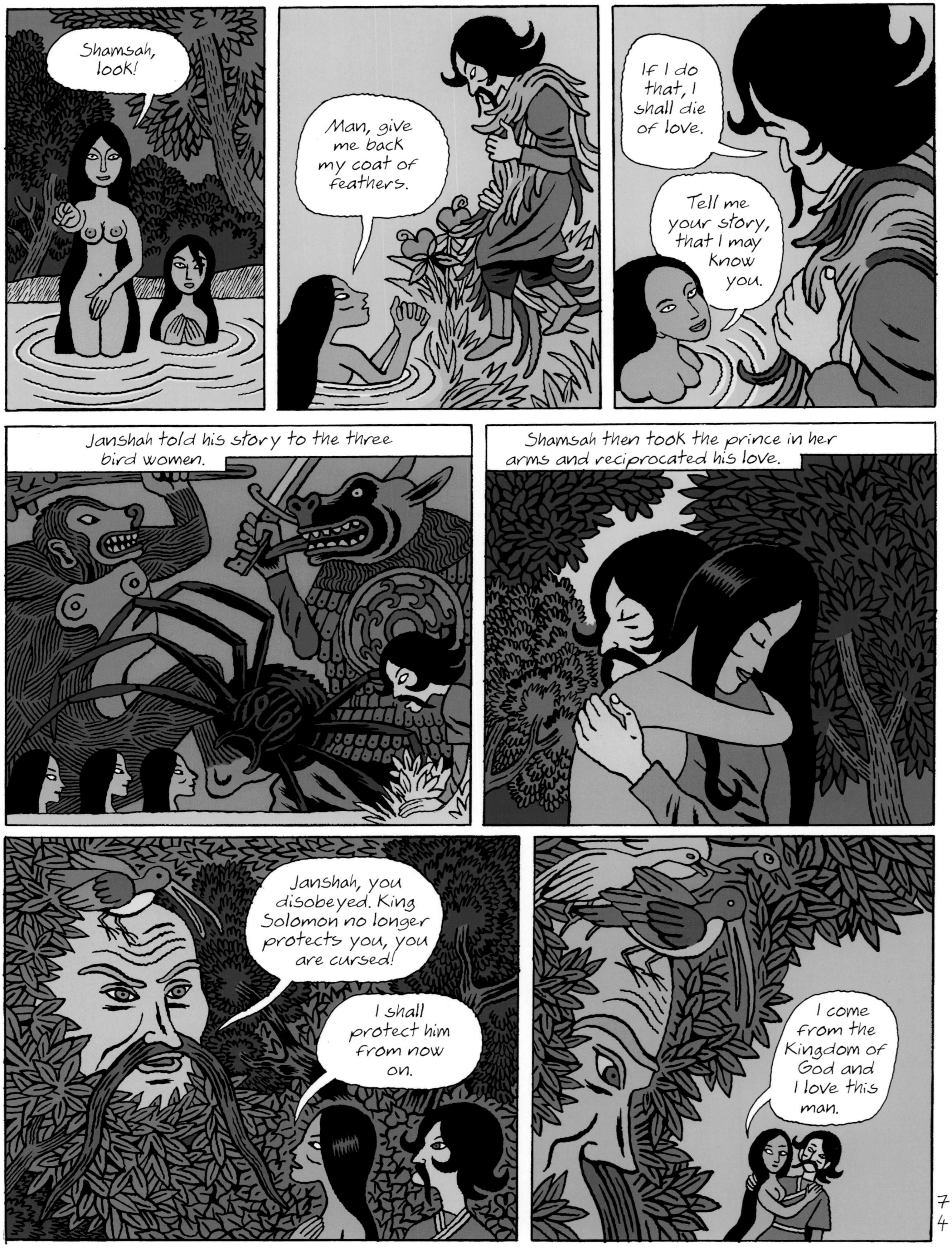
Shamsah, look!
Man, give me back my coat of feathers.
If I do that, I shall die of love.
Tell me your story, that I may know you.
Janshah told his story to the three bird women.
Shamsah then took the prince in her arms and reciprocated his love.
Janshah, you disobeyed. King Solomon no longer protects you, you are cursed!
I shall protect him from now on.
I come from the Kingdom of God and I love this man.
74

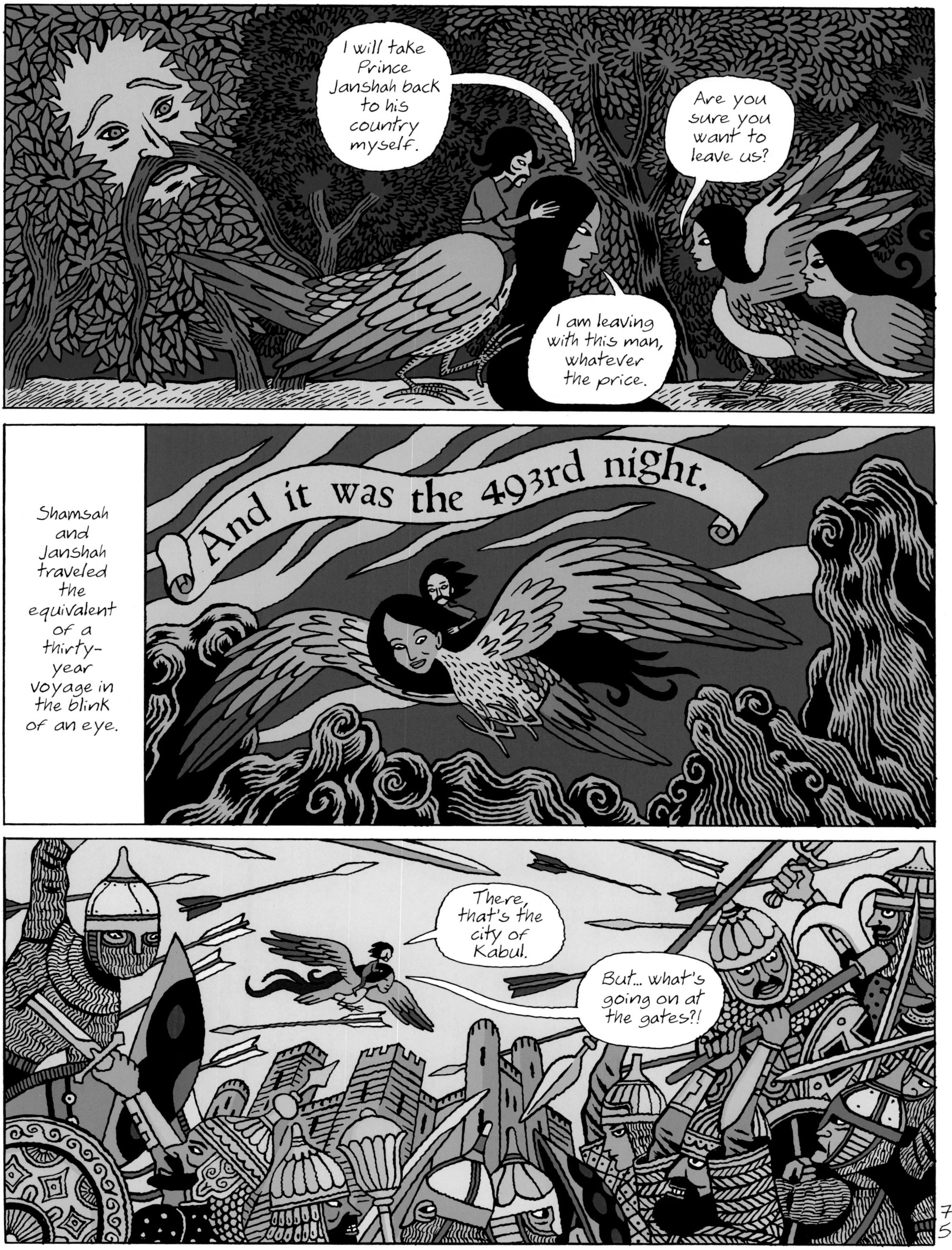

I will take Prince Janshah back to his country myself.
Are you sure you want to leave us?
I am leaving with this man, whatever the price.
Shamsah and Janshah traveled the equivalent of a thirty-year voyage in the blink of an eye.
And it was the 493rd night.
There, that's the city of Kabul.
But... what's going on at the gates?!
75

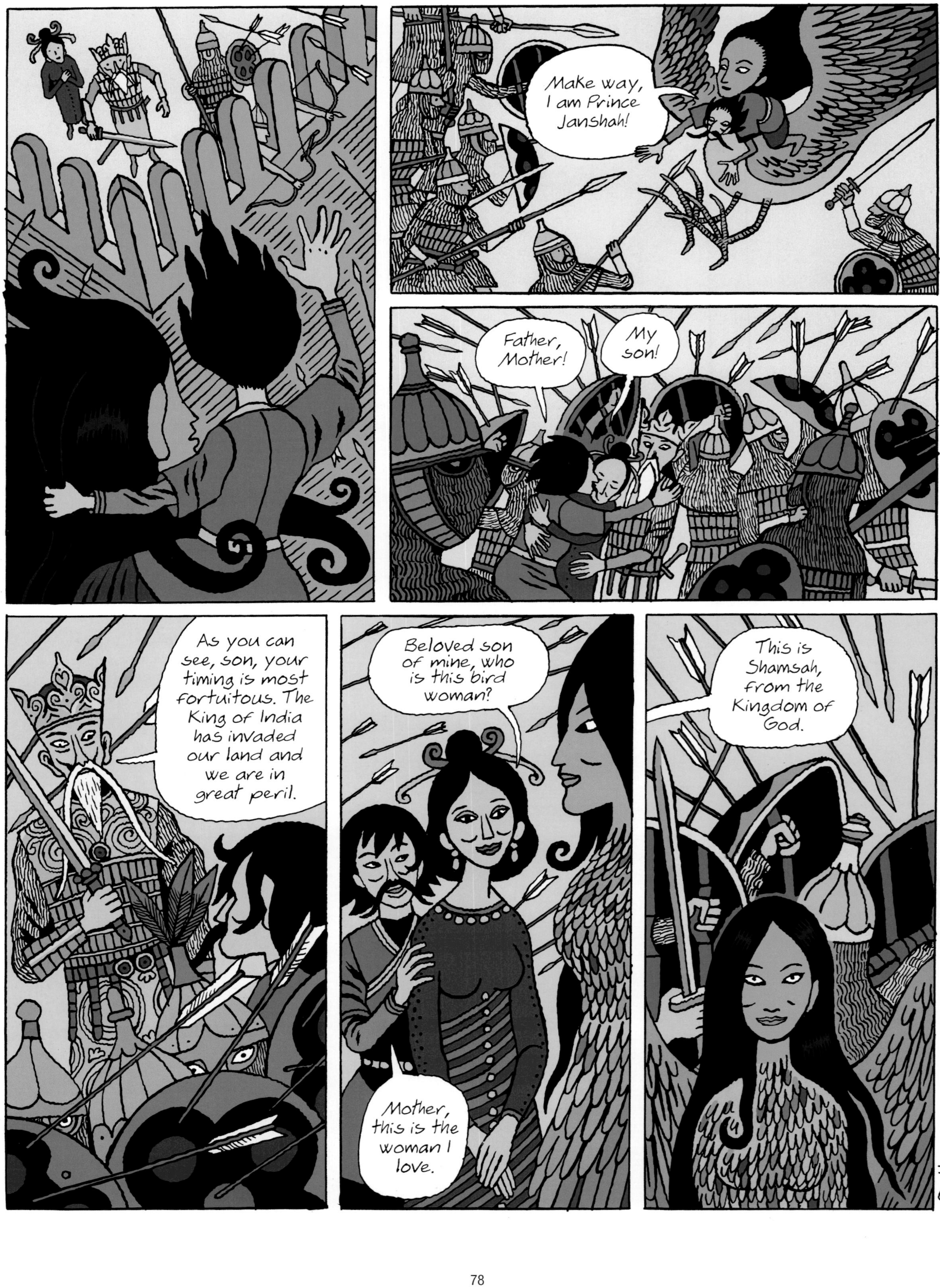
Make way, I am Prince Janshah!
Father, Mother!
My son!
As you can see, son, your timing is most fortuitous. The King of India has invaded our land and we are in great peril.
Beloved son of mine, who is this bird woman?
Mother, this is the woman I love.
This is Shamsah, from the Kingdom of God.

76

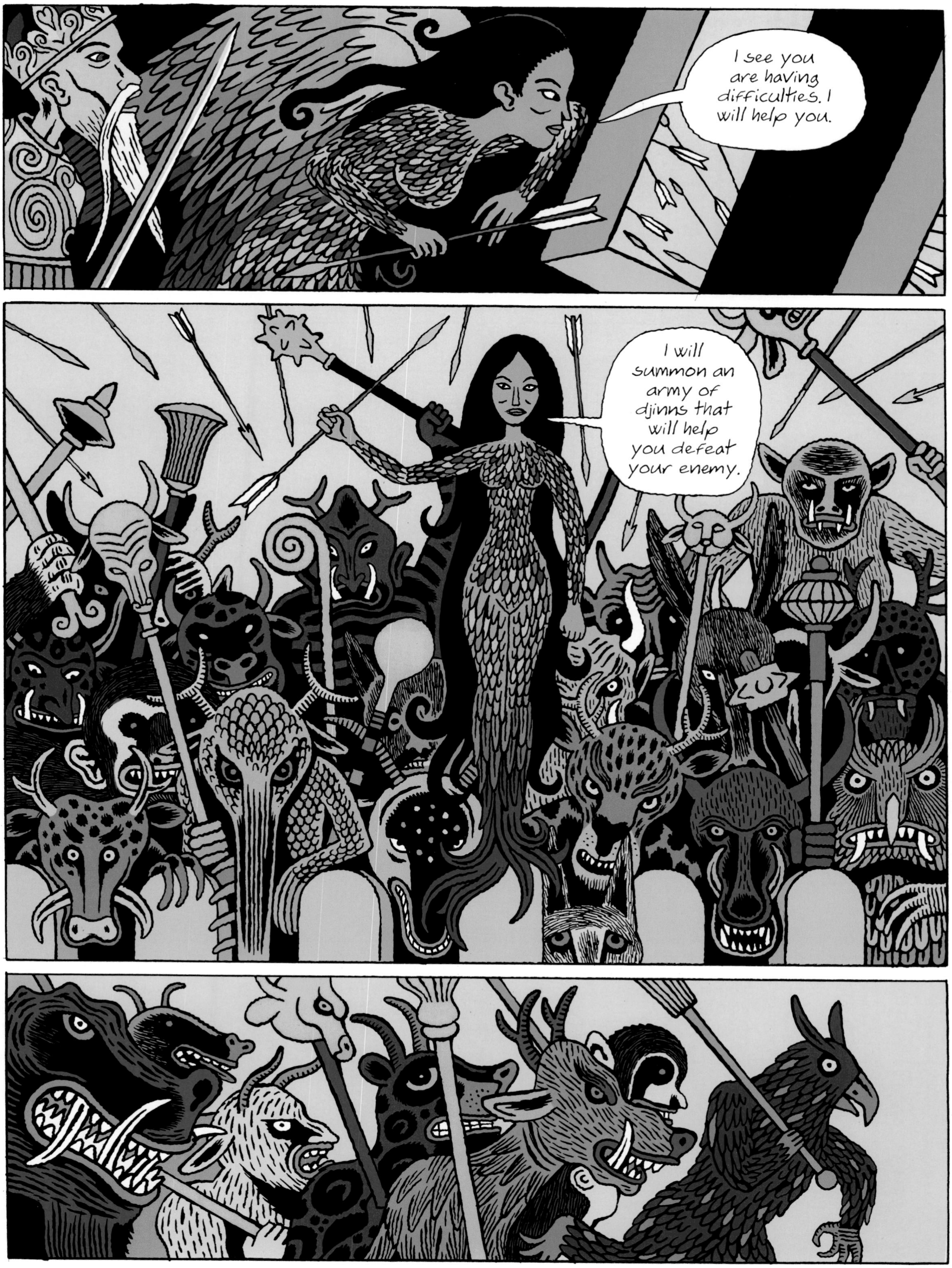
I see you are having difficulties. I will help you.
I will summon an army of djinns that will help you defeat your enemy.

7
7

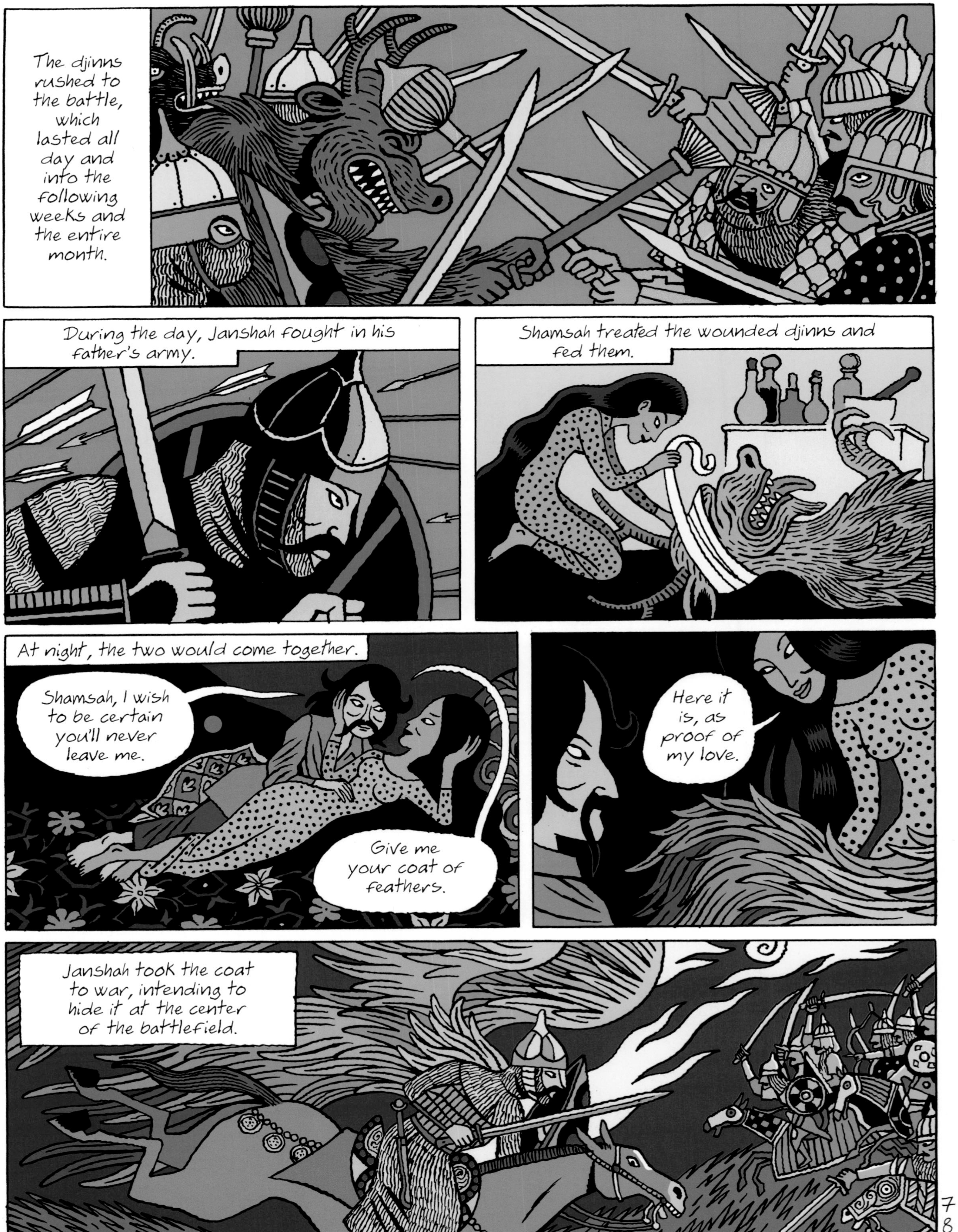
The djinns rushed to the battle, which lasted all day and into the following weeks and the entire month.
During the day, Janshah fought in his father's army.
Shamsah treated the wounded djinns and fed them.
At night, the two would come together.
Shamsah, I wish to be certain you'll never leave me.
Give me your coat of feathers.
Here it is, as proof of my love.
Janshah took the coat to war, intending to hide it at the center of the battlefield.
7
8

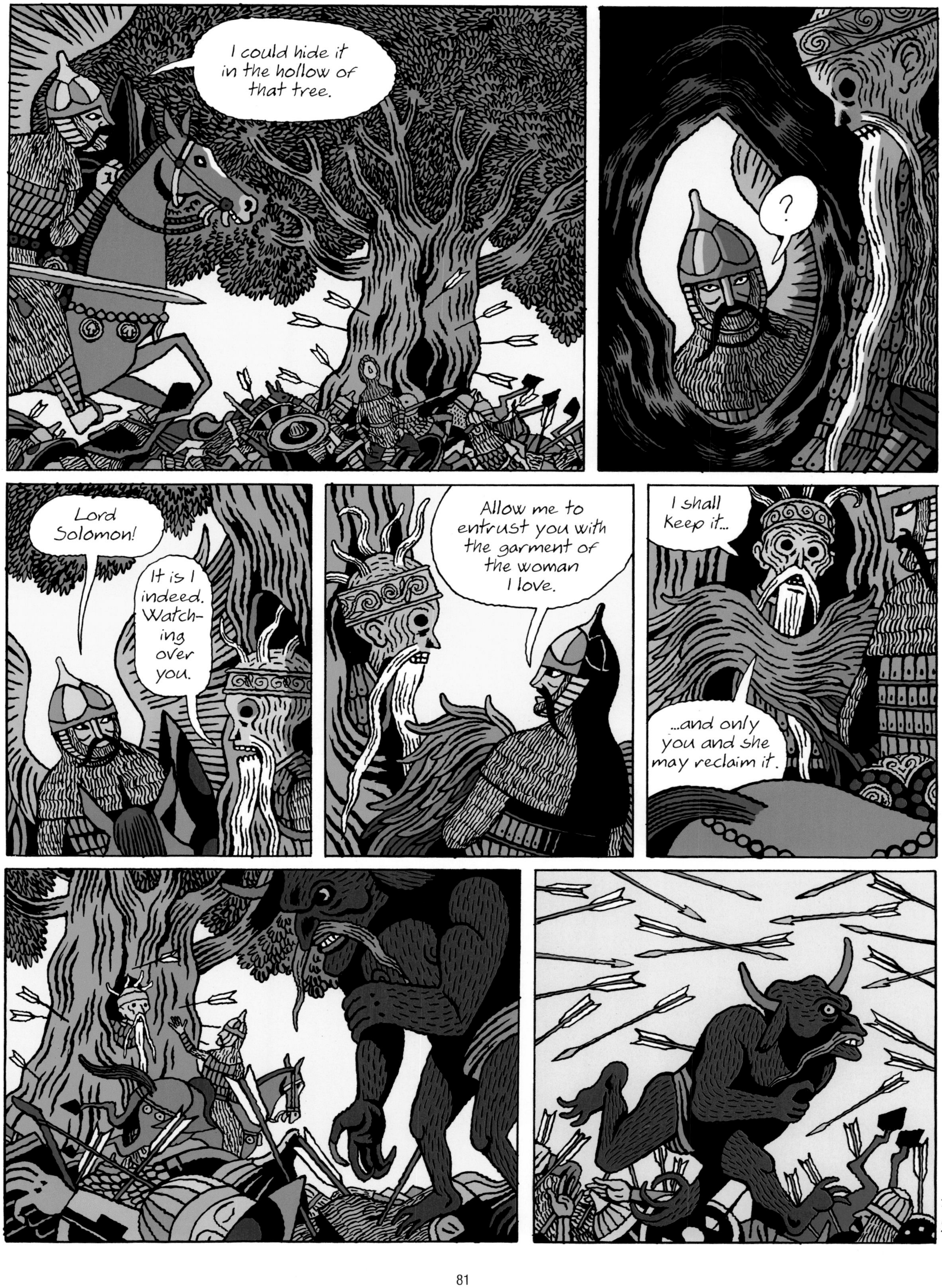
I could hide it in the hollow of that tree.
?
Lord Solomon!
It is I indeed. Watch-ing over you.
Allow me to entrust you with the garment of the woman I love.
I shall keep it...
...and only you and she may reclaim it.

79

Mistress, I am wounded. Heal me, for pity's sake.

Thank you for tending to us. In return, I shall tell you where Prince Janshah hid your coat of feathers.

In the middle of the battle-field is a tree.

In that tree is King Solomon.

It is he who has your garment.

Thank you, O Djinn, for this great favor.

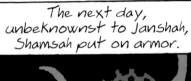

The next day, unbeknownst to Janshah, Shamsah put on armor.

She threw herself into the thick of the battle.

I've been expecting you, Shamsah.

It is killing me not to see my sisters. I beg you to give me back my coat of feathers.

I vow to bring it back, so that Janshah won't know.

Here it is.

Shamsah!

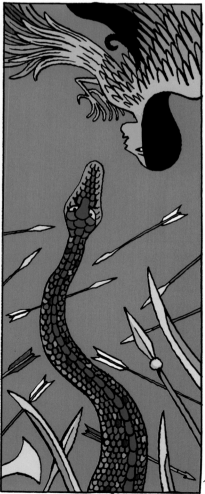

81

Shamsah, beware!

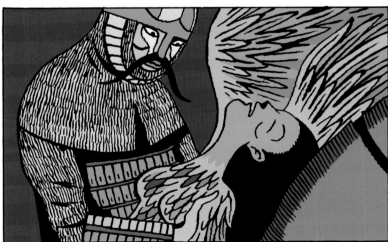

I don't want to live without her. I shall wither and die upon her grave.

Now leave me.

Bulukiya returned to the seashore.

He rubbed the sole of his feet with the sap from the magical plant and made his way through the waves.

And it was the 494th night.

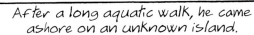

After a long aquatic walk, he came ashore on an unknown island.

8
3

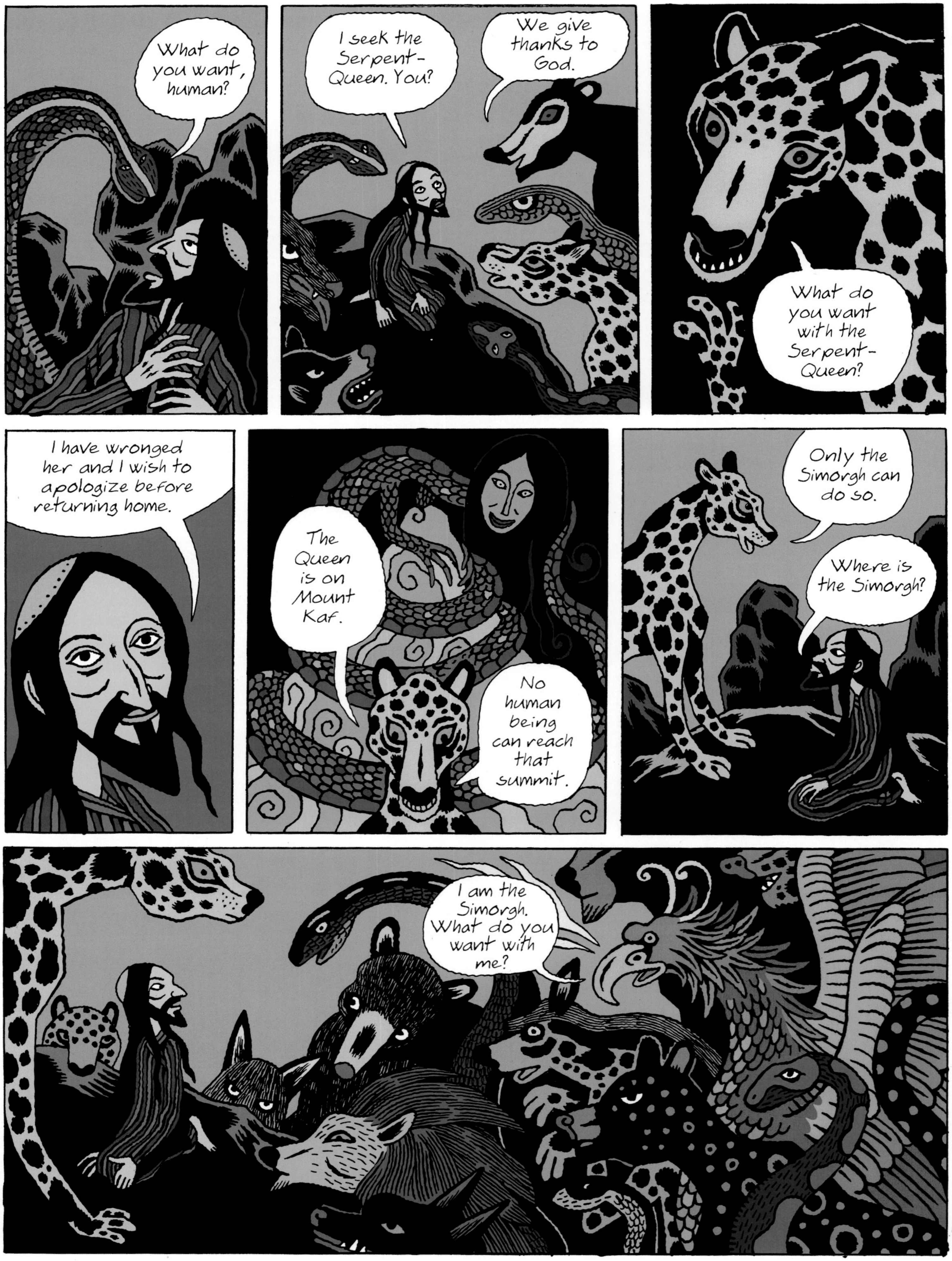
What do you want, human?
I seek the Serpent-Queen. You?
We give thanks to God.
What do you want with the Serpent-Queen?
I have wronged her and I wish to apologize before returning home.
The Queen is on Mount Kaf.
No human being can reach that summit.
Only the Simorgh can do so.
Where is the Simorgh?
I am the Simorgh. What do you want with me?

84

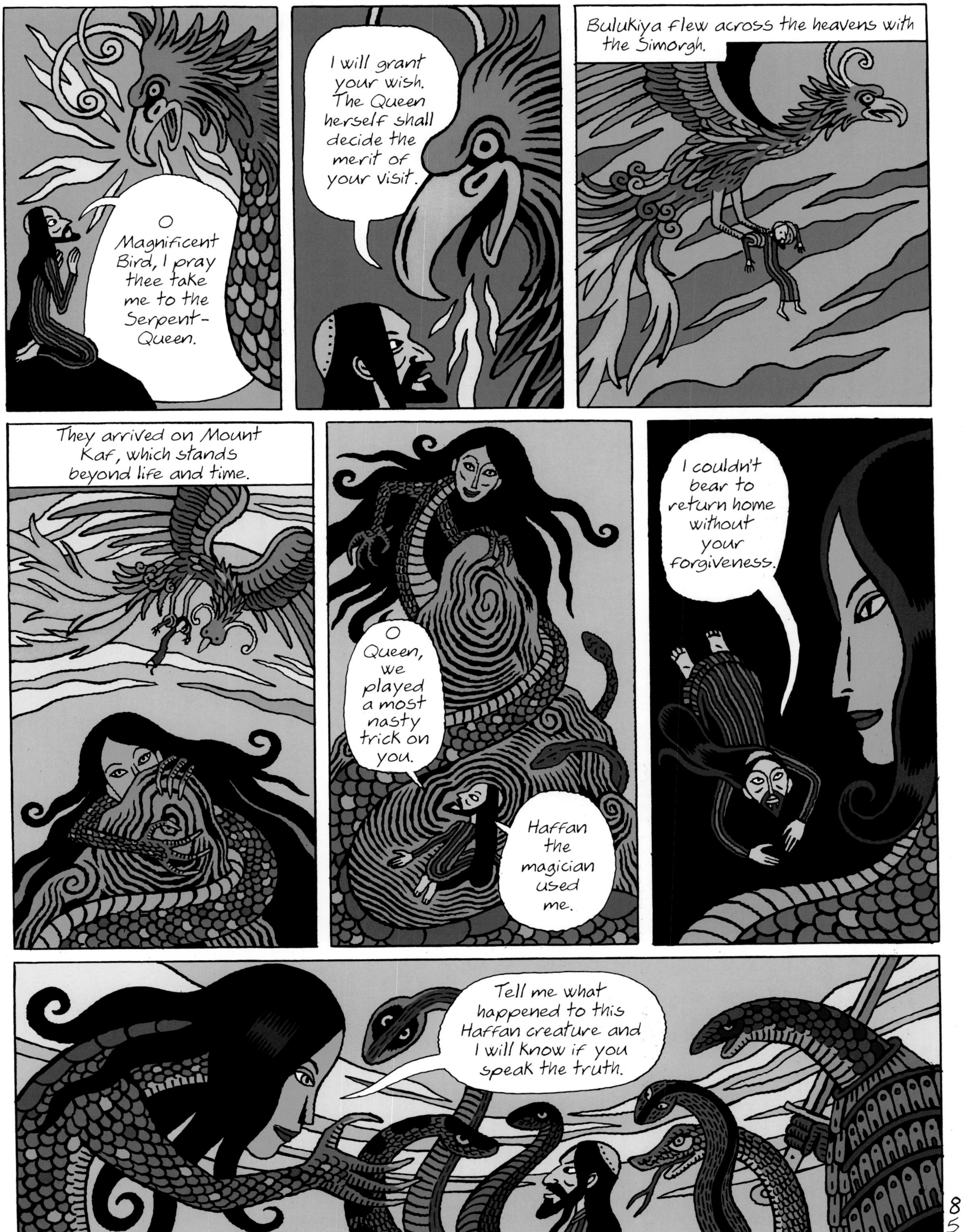
O Magnificent Bird, I pray thee take me to the Serpent-Queen.
I will grant your wish. The Queen herself shall decide the merit of your visit.
Bulukiya flew across the heavens with the Simorgh.
They arrived on Mount Kaf, which stands beyond life and time.
O Queen, we played a most nasty trick on you.
Haffan the magician used me.
I couldn't bear to return home without your forgiveness.
Tell me what happened to this Haffan creature and I will know if you speak the truth.
85

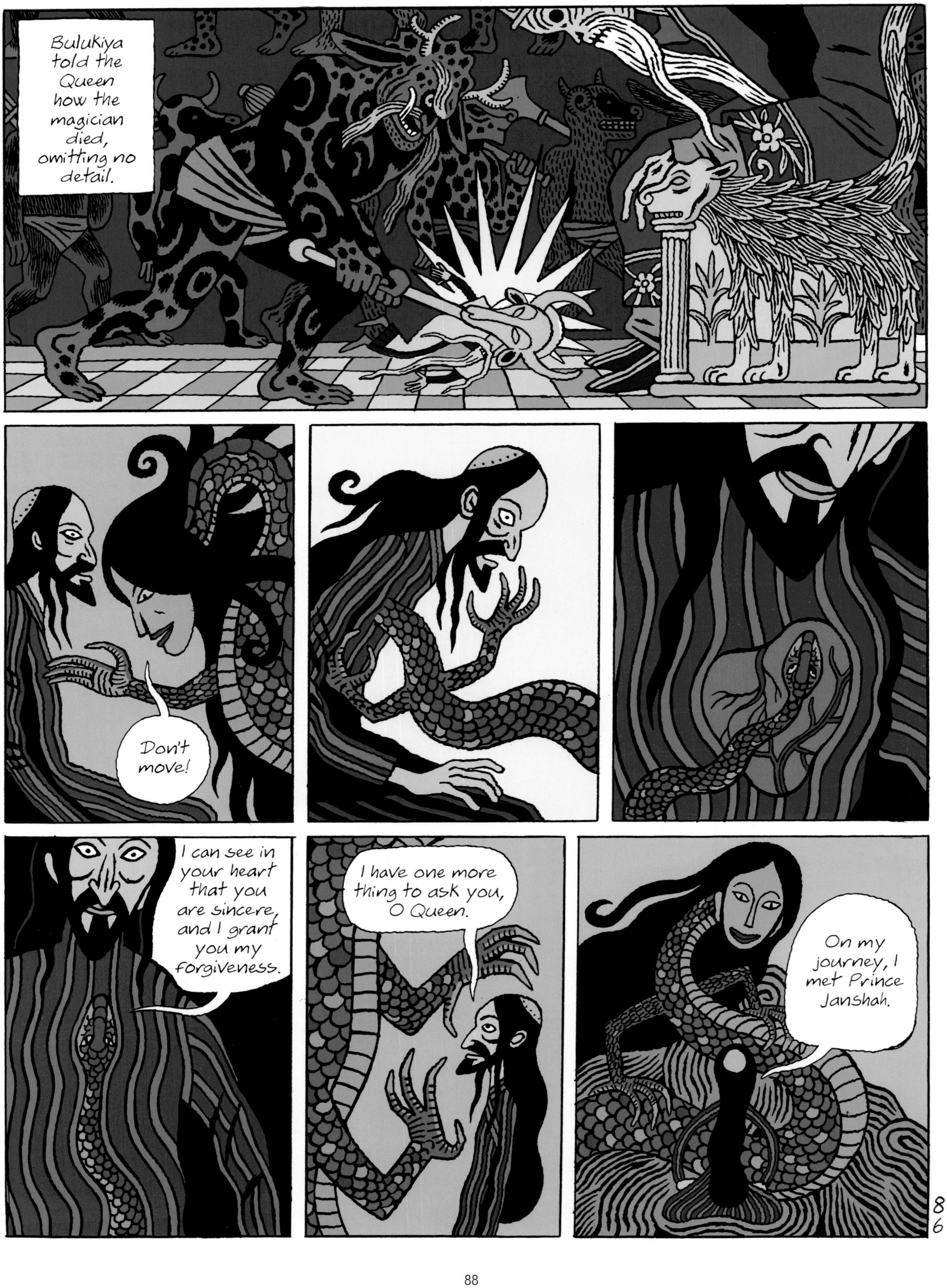
Bulukiya told the Queen how the magician died, omitting no detail.
Don't move!
I can see in your heart that you are sincere, and I grant you my forgiveness.
I have one more thing to ask you, O Queen.
On my journey, I met Prince Janshah.
86

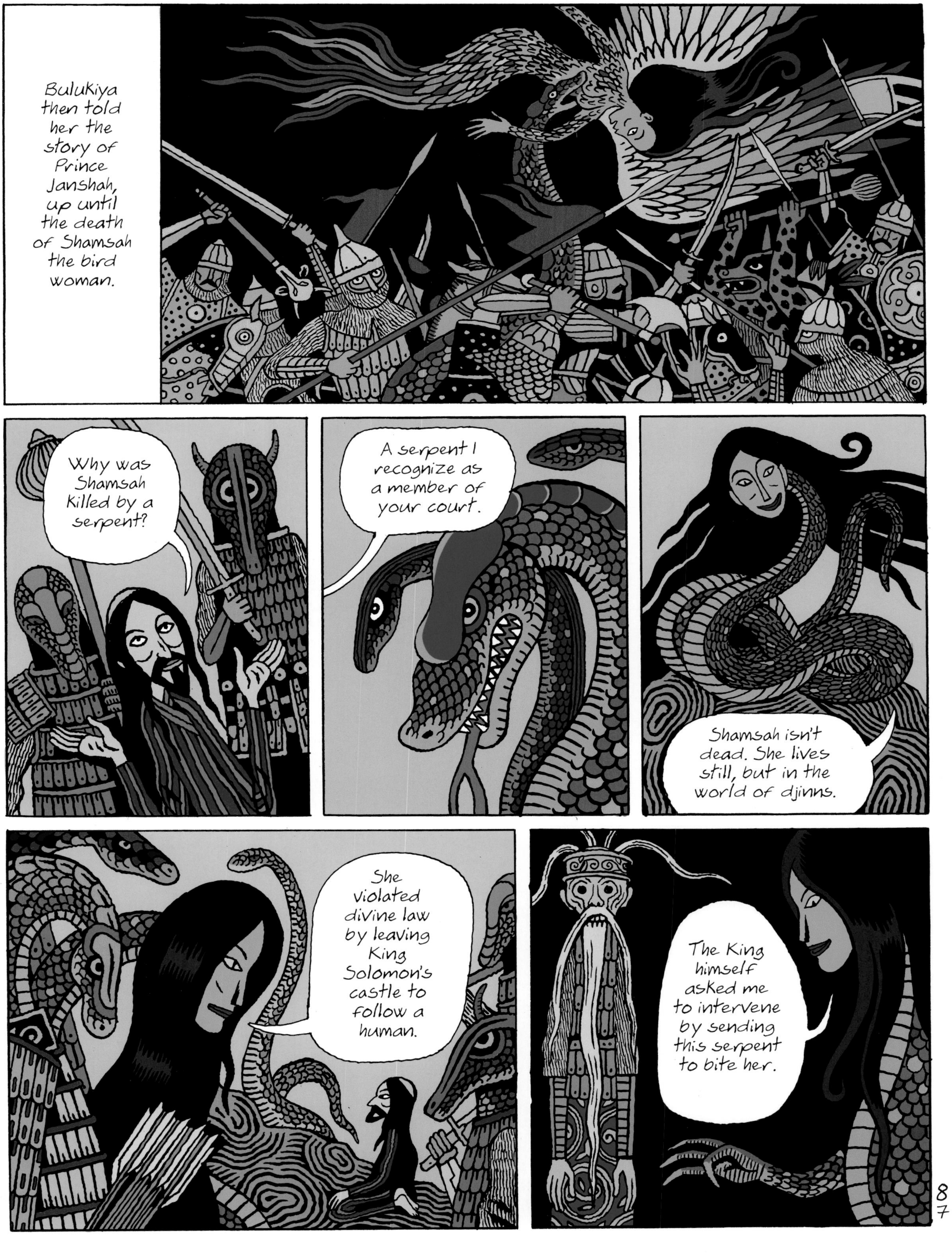
Bulukiya then told her the story of Prince Janshah, up until the death of Shamsah the bird woman.
Why was Shamsah killed by a serpent?
A serpent I recognize as a member of your court.
Shamsah isn't dead. She lives still, but in the world of djinns.
She violated divine law by leaving King Solomon's castle to follow a human.
The King himself asked me to intervene by sending this serpent to bite her.
87

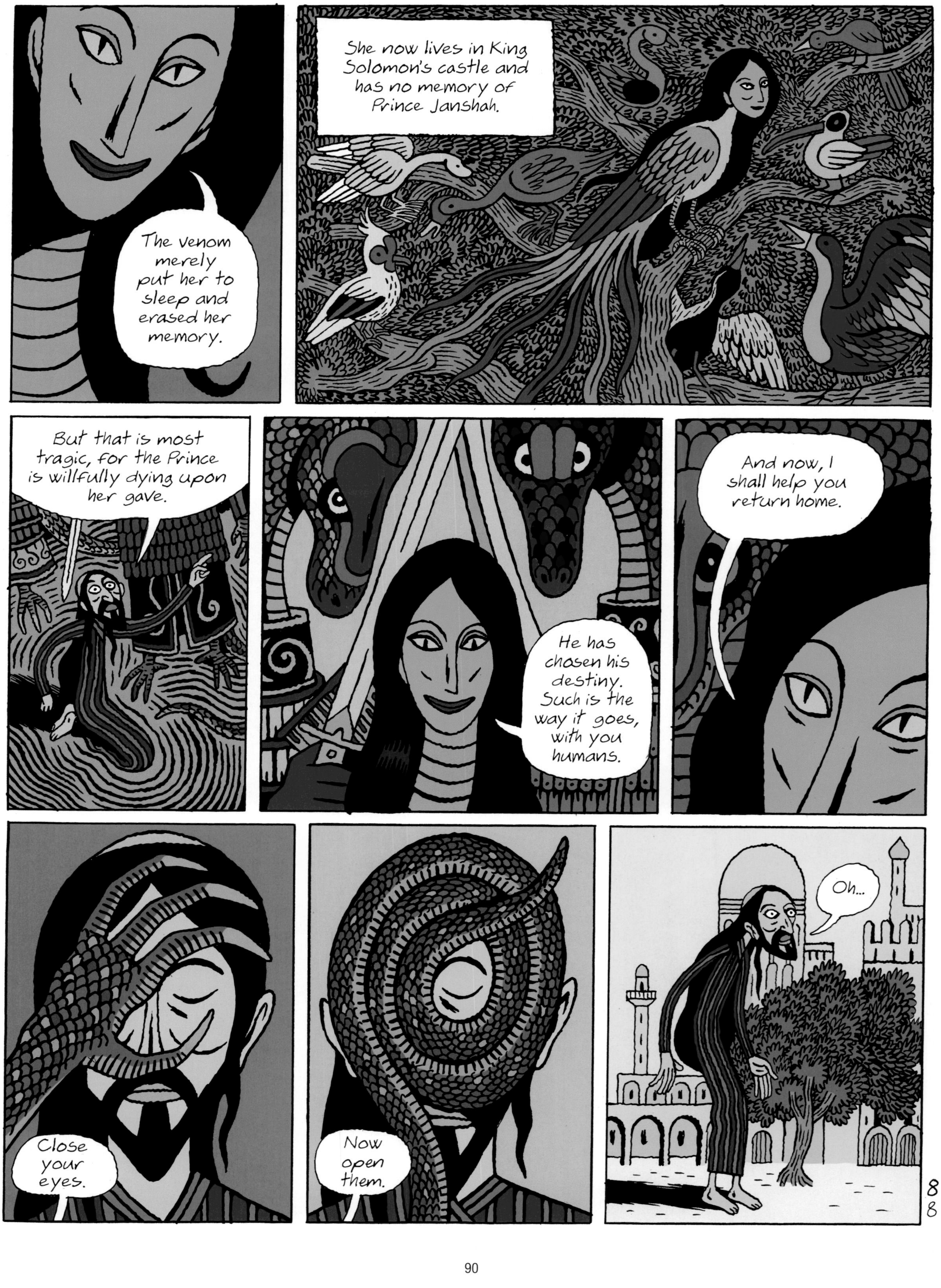

The venom merely put her to sleep and erased her memory.
She now lives in King Solomon's castle and has no memory of Prince Janshah.
But that is most tragic, for the Prince is willfully dying upon her gave.
He has chosen his destiny. Such is the way it goes, with you humans.
And now, I shall help you return home.
Close your eyes.
Now open them.
Oh...

Bulukiya opened his eyes and, much to his great surprise, found himself back in Cairo, at the door to his palace.

Master, is that you?

His mother and all the courtiers celebrated his return, and he ruled with wisdom until the day God called him home.

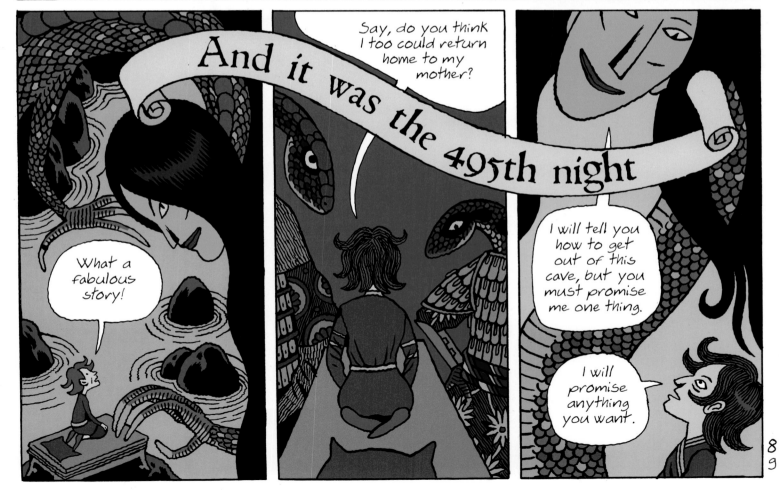

What a fabulous story!

Say, do you think I too could return home to my mother?

And it was the 495th night

I will tell you how to get out of this cave, but you must promise me one thing.

I will promise anything you want.

8
9

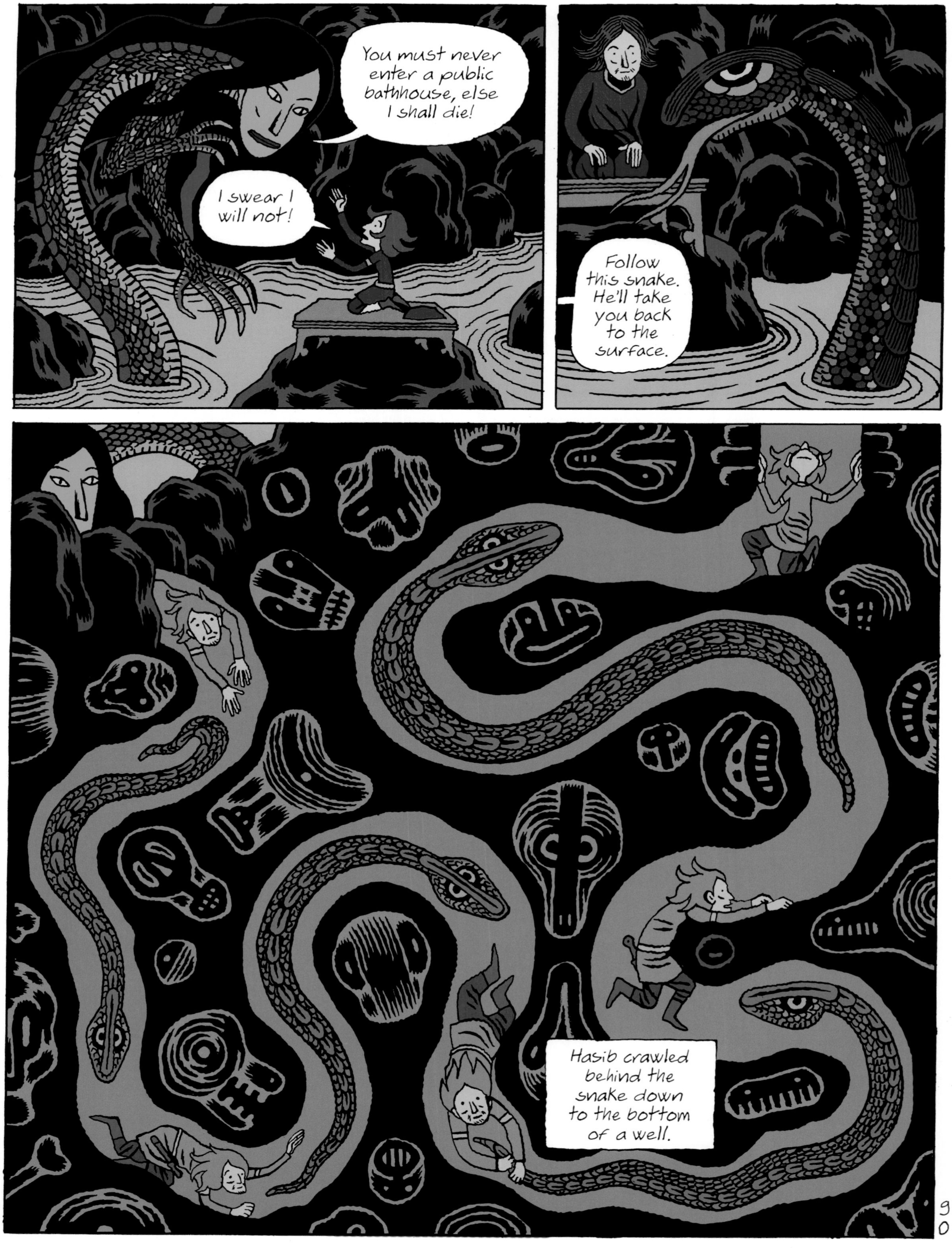
You must never enter a public bathhouse, else I shall die!
I swear I will not!
Follow this snake. He'll take you back to the surface.
Hasib crawled behind the snake down to the bottom of a well.
90

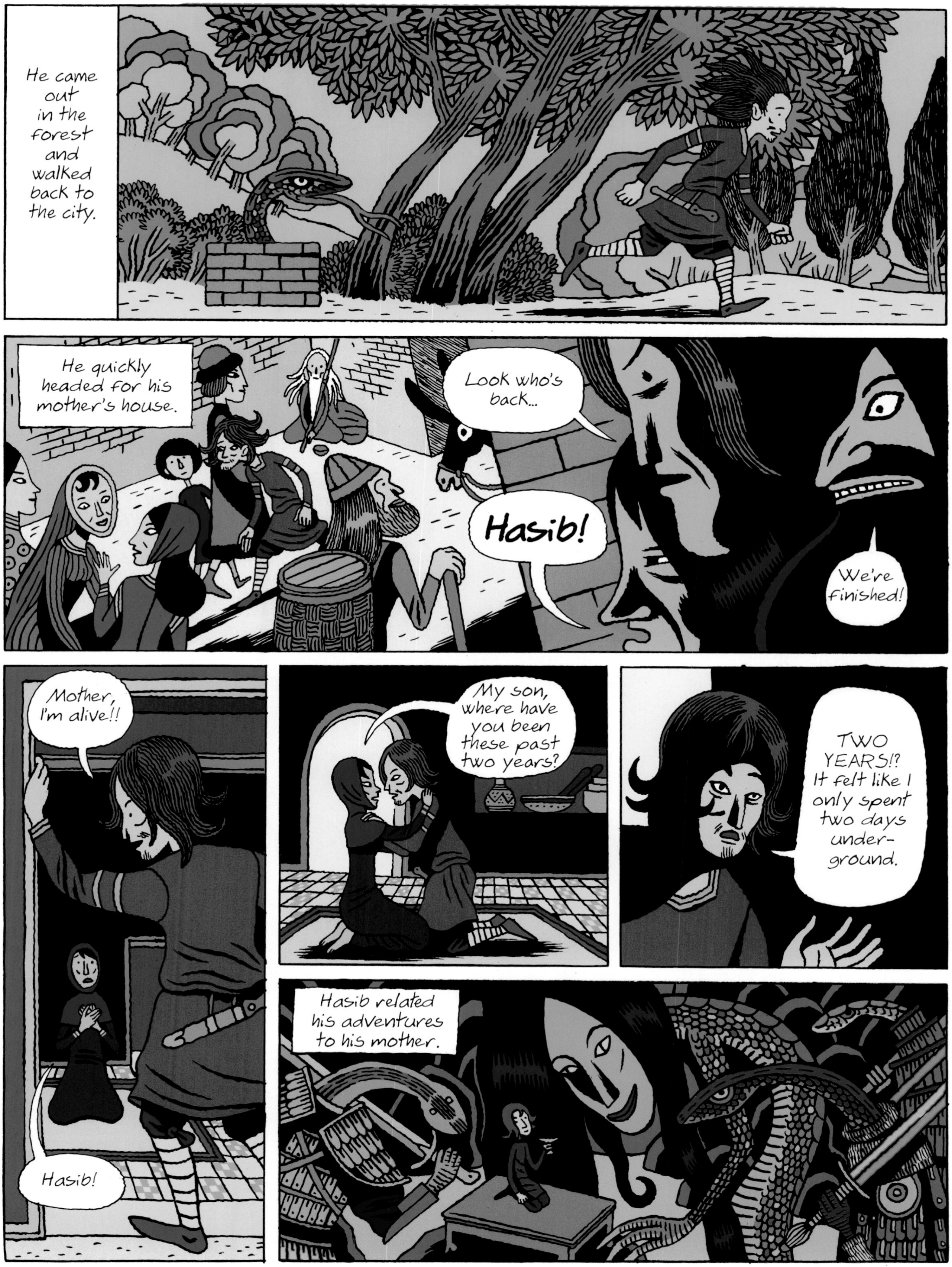
He came out in the forest and walked back to the city.
He quickly headed for his mother's house.
Look who's back...
Hasib!
We're finished!
Mother, I'm alive!!
Hasib!
My son, where have you been these past two years?
TWO YEARS!? It felt like I only spent two days under-ground.
Hasib related his adventures to his mother.
91

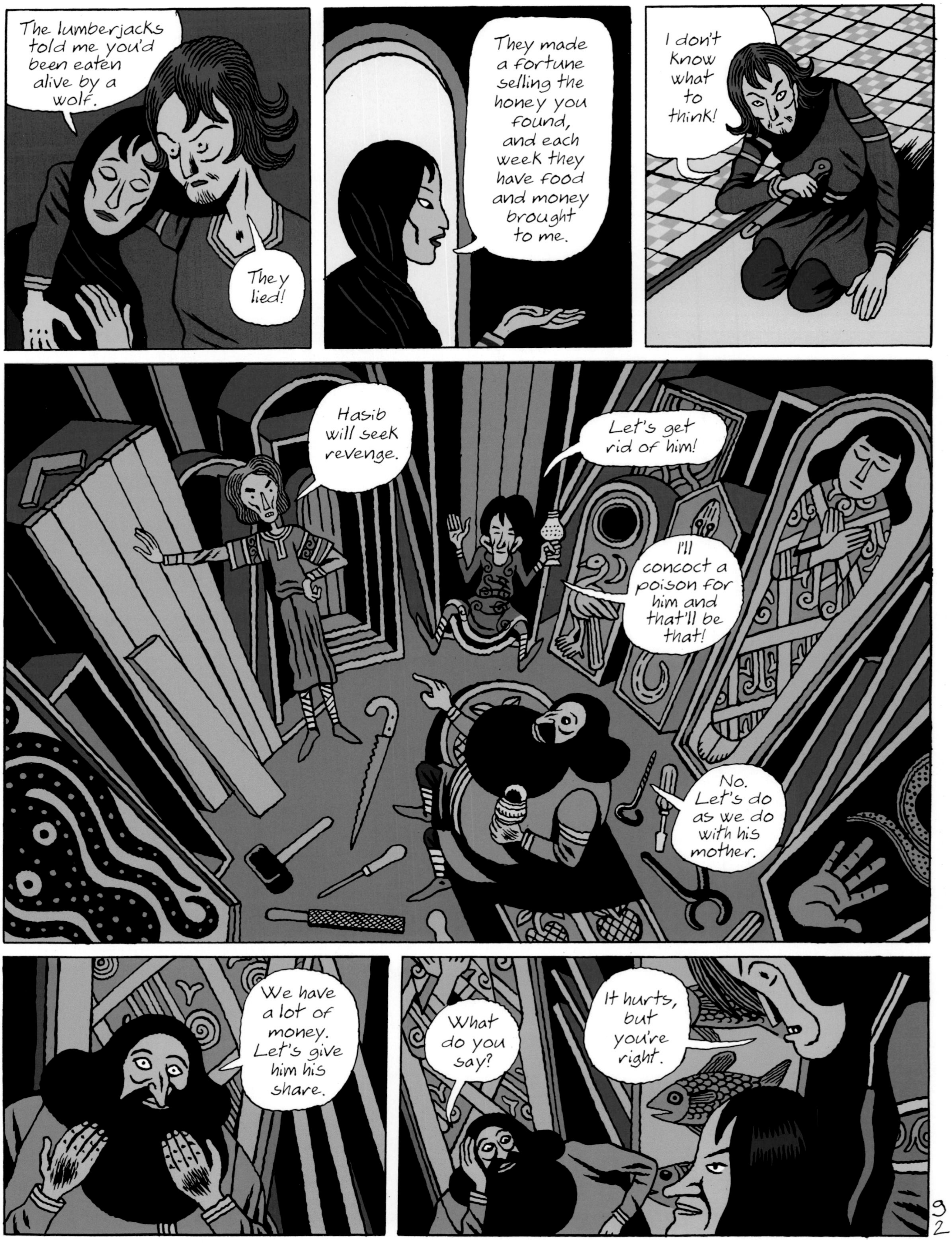
The lumberjacks told me you'd been eaten alive by a wolf.
They lied!
They made a fortune selling the honey you found, and each week they have food and money brought to me.
I don't know what to think!
Hasib will seek revenge.
Let's get rid of him!
I'll concoct a poison for him and that'll be that!
No. Let's do as we do with his mother.
We have a lot of money. Let's give him his share.
What do you say?
It hurts, but you're right.
92

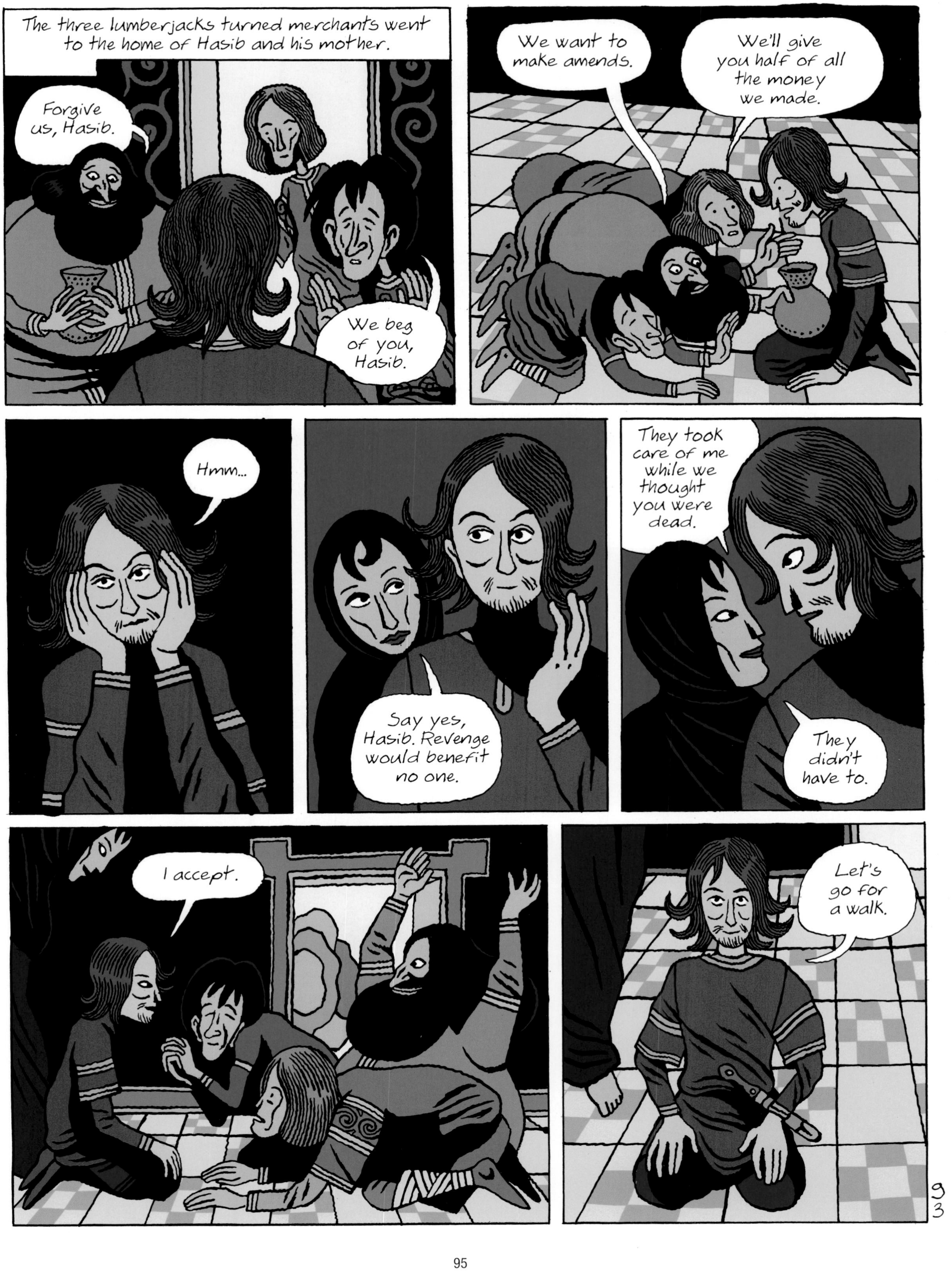
The three lumberjacks turned merchants went to the home of Hasib and his mother.
Forgive us, Hasib.
We beg of you, Hasib.
We want to make amends.
We'll give you half of all the money we made.
Hmm...
Say yes, Hasib. Revenge would benefit no one.
They took care of me while we thought you were dead.
They didn't have to.
I accept.
Let's go for a walk.
93

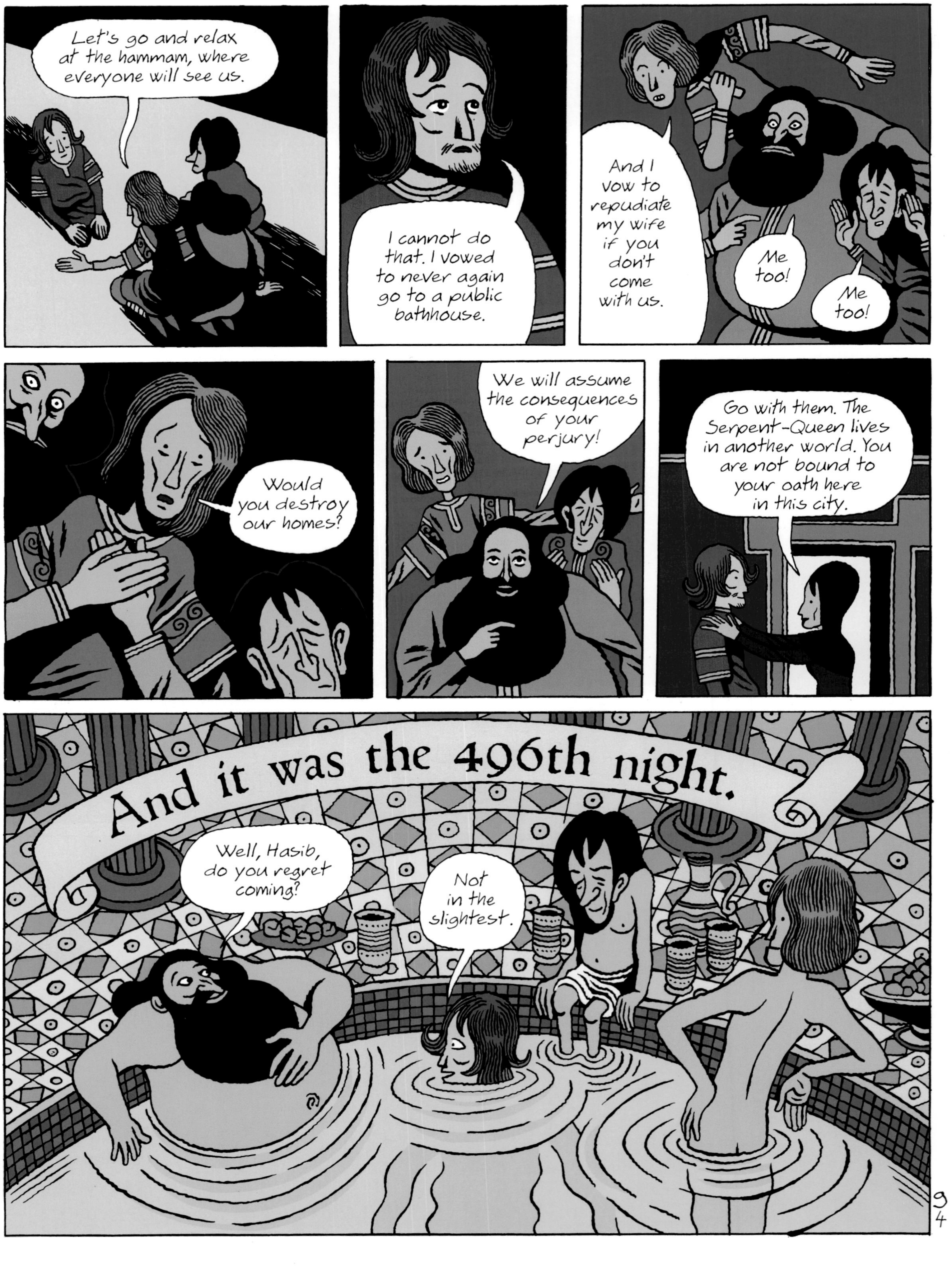
Let's go and relax at the hammam, where everyone will see us.
I cannot do that. I vowed to never again go to a public bathhouse.
And I vow to repudiate my wife if you don't come with us.
Me too!
Me too!
Would you destroy our homes?
We will assume the consequences of your perjury!
Go with them. The Serpent-Queen lives in another world. You are not bound to your oath here in this city.
And it was the 496th night.
Well, Hasib, do you regret coming?
Not in the slightest.
94

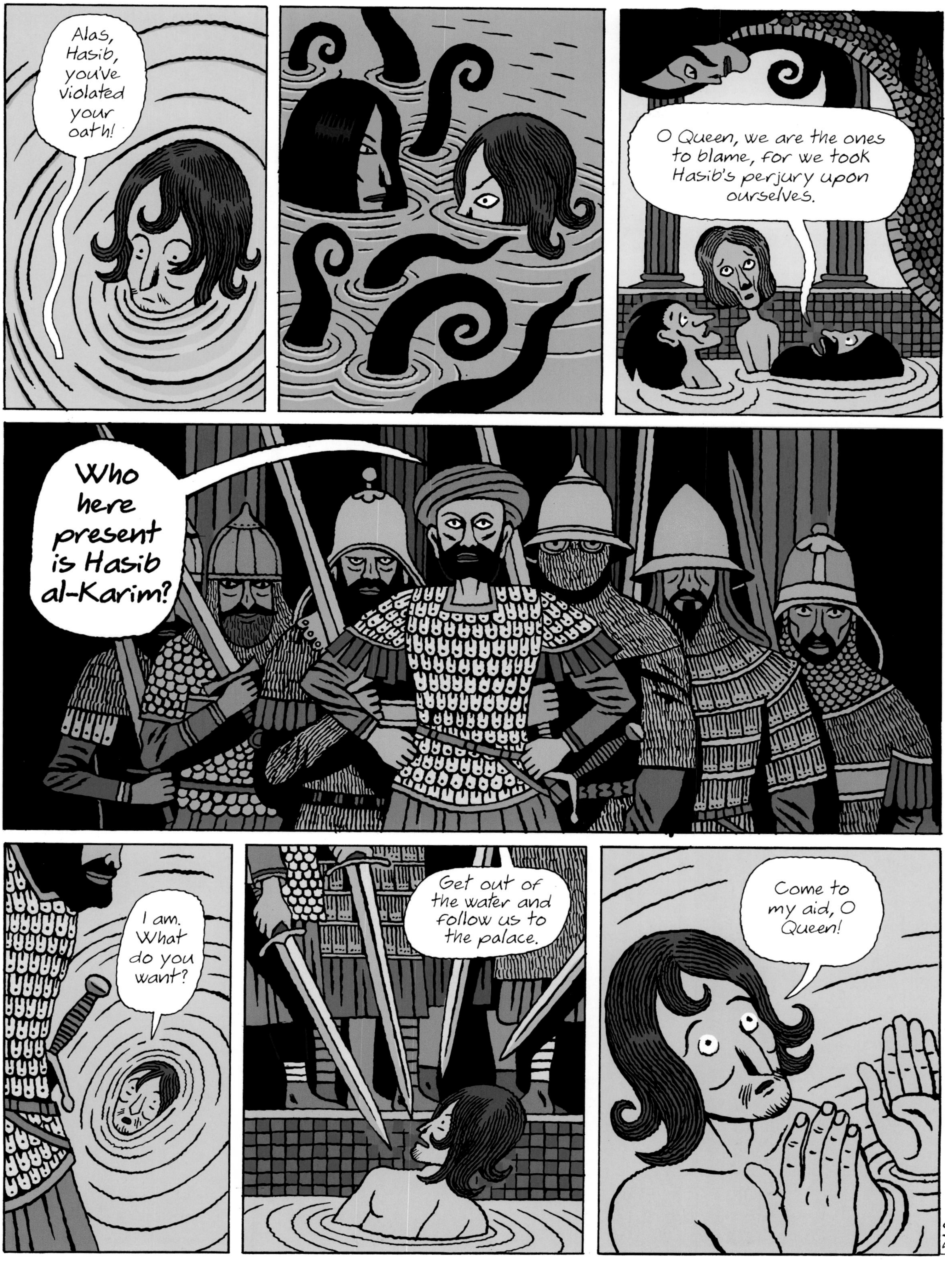

Alas, Hasib, you've violated your oath!
O Queen, we are the ones to blame, for we took Hasib's perjury upon ourselves.
Who here present is Hasib al-Karim?
I am. What do you want?
Get out of the water and follow us to the palace.
Come to my aid, O Queen!
95

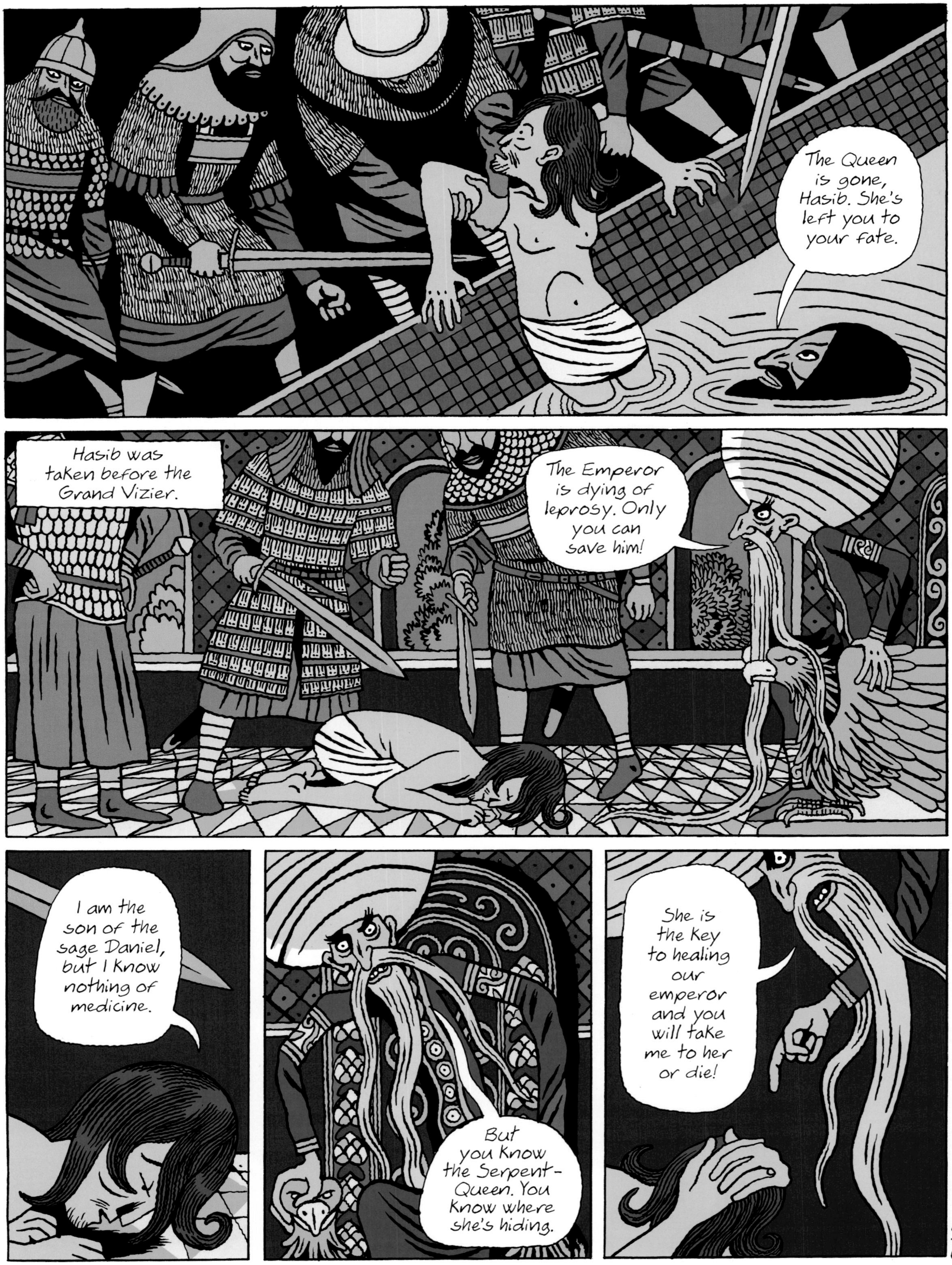

The Queen is gone, Hasib. She's left you to your fate.
Hasib was taken before the Grand Vizier.
The Emperor is dying of leprosy. Only you can save him!
I am the son of the sage Daniel, but I know nothing of medicine.
But you know the Serpent-Queen. You know where she's hiding.
She is the key to healing our emperor and you will take me to her or die!

96

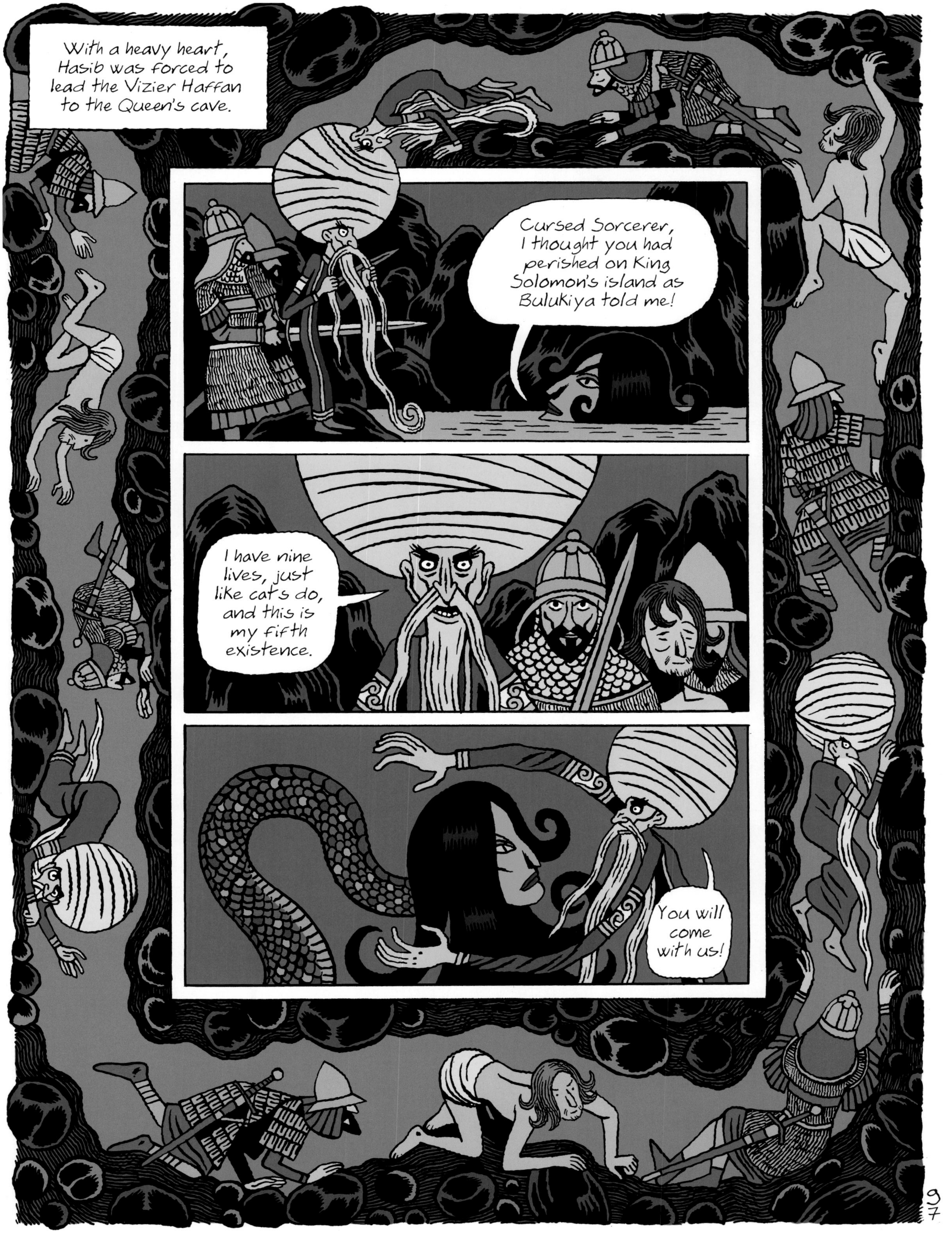
With a heavy heart, Hasib was forced to lead the Vizier Haffan to the Queen's cave.
Cursed Sorcerer, I thought you had perished on King Solomon's island as Bulukiya told me!
I have nine lives, just like cats do, and this is my fifth existence.
You will come with us!
97

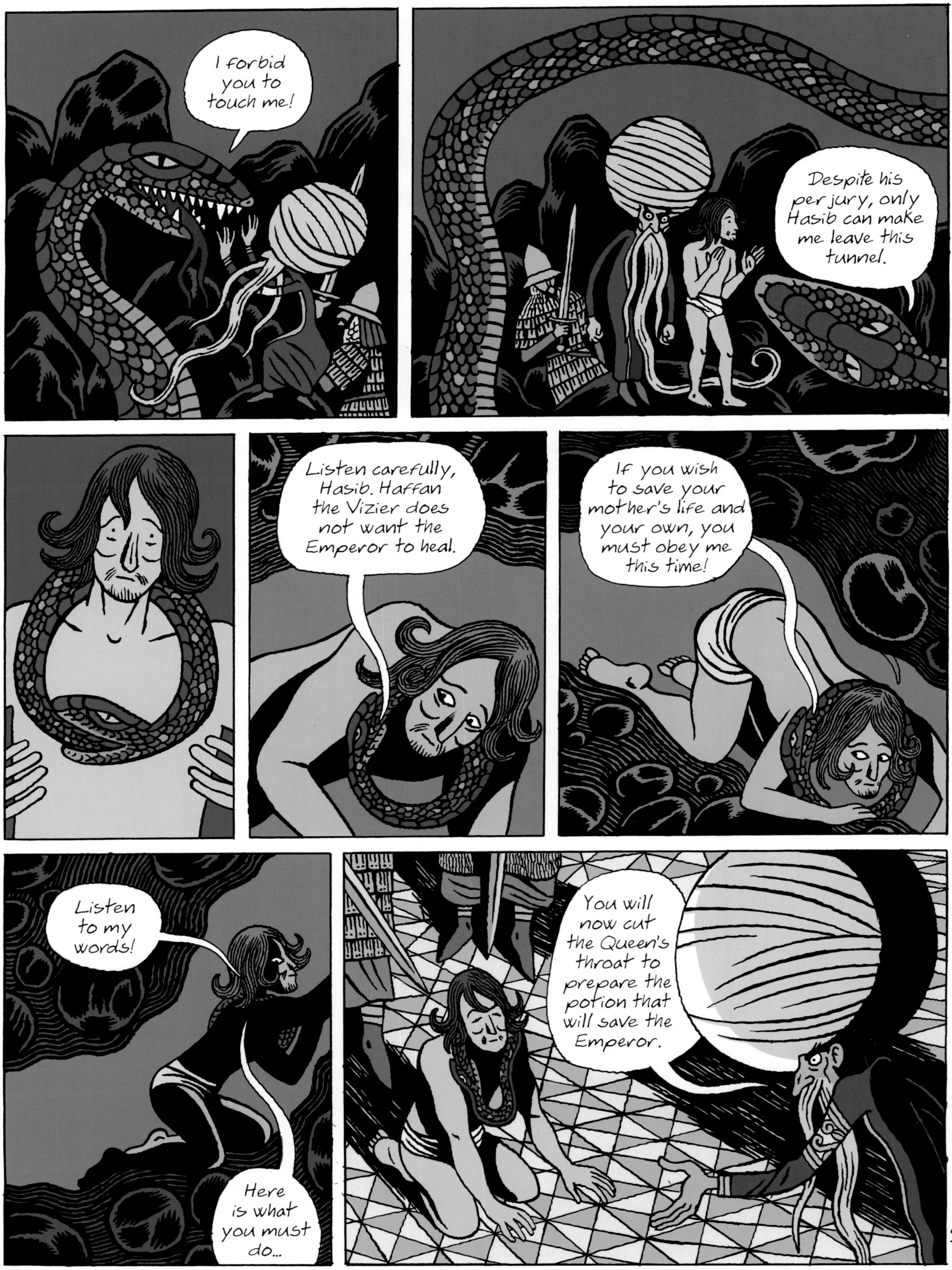
I forbid you to touch me!
Despite his perjury, only Hasib can make me leave this tunnel.
Listen carefully, Hasib. Haffan the Vizier does not want the Emperor to heal.
If you wish to save your mother's life and your own, you must obey me this time!
Listen to my words!
Here is what you must do...
You will now cut the Queen's throat to prepare the potion that will save the Emperor.
98

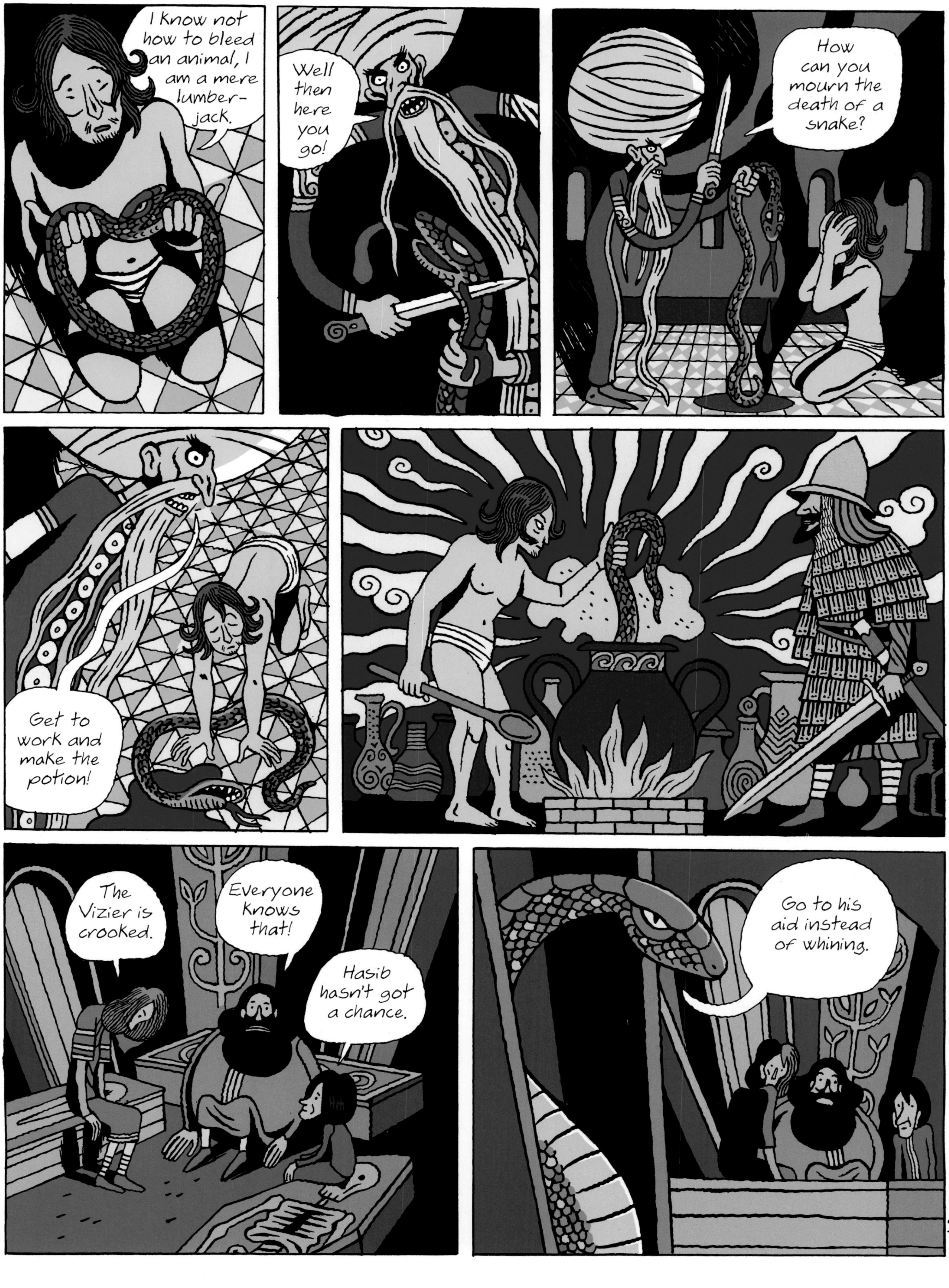
I know not how to bleed an animal, I am a mere lumber-jack.
Well then here you go!
How can you mourn the death of a snake?
Get to work and make the potion!
The Vizier is crooked.
Everyone knows that!
Hasib hasn't got a chance.
Go to his aid instead of whining.

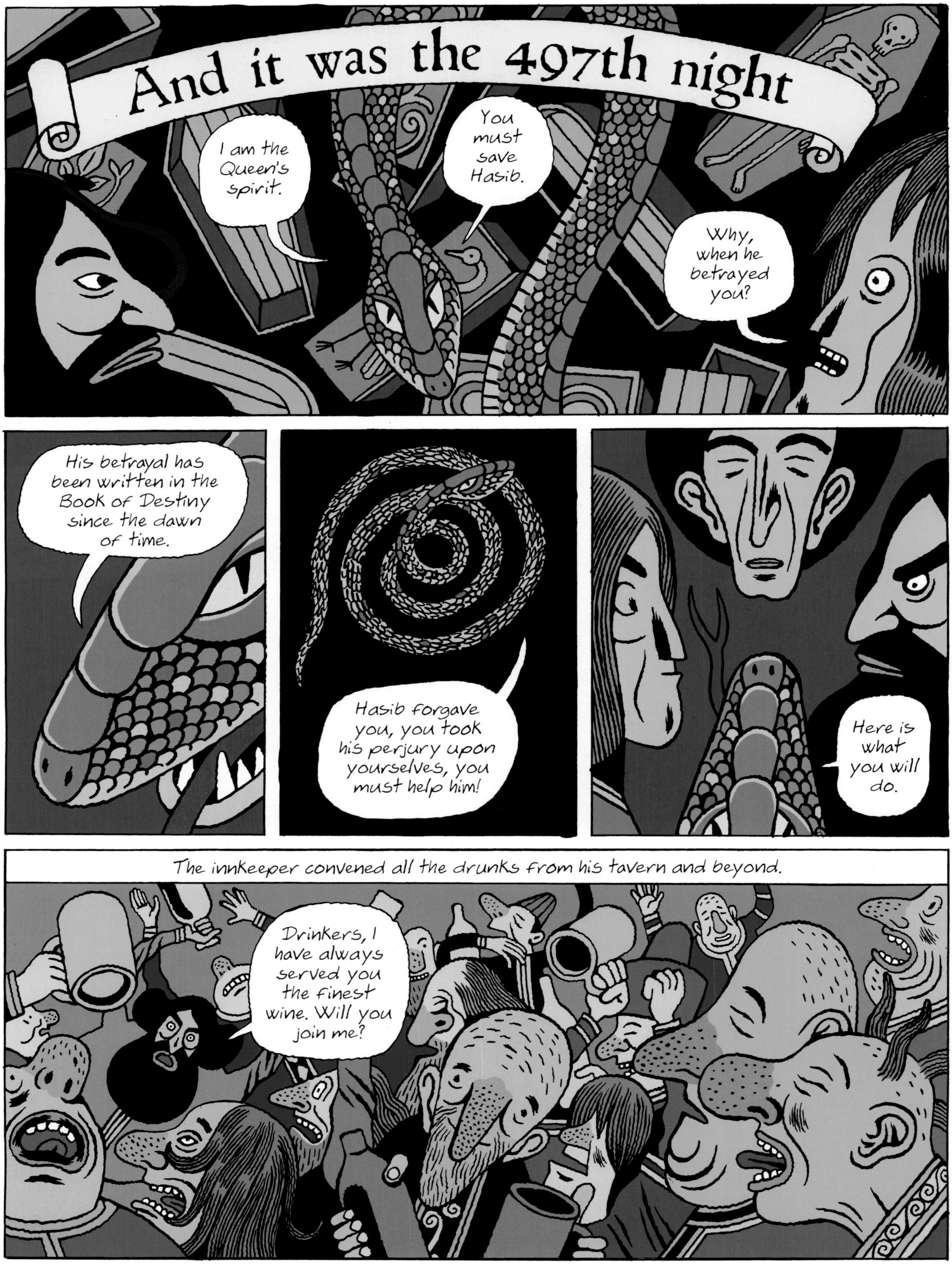
And it was the 497th night
I am the Queen's spirit.
You must save Hasib.
Why, when he betrayed you?
His betrayal has been written in the Book of Destiny since the dawn of time.
Hasib forgave you, you took his perjury upon yourselves, you must help him!
Here is what you will do.
The innkeeper convened all the drunks from his tavern and beyond.
Drinkers, I have always served you the finest wine. Will you join me?

100

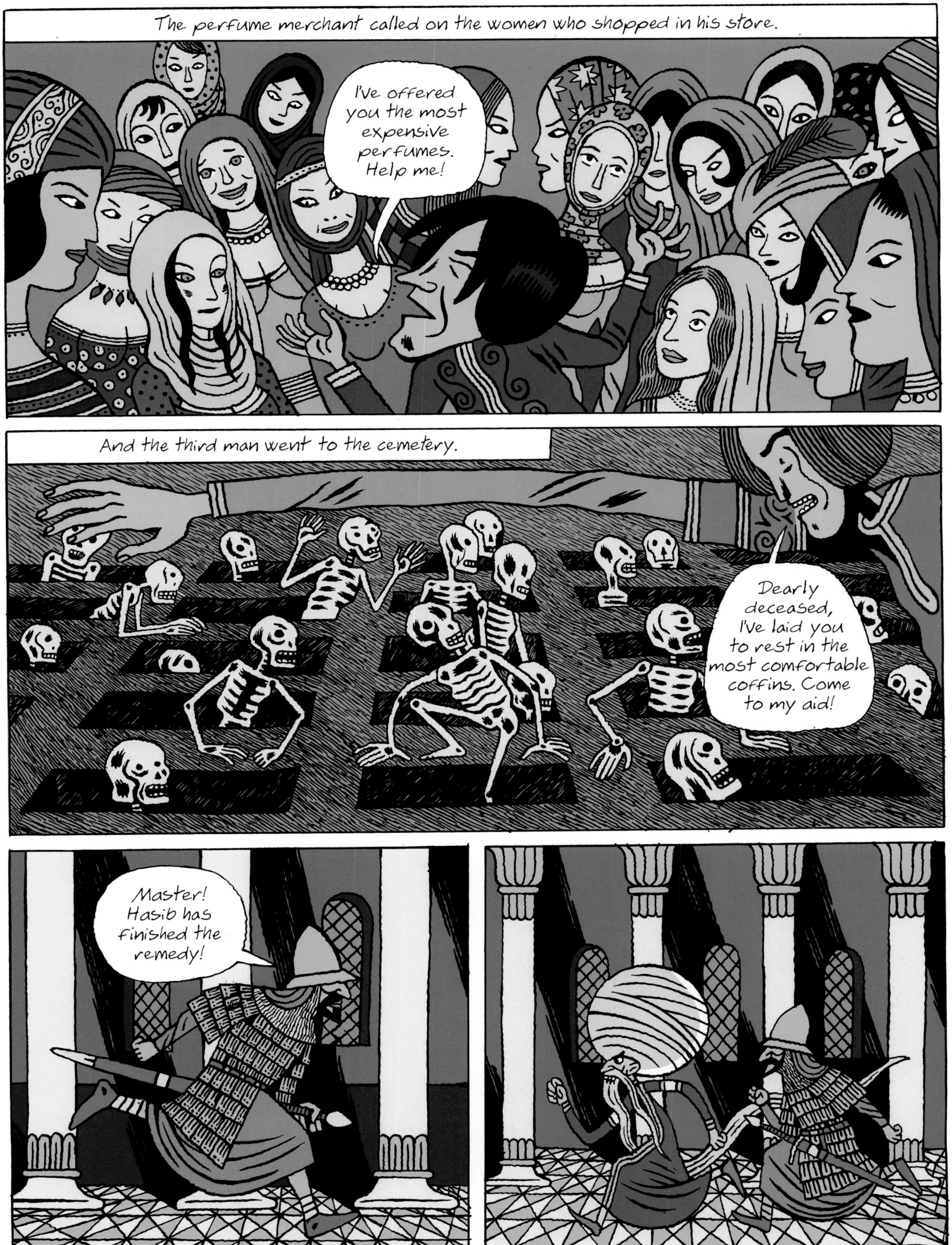
The perfume merchant called on the women who shopped in his store.
I've offered you the most expensive perfumes. Help me!
And the third man went to the cemetery.
Dearly deceased, I've laid you to rest in the most comfortable coffins. Come to my aid!
Master! Hasib has finished the remedy!

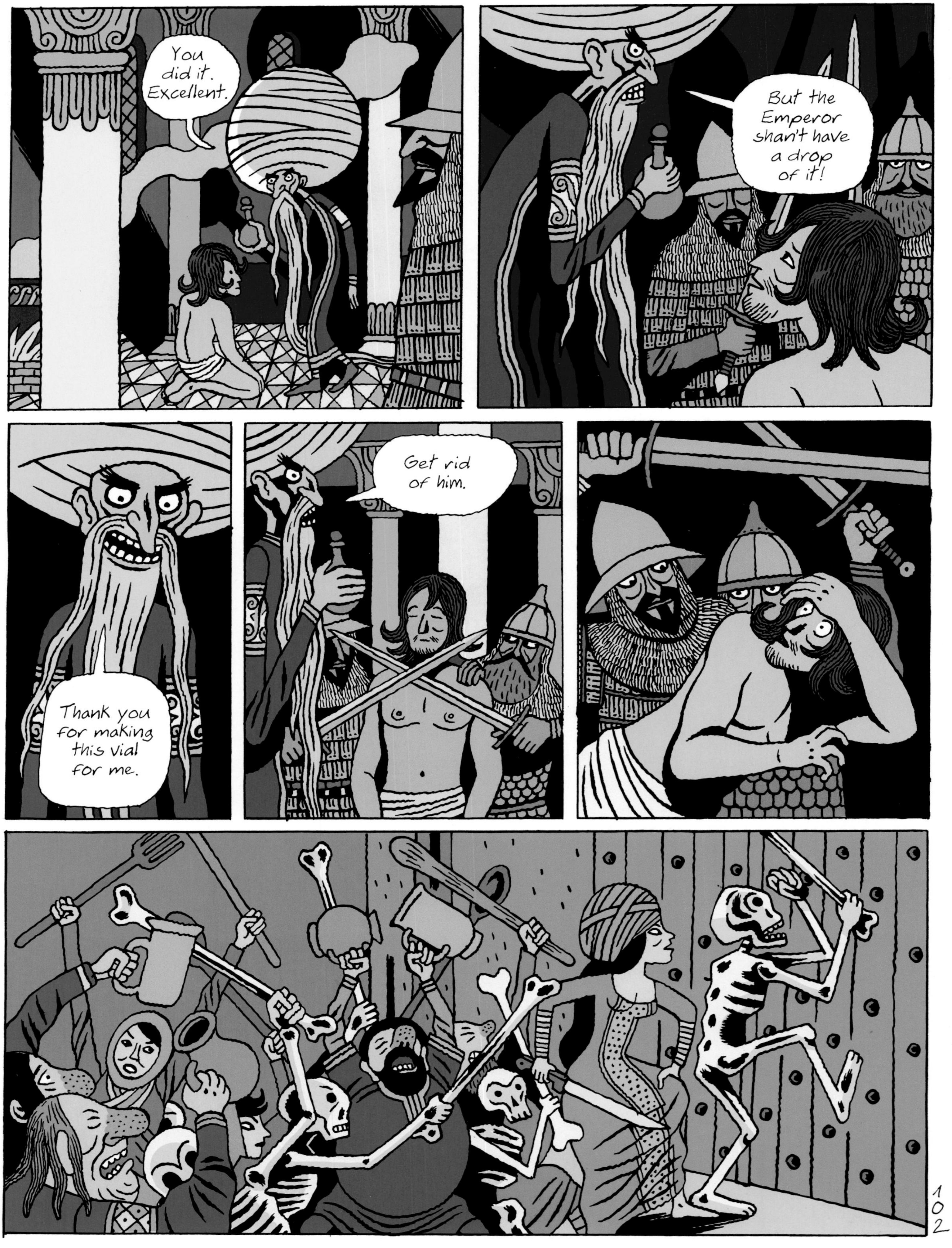
You did it. Excellent.
But the Emperor shan't have a drop of it!
Thank you for making this vial for me.
Get rid of him.
102

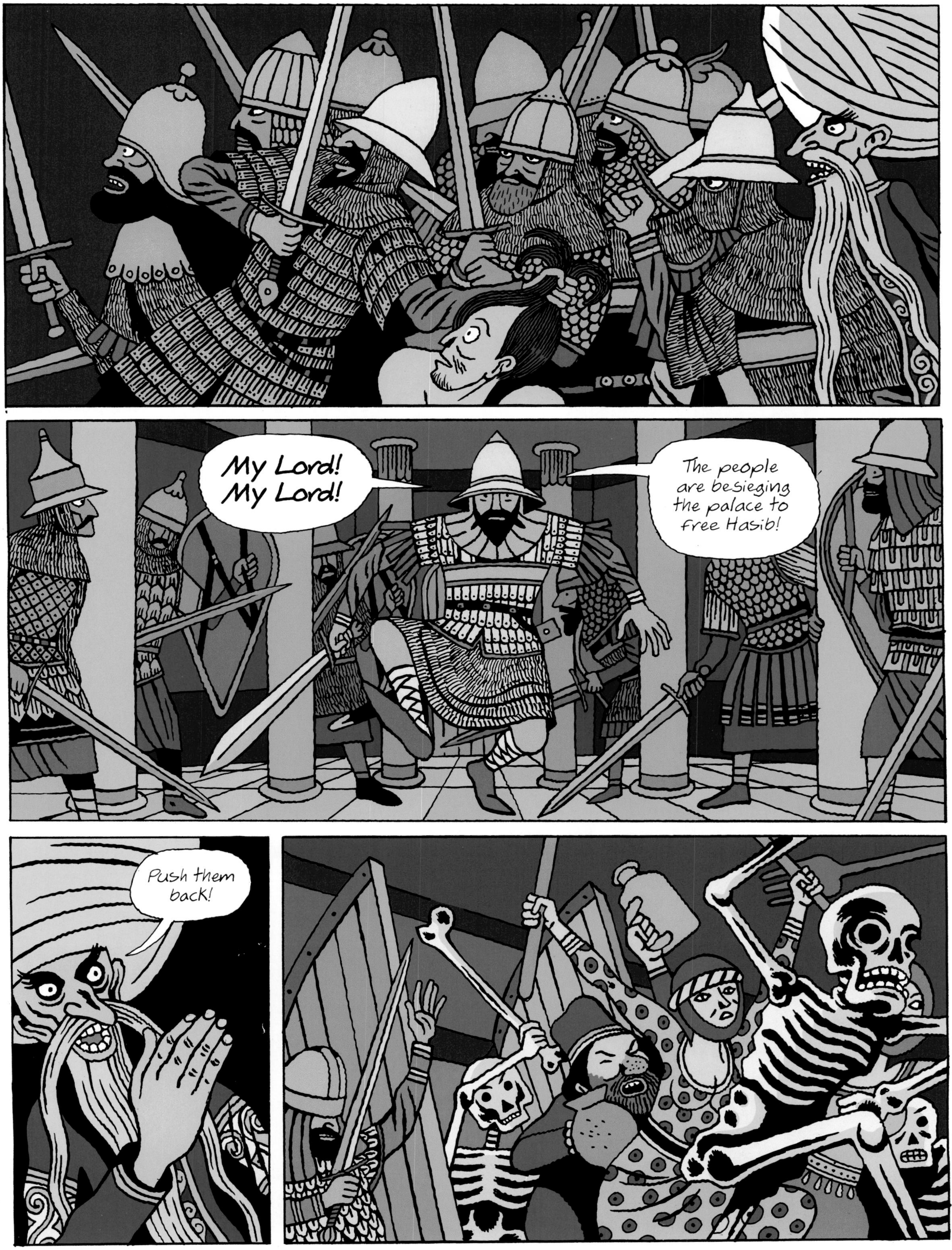
My Lord! My Lord!
The people are besieging the palace to free Hasib!
Push them back!

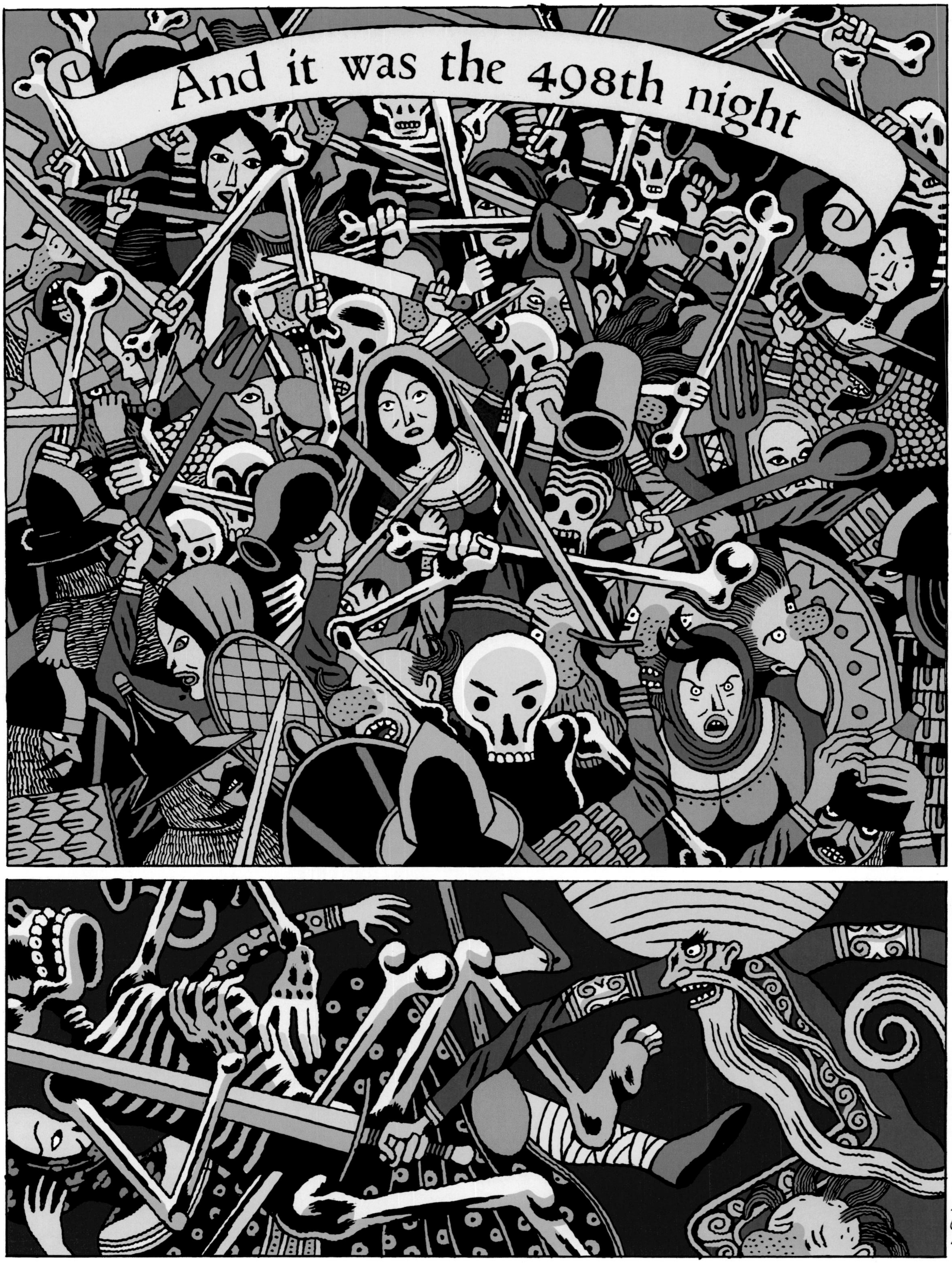
And it was the 498th night

104

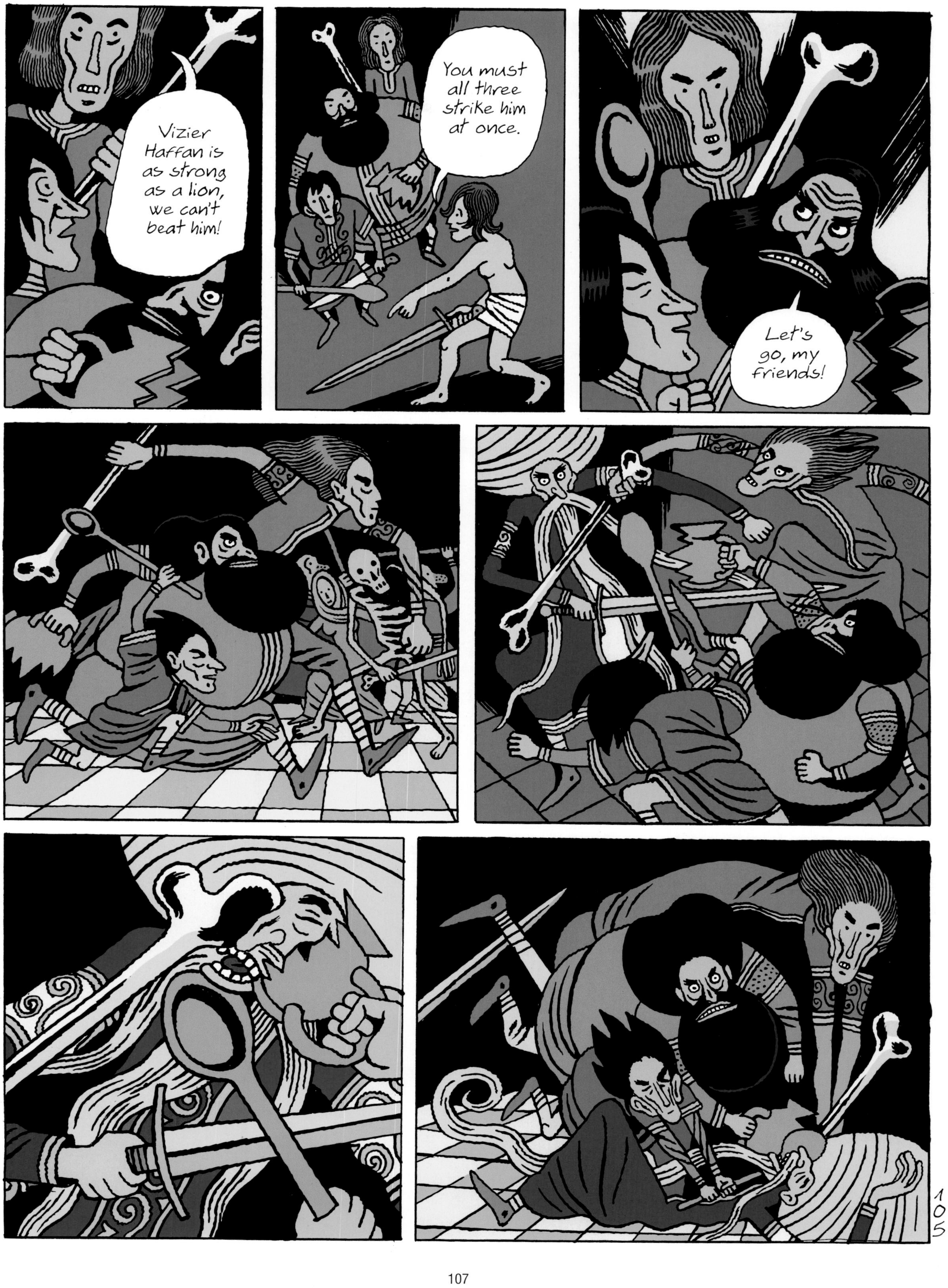
Vizier Haffan is as strong as a lion, we can't beat him!
You must all three strike him at once.
Let's go, my friends!
105

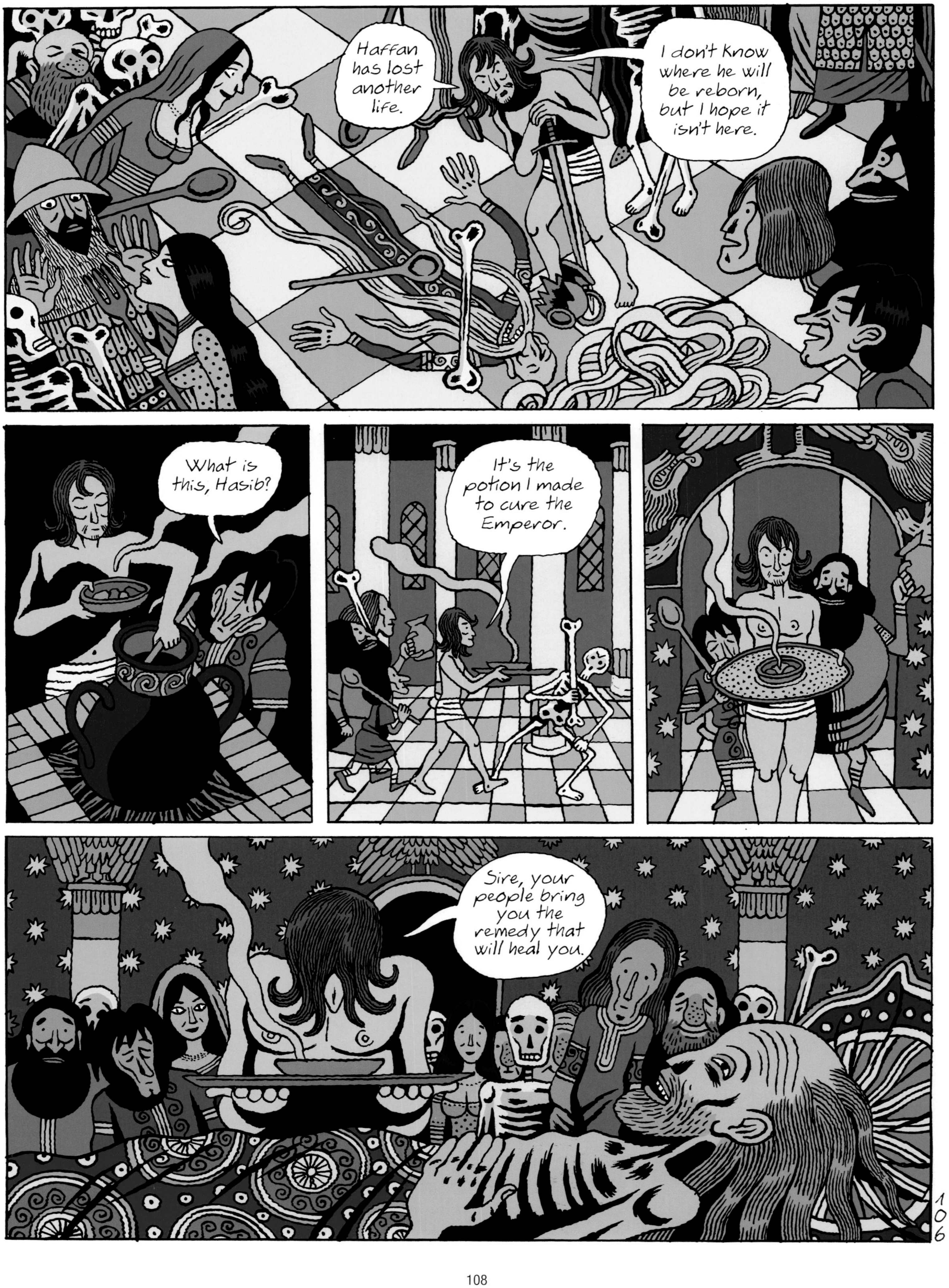
Haffan has lost another life.
I don't know where he will be reborn, but I hope it isn't here.
What is this, Hasib?
It's the potion I made to cure the Emperor.
Sire, your people bring you the remedy that will heal you.
106

Eat, Sire.

Hasib, you have brought me back to life.

Sire, all credit goes to the Serpent-Queen, who gave her life for you.

I knew Vizier Haffan was betraying me.

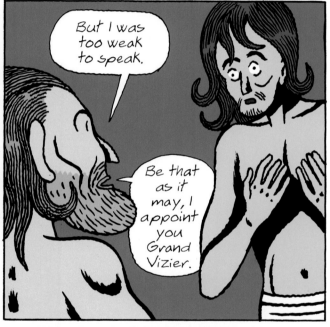

But I was too weak to speak.

Be that as it may, I appoint you Grand Vizier.

Vizier? Me? But I am not qualified.

Accept, Hasib. I shall go on protecting you, for the common good.

107

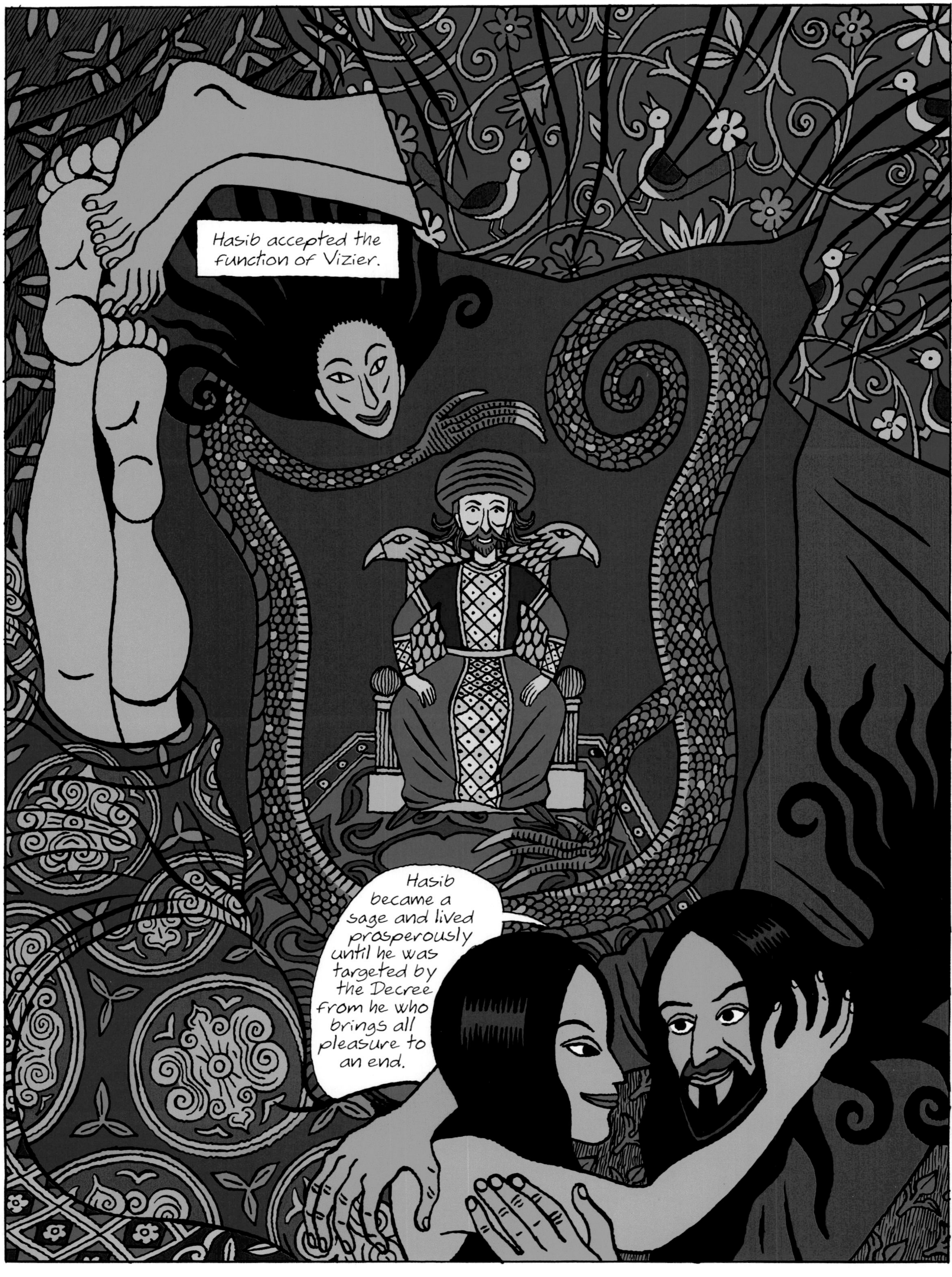
Hasib accepted the function of Vizier.
Hasib became a sage and lived prosperously until he was targeted by the Decree from he who brings all pleasure to an end.
108

David B. is one of France's finest cartoonists and a co-founder of the legendary L'Association collective. He is the author of many books of comics including The Armed Garden, Nocturnal Conspiracies, and Epileptic which was awarded the Angoulême International Comics Festival Prize for Scenario and the Ignatz Award for Outstanding Artist. Nocturnal Conspiracies was nominated for the L.A. Times Book Prize and the Eisner Awards. He lives and works in Orléans, France.

If you liked this, you'll also like from NBM Graphic Novels:

The Dungeon series, multiple volumes
Written by Lewis Trondheim and Joann Sfar
Art by various artists
"The humor can be biting and sly. And precisely because it is so light and warmhearted, the moments of melancholy and actual profundity reach into your chest, pull out your heart and keep it hostage."
-The New York Times Book Review

Glacial Period
By Nicolas de Crecy
In The Louvre Collection.
"De Crecy is a gifted storyteller whose eye for body language and ear for a funny line never fails him. He deftly combines art history, science fiction and simple philosophizing in a short but very sweet tale."
-Publishers Weekly

See many more graphic novels
with previews at
NBMPUB.COM

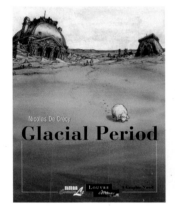

NBM
160 Broadway, Suite 700, East Wing,
New York, NY 10038
Catalog available upon request

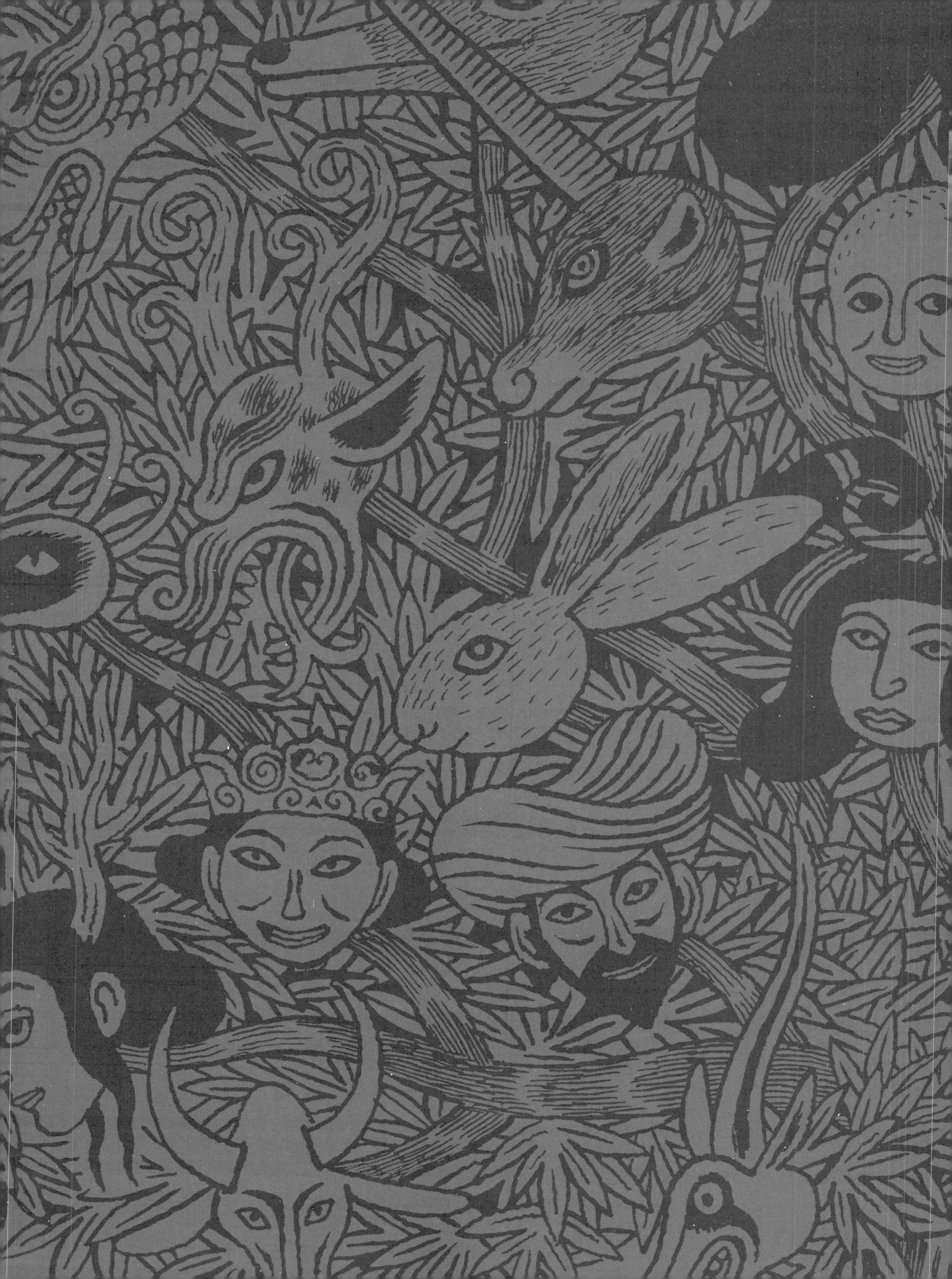